D1603696

A man said to the universe,
"Sir, I exist,"
"Yes" replied the universe,
"But that has not created in me
a sense of obligation."

—Stephen Crane

Printed in the United States of America

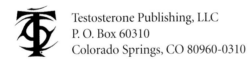 Testosterone Publishing, LLC
P. O. Box 60310
Colorado Springs, CO 80960-0310

Phone: Toll-Free 800-530-1940;
Outside the US and Canada 719-473-5500

10 9 8 7 6 5 4 3 2 1

Library of Congress Control Number: 2006907912
ISBN-13: 978-0-9773063-1-2
ISBN-10: 0-9773063-1-3

Visit www.t-nation.com.

A SPECIAL THANKS TO LAURIE GOLDER AND TIM PATTERSON, without whom this book wouldn't have been possible. Plain ol' regular thanks to Philippé Abel, Muhammad Ali, Jason Alexander, David Attenborough, Woody Allen, Michael Amorillo, Joel Bernstein, Corey Blake, Glynn Bolitho, David Borack, Paul Bruss, Walter Brylowski, Bubbles, James Burke, Edgar Rice Burroughs, Johnny Carson, William Jefferson Clinton, Jerry Coleman, Sean Connery, Steven Crane, Elvis Costello, ee cummings, Ted Danson, Rodney Dangerfield, Racquel Darrian, Larry David, Jason Deitch, Ralph DeHaan, Charles Dickens, Maureen Dowd, Mike Downey, Julia Louis Dreyfuss, Clint Eastwood, TS Eliot, Chris Farley, F. Scott Fitzgerald, James Gandolfini, Bob Gibson, David Golder, Kathie Golder, Dick Golder, Janice Golder, Cary Grant, Rob Grishow, Tony Gwynn, Tom Hall, Ray Harryhousen, David Halberstam, Phil Hartman, Ernest Hemingway, Denny Hickman, Tom Horgan, John Irving, Mick Jagger, Michael Jordan, Larry Katz, Garrison Keillor, John Fitzgerald Kennedy, Jack Kerouac, Keith Keveney, Stephen King, Frances King, James Tiberius Kirk, Chris Kochmanski, Jerzy Kosinski, Stan Lee, David Letterman, Ted Leitner, Adriana Lima, Shelly Long, Mario Logger, Bela Lugosi, Tim Luoma, John McCain, Ron McCallum, Jerry Meredith, Dennis Miller, Marilyn Mills, Mom and Pop, Marilyn Monroe, Mickey Mantle, Fred Morck, Van Morrison, Brian Moss, Bill Murray, Vladimir Nabokov, James Newcomb, Barack Obama, Caroll O'Connor, Tom Overton, Camille Paglia, Charles Poliquin, Richard Pryor, Ernesto Ramos, Ayn Rand, Robert Redford, Riley, Michael Richards, EA Robinson, Matt Sanders, JD Salinger, Lou Schuler, Jerry Seinfeld, Sara Silverman, Chris Shugart, Phil Stevens, Claudia Schiffer, Arnold Schwarzenegger, Seven of Nine, Adam Sorkin, Stephen Spielberg, Spock, Curtis Stadtfeld, Patrick Stewart, Jon Stewart, Tanner, JRR Tolkien, Toney, Grant Tonkin, Julianne Van Valkenburg, Wallace, Chad Waterbury, Peter Watry, Gary Williams, Robin Williams, Ted Williams, Frank Lloyd Wright, Tom Wolfe and Testosterone readers.

Foreword: A Return to Manhood
by Chris Shugart

You're a wimp. That's right, I said it. A wimp, a sissy, a panty-waist, and a *wussy*. And the worst part is, you probably don't even know it.

Over the last few years, the manhood of the North American male has been under attack. It's been chipped at and eroded by a relatively new form of political correctness: the movement to demonize and suppress Testosterone.

Somehow, this innocent hormone (which women possess too, by the way) has come to represent many negative aspects of society. Just watch the nightly news. Any time a bunch of violent, stupid people collectively do something violent and stupid in a public setting, you're sure to hear the phrase "too much Testosterone" come up in the discussion that follows. Why is that? After all, science tells us that many men who are prone to violence have just the opposite problem—they have *low* T levels.

Closer to home, a young man I know was asked by high school administrators to go home and change his "inappropriate and offensive" T-shirt. The single naughty word printed on the front of the shirt? *Testosterone*. Gosh, it's a good thing he was made to change clothes. Otherwise, there might have been a riot or an outbreak of otherwise dormant sexual thoughts among the teenagers at his school! What would have happened if his shirt had read *Estrogen*? Why, he'd have probably been patted on the head and rewarded for being so sensitive and empathic and, well, so *responsibly castrated*.

What's wrong with Testosterone anyway? And what's so wrong with being masculine? Testosterone, after all, is the elixir of heroism, passion, drive, energy, and intensity. Didn't you know that? Or has all that "primitive" stuff been sucked out of you by a society that would like to keep your testicles safely locked up in a jar under the bed, only to be removed during times of war and procreation (which you'd better not enjoy)?

Luckily for Testosterone-fueled men and the women who love them, this maligned hormone has a crusader. It began eight years ago in an online magazine called, you guessed it, *Testosterone Nation*. In his *Atomic Dog* column, TC began to define and outline the masculine ideal for the new millenium.

Is TC an edgy humorist? Yes. Is he an advocate, defender, and reveler in all things Testosterone? Yes, that too. Is he a sensitive intellectual? Yep. A motivational guru for people who hate those pansy-assed motivational gurus? Roger that. A firebrand for unabashed manhood in an increasingly sissified society of wimps? Ditto.

Thousands of people now visit T-Nation.com every week to see what TC has to say. This book is a "best of" collection from those weekly columns. It will no doubt make a lot of people angry. It will no doubt be highly offensive to many individuals.

Good.

It's time to piss some people off, reclaim healthy masculinity, and set the record straight about Testosterone. It's time to be men again.

CS

Contents

SECTION 4. Man vs. Woman

SECTION 5. Testosterone—The Essence of Man

SECTION 6. SEX

A Kick in the Pants

SECTION

1

Chapter 1

10 Secrets for Living Well

"Testicularity is the last vanguard of civilization; what ties us to nature, what makes us want to excel, what makes us want to discover, invent, and conquer. Don't let your balls go the way of the appendix."

❝ *I've drank more beer, pissed more blood, and banged more quiff than all you numb-nuts put together.*"

— Clint Eastwood in, *Heartbreak Ridge*

Let's get one thing straight, damn straight. I've never felt any physical attraction to a man. The only penis I ever want to see flapping in the wind is mine. Sure, sure, I admire and appreciate the artistry, for lack of a better word, of the occasional muscular male body, but that's as far as it goes.

That being said, I have at times in the past felt *something* for Clint Eastwood. What that something was, I'm not exactly sure, but it was a combination of admiration, idol worship, and a strange warm fuzzy feeling that emanated from my balls and spread out and enveloped the more primitive centers of my brain. No, I don't have a desire to, as Clint once said in a movie, "swap spit in the shower," but I admired the way he looked—at least before age turned his face into an old catcher's mitt. It was as if one of the archangels had challenged God to personify masculinity and God had come through in spades.

And of course I liked the way he acted in tough situations because it's the way I wanted to act in tough situations. I'm a hothead, the kind of guy who gets all red with teeth clenched and veins sticking out of his forehead and neck when some peckerwood infringes on the integrity of my universe. Any chance of saying something clever to an adversary is always completely extinguished by an overflow of epinephrine. Clint, on the other hand, got mad but he always stayed *cool.* Oh, he did his share of teeth clenching alright, but he never raised his voice and you sure as hell didn't see his hands shaking from excitement. And he always verbally chilled the shit out of anybody who had the temerity to be born on the same planet as he was:

"I know what you're thinking. Did he fire six shots or only five? Well, to tell you the truth, in all this excitement, I've kinda lost track myself. But being as this is a .44 Magnum, the most powerful handgun in the world, and would blow your head clean off, you've got to ask yourself one question: Do I feel lucky? Well, do ya punk?"

Trouble is, Clint's just a damn actor. Some acne-riddled writer with glasses as thick as the windshield of a Hummer dreamed up the things he did and said. The real Clint Eastwood is probably a cool guy on his own merits, but he couldn't possibly match up to his screen personae. That's why I'm usually not wild about reading articles about people who I like or admire; better to let the fantasy live on rather than see it annihilated by some reporter shining a battery of halogen lights on his or her wart-riddled personality.

But I can't always avoid these articles, either. Case in point, this month's *Men's Journal* published an article detailing Clint's "10 Secrets for Living Well." I was intrigued so I read it.

After reading the article, I don't think that Clint actually came up with this list. Instead, I think it was just the work of yet another writer who gleaned these secrets based on his observations of Clint. Case in point, I can't imagine Clint believing that a *car* can make a man. Surely he doesn't think a man who suffers from testicle deprivation can cure his problems by hopping behind the wheel of a Ford F150.

Regardless, the list is kind of fun to read, particularly when Clint pontificates on what would happen to him if he were on *Queer Eye for the Straight Guy.*

"Those guys would put me in a pair of Britney Spears jeans—you know, the ones that show the crack in your ass. Maybe throw a tattoo on my tailbone."

Good, manly stuff that makes your balls tingle in harmony.

Here's the exact list:

1. Call your own shots.
2. Be fearless.
3. Keep moving.
4. Love your job.
5. Speak softly…you know the rest.
6. Don't be predictable.
7. Find a good woman.
8. Learn to play the piano.

9. You are what you drive.

10. Avoid extreme makeovers.

However, in what's probably a supreme act of hubris, I couldn't help attempting to come up with my own "10 Secrets for Living Well." Here they are in no particular order:

1. Don't apologize for something unless you mean it.

All too often, some politician or celebrity says or does something that's disagreeable to schoolmarms only to do a mea culpa a few days later. Bullshit. If you say something that begs an apology, do it right away before thoughts of possible financial retribution force you to issue a false apology. Why? It's called integrity.

We're being bombarded by apologies lately: a drunk Joe Namath is interviewed on *Monday Night Football* and he slurs on about some silly point and tells Suzy Kolber on live TV that he'd like to kiss her; Crocodile Hunter Steve Irwin feeds a crocodile with one hand while holding his infant son in the other; one politician after another says something he or she didn't mean to. As a result, nannies and similarly Testosterone-challenged beings around the world go crazy, forcing everyone and everything to apologize for their "egregious and insensitive" actions or comments.

Namath's a drunk and Irwin was a moron. The politician expressed a legitimate opinion, any one of which would piss off somebody, somewhere. Can't we just leave it at that?

Democratic presidential wannabe General Wesley Clark was asked by a civilian how he'd respond if President Bush or Clark's own Democratic rivals questioned his patriotism or military record. Clark didn't know the television cameras were on so he said, "I'd beat the shit out of them." A few more sensitive types demanded an apology so a few hours later Clark's people acknowledged that he had misspoken and what he really meant to say was that he'd "beat the *living* shit out of them."

Now that's an apology I can admire.

2. Be a Superhero.

Everyone was born with some super powers. Me? I know exactly when meat is cooked just by looking at it. It's not like having X-ray vision but hey, it's something. I can also perfectly imitate a sofa chair by throwing a sheet over my body and crouching with outspread arms. Neither of these would make me an ideal crime fighter, but you gotta go with what you've got.

Anyhow, superheroes stand for justice and invariably do what's necessary to protect the people. They don't do it for financial gain; they only do it because it's the right thing to do. And, of course, a superhero needs a body to match his high ideals so he can carry out the force of his will.

What better reason to work out?

3. Embrace pain.

Nothing really good comes too easy. Physical pain, emotional pain, that special kind of pain that comes with seeing Norwegian nanny Elin Nordegren get engaged to a dweebylooking guy like Tiger Woods, it's all good. It's all part of life and it all builds character.

Wallow in it. It makes life's inevitable pleasures all the more sweet.

4. Practice humility.

Practicing humility isn't just for the sake of the sons of bitches around you; it's for your benefit, too. You might be the most confident, overbearing punk on the planet but sooner or later this thing we call life is going to bite you on your proud ass. I was standing in line for a cup of coffee the other day behind this tough looking guy in his middle to late fifties and his stammer was so bad that he couldn't make his order clear. Compared to him, Porky Pig is a gifted orator. But the strange thing was that the stutterer was so embarrassed he had to leave the coffee shop. You'd think that a man of that age had at some point come to grips with his stutter, but not this guy.

He came back a few minutes later, though, and began speaking to the owner of the shop in barely audible tones. The shopkeeper later told me that for some reason the guy was able to speak without much of a stammer if he whispered. What the stutterer had explained was the he was a former lieutenant colonel in the Marines who'd recently come back from Iraq where he'd been bit in the hand by a poisonous snake. The venom had damaged his nervous system and affected his speech so that he now has a machinegun-like stammer. He was otherwise unaffected.

As such, this once-proud man, a leader of men, had suffered a severe blow to his self-esteem. Whereas his voice had once inspired and commanded, it was now an object of pity and derision.

The previous example is of course rather benign when you compare it to all the other problems that can befall a person. Any new day can bring disease, injury, or disability and no one is immune. As such, try to remember that your shit doesn't stink any less than anyone else's and act like it. The only people who deserve to act cocky are those who have won both a gold medal in the Olympics *and* a Nobel Prize and at last count there wasn't anyone who fit that bill.

5. Try not to lie.

At the risk of sounding like a Boy Scout, lying has become a national pastime.

Those who had to deal with the old Soviet Union long enough learned a simple fact: Most Soviets were itinerant liars and what's more, the Soviets didn't consider it to be a character fault. It was just part of doing business, political or otherwise.

Unfortunately, the custom seems to have been adopted by the U.S. government and its people. Lying is fashionable. If you get caught, all you've got to do is issue an apology, no matter how long after the fact.

It's really quite effective.

Too bad it diminishes the spirit.

6. Experience sex.

I'm telling you right now, when I'm on my deathbed, I'm in all likelihood not going to lament the fact that I missed a couple of workouts in June of 2003. Instead, I'm going to regret that I didn't get to screw any Victoria's Secret models; didn't romp naked through fields of wheat with any NFL cheerleaders; didn't spin a lovely naked quadruple amputee across my satin sheets as if she were a dreidel.

Sure it's superficial, but to deny these urges is to deny my essence. I like sex and only have sex with women who feel the same way and I make no apologies.

If I were to do it all over again, I would be much more forthright in stating my wants to women. I wouldn't waste so much time discussing excruciating minutiae in the hopes of striking some chord that would convince them to allow me to bed them. I learned that fact eventually, but I think of all that pussy I wasted. What a tragedy.

7. Don't do anything you don't want to do.

A few months ago, I was doing some serious, major-league bitching to Tim Patterson about having to attend some boring meeting where I'd have to make nice with people I'd prefer to shove through a meat grinder. Tim then said something that changed my life: "TC, we've worked hard and we're at a point that we don't have to do anything we don't want to do." And then the clouds parted and from the heavens sprung forth a beautiful light. Birds came out of the trees and placed a garland made of mountain flowers upon my brow. Female pixies arose from the heather and tickled my genitals with ferns until I giggled with glee.

It won't always be possible to only do things that I want to do. Obviously, no male/female relationship can exist without making some sacrifices, but damn, trying to follow this piece of advice has made life a helluva lot more enjoyable.

8. Take big chances.

If Tim Patterson didn't take chances, he'd still be the chief colorist at the Jackie Stallone School of Cosmetology in Miami Beach instead of CEO of Biotest and executive editor of Testosterone Magazine. Likewise, I'd still be at General Dynamics, working on cruise missiles and spending my lunchtime playing football with a football-shaped nuclear payload and wondering why, later, my pee was bright blue and glowed in the dark, instead of being chief flunkie to Tim Patterson, CEO of Biotest and executive editor of Testosterone Magazine.

See? With great risk comes great reward.

Actually, I'm a little better off than I let on, but it's absolutely true that taking chances often leads to huge rewards, both financially, physically, personally, and in every way possible.

If you're unhappy in any way in your life or chosen career and the prospects for natural change seem dim, you owe it to your goddam soul to change things. Figure out what it is you need to do, plan it out, and do it.

What's the worst that could happen?

9. Read everything.

In the movie *Three Days of the Condor*, Robert Redford reads books for the CIA. His job is to find codes or messages being relayed via text by hostile foreign operatives. As a result of the knowledge he's gained by reading anything and everything, he's able to piece together why a renegade CIA within the CIA is trying to kill him. He can tap phones, run evasive patterns while being shot at, and even figure out how a man was murdered when forensics found a dead body with a hole in it but no bullet and only a few drops of water (the killer made a bullet out of ice).

It's fiction, but the lesson wasn't lost on me. Knowledge is cool. It's like a cosmic lock-picking kit. With it, you can figure out almost anything or at least figure out an acceptable solution to everything. Too bad smarts don't earn a lot of respect. It's only when Americans start giving the smartest kid in the class the same accolades as they do their star athletes that we'll see all our problems disappear like so much sausage at a Polish wedding.

Most weight trainers think nothing of spending 15 to 20 hours a week training their body but hardly spend any time training their mind. Give the mind equal time.

10. Try to have some balls.

I was driving home the other day when I saw the following vanity license plate:

CMDR 007

Only it was affixed to a Toyota Camry. Yep, Commander James Bond—Agent 007—traded in his Aston Martin for a freakin' Toyota Camry. Can the apocalypse be far behind?

Alright, so it's just a yuppie nerd who likes to think of himself as Bond, albeit a low-budget, pussified Bond. It probably doesn't mean anything, but it somehow struck me as symbolic of our Testosterone-deprived times.

For God's sake, if you know what mileage your car gets or who has the best deal on patio furniture, it's time to stop microwaving your testicles or whatever it is you do to sterilize them. Look above you. There are stars in the heavens above. Look around you. There are trees, mountains, and rivers to explore, women to fuck, adventures to be had. Screw your car's mileage.

Testicularity is the last vanguard of civilization; what ties us to nature, what makes us want to excel, what makes us want to discover, invent, and conquer. Don't let your balls go the way of the appendix.

That's it. That's my list. So maybe it's not the Tao of Lao Tse, but following my own recommendations—or at least trying to follow them—has served me well so far.

Chapter 2

Let Go of the Rock

"The only people who lose are the ones who cash in their chips and refuse to play another hand."

E very once in a while, I slip into this David Copperfield mode where I start looking back on my life. It doesn't take much to make me start reminiscing like an ex-high school quarterback whose current dose of daily glory is restricted to being the only one at the plant who can throw a 50-pound sack of manure clear to the top of the truck.

Don't get me wrong; it's not like I'm looking back bitterly on any glory days of yesteryear. As far as I'm concerned, these are the glory days, right here, right now and, as a matter of fact, I think I'm the only one at the office who can hurl sacks of manure onto Tim Patterson's truck. (He uses it to fertilize his beloved asparagus plants, shoots of which he gnaws continuously so that he can leave pungent urine in our offices. Apparently, it's just his way of letting us know that he's thinking about us. Personally, I think it'd be easier if he left a Post-it note, but hey, he's the boss.)

It was a breakfast with a friend that triggered this particular walk down memory lane. Harry and I had first met about 12 years ago when I got a job at General Dynamics in San

Diego. We were both technical writers, and our job was to write manuals on how to take apart a top-secret variety of nuclear cruise missiles.

(And to think, most of you slept peacefully at night, not knowing that there was a looney-toon involved in U.S. security. I thought about taking one of the payloads home in my lunchbox so I could use it to threaten retaliation against my landlord for raising my rent, but I thought better of it, considering that he had just attained nuclear capability himself.)

Harry had taken me under his wing and showed me the ropes. We worked together for a couple of years, but I knew from day one that punching a clock to write dull books that no one would ever read wasn't exactly what I wanted to do with my life. We went our separate ways, but we've always stayed in touch. When we met last week for breakfast, we reminisced about our days at General Dynamics. In between bites of his poached eggs, he said, almost wistfully, that that was the last time he'd made more money than me.

Now, Harry's a great guy, a talented guy. He's a good writer, and he's got scores of half-finished books lying around his study. He's also got plans for all kinds of inventions, and most of them aren't half-bad. He never carries through with much of anything, though. Instead, he's stayed pretty much in the same line of work. He now writes about computers instead of cruise missiles but, other than that, not much has changed.

Harry is cursed with an affliction that I call *inertia*. He's one of those guys who'll say things like:

"I'm going to start going to night school so I can get another degree and get a real job."

or...

"I'm going to start working out and dieting next week so I'll be in shape for that reunion."

or even...

"Oh, yeah, one of these days I'm going to get that penis extension, and *then* the girls will come running."

The trouble is, he never does those things. Well, he did get the penis extension but, like a lot of guys, he tried to save some money by doing it himself. Personally, I think it was a mistake to use a bowling ball tied to a bungee cord, but what do I know? It is a lot longer now, but it's not good for much of anything except tying sheets of plywood to the roof of his car. Despite that, Harry is reasonably happy, but I don't think he ever came close to fulfilling his potential.

Now, I'm by no means a big success story in terms of financial riches, but I think I'm a success in *life*. No, no, I'm not going to tell you about all the love in my life for the children and how money can't buy you happiness or any of that, hippie anti-materialism that's now resurfaced as New Age philosophy, so don't worry. It's just that I keep rolling the dice until they come up my way, and when I say I'm going to do something, I generally do it.

It sure wasn't easy, though.

Back in the '80s, I was teaching freshman composition at Eastern Michigan University while working toward my masters in American lit. I was also dinking around the science lab a little bit, contemplating the almost insane wish to work on my master's in microbiology at the same time. I knew, though, that school had given me all it was going to give me. I certainly wasn't going to get a job where I had to spend my evenings reading themes on how some pasty-faced kid spent his summer vacation, and I sure as hell wasn't going to spend my life sitting in a lab somewhere preparing fecal smears for some stick-up-his-ass doctor. No, if I was going to prepare fecal smears, it was going to be for *me* and *me only*!

I knew only two things: I wanted to be "my own man," and I wanted to write. So I rolled the dice. I moved out to Albuquerque to live with my brother. I took my tennis racket, a gym bag full of clothes, and my cheap, pathetic polyester suit, and drove my broken-down Oldsmobile Delta '88 Royale out West.

Of course, Albuquerque wasn't necessarily the city of my dreams, but it was a start, and it was someplace different. I got a job almost immediately working for a small newspaper. Trouble was, it was the *Penny Saver*, and my job had nothing to do with editing or writing; instead, I had to sell ad space. Jobs were hard to come by then, and I couldn't afford to be choosy.

My route was the old section of Albuquerque where hardly anyone spoke English. Unfortunately, I didn't speak Spanish. I sold one ad in four weeks and got fired from the *Penny Saver*. Of course, every experience teaches you something—even the bad ones—and I now know how to say "Go home, you stupid Anglo" in Spanish.

I then got a job selling used cars, at an interest rate of around 18 percent. I worked there for about three months, and I think I sold a total of six cars. I ended up quitting that one, even though they were probably damn close to firing me.

After that, I registered at an employment agency. The job offers came *rolling* in. I got offered a job playing Santa Claus at the mall, even though I weighed all of 160 pounds at the time. I was offered a job as a fertilizer salesman (so the bit about the manure in my opening paragraph isn't far from the truth). I was even interviewed for one job by a guy wearing a gorilla suit (it took me a few shocked minutes to figure out that it was Halloween).

The coup de grace came when I was offered a job as an exterminator. Six years of college and a dual major had taken me to this: sitting in Albuquerque, wearing a suit made of space-age polymers, kissing the ass of a guy who wants to hire me to kill cockroaches. I think fate intervened, though. I had gotten kicked in the right nut about a week before when I was jumped in a parking lot (that's another story), so my scrotal sack looked about the same size and shape as an old Spalding football. So when the guy says to me, "Yeah, you gotta take a physical, but don't worry about it ... we just wanna' make sure you got both nuts," the irony sinks through me like battery acid.

I wasn't even qualified to kill vermin.

I drove my good nut and his friend, Puffy, home from the interview and, as I was cruising back toward my brother's apartment down I-25, some bastard rolled down his window and yelled, for no goddam reason, "Go blow!!!" It wasn't until months later that I figured he had seen my Michigan license plates and was, in fact, yelling "Go Blue!" in a homage to the University of Michigan football team, but my damaged psyche interpreted it as just more proof that the whole world was against me.

When I woke up the next morning, I toyed with the idea of checking out over the nearest cliff, Thelma and Louise–style, but someone had slashed all my tires the night before.

Things picked up the following week, though. A woman—a real hot number, I might add—hired me to be an advertising salesman for *Albuquerque Monthly* magazine. After the interview, she asked me, rather nonchalantly, "You ever fuck your boss?" No, I hadn't, but I didn't think that Leonard, the chief exterminator, was into that sort of thing.

Well, there's always a first time for everything. I got laid that night. Most jobs, I don't even get a blowjob. The next morning, I showed up to work only to find that the doors were padlocked. The owner had decided to close down the place without giving anybody any notice.

Every day, despite all of the crap that was happening to me, I dragged my ass over to Liberty Gym and took out my frustrations on the weights. I was still determined to fix things, and I knew that any job I got was just a stepping stone, or at least something to hold me over until I was able to do what I wanted.

Soon after, I met my future wife, and she believed in me and allowed me to stay home and work on a book about cancer. She also set it up so that I was able to go back to school and take some grad courses in microbiology. The book didn't get picked up, and the courses were only to keep me "in the game," so to speak, but I was slowly getting my self-respect back. I eventually got a job working for a defense contractor as a technical writer and, one day, I applied for a job at General Dynamics in San Diego. They hired me, and Albuquerque was history for us.

That's where I met Harry. I could go on and on and probably bore the shit out of you but, after a couple of years, I got the bright idea of submitting some articles to the bodybuilding magazines. Wonder of wonders, they bought one for a hundred-and-twenty-five bucks! Then they bought another. I sent stuff to *all* of the mags. Soon, I was writing about three or four articles a week and was actually tapping out a meager living on my computer.

After discussing it with my wife, I decided to take a chance and quit my job at General Dynamics to try writing full-time. We set a goal, though: If I wasn't editor-in-chief of a magazine in three years, I was going to quit and try another route. No matter that I had to subjugate my own opinions about bodybuilding and instead report the mostly absurd workout recommendations of what worked out to be close to 500 competitive bodybuilders; I knew I was paying my dues and that some day I'd get to write my own stuff. Eventually, a bloke by the name of Bill Phillips found me, and I fulfilled my goal, a full year early.

That job is ancient history now, but I was able to establish a name for myself in the business. When I left *Muscle Media*, I received no less than five offers to head up different bodybuilding magazines. It's not a way to get rich, certainly, but I call my own shots now. I don't have to punch a clock; I work pretty much whatever hours I want; and I have my self-respect. Tim Patterson also gives me chocolate treats and scratches me behind the ears when I do a good job.

But it could have been very different. I might have settled for selling cars way back when. Worse, I might have stayed in Michigan, not having the courage to take a chance, and letting fate control me rather than the other way around. I took chances, and I didn't give up. I resisted *inertia*.

It's sometimes a lot easier to accept things the way they are, to sit back and complain bitterly to anyone who'll listen, but that's the big difference between people who are happy and people who are miserable.

I think these people don't realize that it really doesn't take all that much courage to change their lives. I don't care if we're talking about working out religiously, changing jobs, getting out of a bad relationship, or moving to a different town. Believe me, you *can't lose*.

Whatever you do, provided that you stay focused, works out. The only people who lose are the ones who cash in their chips and refuse to play another hand. It's like the Chinese allegory of the man caught in the rapids. He's managed to grab hold of a rock, but the raging waters are beating him against the rock over and over again. If he doesn't let go, he'll soon die, but he's afraid to let go because he doesn't know what dangers lie downstream.

Let go of the rock.

Chapter 3

A Hard-on for Talent

"At the risk of sounding cheerleaderish, you have talent; you have artistry that deserves to be cultivated. It might require you to be yourself, to embrace nonconformity, to eschew imitation, but it's there. It might require a shot of confidence, bravery, or a good old-fashioned kick in the pants to bring it out, but you owe it to yourself to figure out what it is."

I've always had a hard-on for talented people. I don't care if I'm watching a short-order cook flip pancakes; if he's good at it, can send the pancakes flip-flopping skywards only to stop just shy of sticking on the ceiling and tumble down again onto a hot griddle, it makes me smile and feel I'm in touch with the divine nature of the universe. (Not that the sweaty guy in a batter-stained tank top is an emissary of God, but you get the picture.)

Oddly, our society doesn't always reward talented people for doing what they're good at. As such, they're often hard to spot. I sometimes have to search under occupational rocks to find these talents.

There are plenty of people, though, whose talents are easily discernible because their talents are marketable and highly visible. Take sports, for instance. I never really gave a rat's ass about basketball but I never missed watching Michael Jordan play. There was such artistry in the way the guy played with the ball, played *away* from the ball, and played with his opponents' heads that it's a goddam pity we couldn't somehow capture the essence of each performance and hang it on the wall somewhere so we could appreciate that enormous talent every day.

I felt the same way watching Muhammad Ali, or Gretzky, or Gail Sayers. I feel the same way now watching Tiger Woods or Barry Bonds. I feel the same way seeing someone do a squat or a power clean the way they're *supposed* to be done. And I think I sense this type of talent brewing in a young rookie shortstop for the San Diego Padres named Khalil Greene. He might not yet be breathing the same rarfied air as the other sports giants, but he's taking an occasional deep gasp.

But sport's hardly the sole domain of talent.

The other night, while watching parts of the Democratic convention, I saw a skinny guy from Illinois take the stage to do the keynote speech for his party. I'd never seen or heard of him before. He had the unlikely name of Barak Obama and he's the son of a Kenyan goat herder—yes, a goat herder—who became president of the *Harvard Law Review* during college and now wants to represent the land of Lincoln as a senator.

Oh my brothers, I heard this strong voice channeling the combined spirit and oratorical skills of Winston Churchill, Martin Luther King, JFK, Ronald Reagan, and Bill Clinton. For a moment, I could have sworn I heard a distant choir of angels laying down a heavenly accompaniment. For the duration of his speech and for a little while longer, I felt that the world was good and all things are possible. I breathed in the scent of lilac and I felt puppy dogs licking my ears.

Now *that's* talent.

In short, this guy was *good*, and screw your political leanings. If just one SOB writes to me, "Yeah, but he's a Democrat," I swear I'll reach out my cyber paw and take a bear-like swipe at your head. Talent doesn't discriminate against political affiliation, race, religion, or sex. It is an equal-opportunity employer.

Then there are the writers, musicians, artists, and architects. The Nabokovs and the Wolfes, the Mozarts and the Lennons, the Picassos and the Gehrys—the stuff they've done is every bit as remarkable as anything seen or heard in nature.

The list is gloriously long. But one thing most of these gifted ones have in common is money. For the most part, they've been richly rewarded for what they do.

The trouble is, some people are reading their success all wrong. They're equating their monetary rewards as their true success and not necessarily what they do or what they give to humanity.

When I was at EAS and running *Muscle Media 2000*, there were two "levels" of workers. The first floor of the building was populated by regular people, the guys and girls who worked in the warehouse, answered the phones, and paid the bills. The second floor, however, was infested with the management people, almost all of whom had been high school buddies with Bill Phillips, the owner.

The people on the first floor weren't allowed to go up to the second floor unless summoned. In keeping with this caste system, the people on the second floor made lots of dough. Almost all of those that lived on the top floor had shiny new BMWs, and when you drove up in the morning and saw all of them lined up in their reserved parking spaces, you could easily see how a lot of passersby thought we were an automobile dealership.

Hardly any of these management types had any discernible amount of talent. Many of them, were it not for Bill, would have, after years of ass kissing, risen to the level of middle management at Woolworth's.

I can remember several conversations where these ersatz Masters of the Universe ridiculed people who made less money than they did, in one instance making fun of a husband of one of the secretaries, a guy I happened to know and like. While he had a degree from college, he had a low-paying job assembling wheelchairs. What they ignored, though, was that this guy was a consummate outdoorsman, a naturalist, hunter, hiker, ecologist. He just liked being outside, felt better and more at ease out of doors, and for that they ridiculed him.

If the apocalypse comes and you're relegated to eating berries and want to know which ones will kill you and which ones won't, this is the guy you want at your side, not some obsequious ass kisser with a shiny BMW.

The outdoorsman had talent, but it wasn't a marketable talent; at least he hadn't yet figured out how to market what he knew and could do. It didn't matter much to him anyhow because he didn't spend a lot of time thinking about money.

Ol' Ralph Waldo Emerson described these EAS pinheads perfectly:

"They measure their esteem of each other by what each has, and not by what each is."

The world is full of these people, the occasionally well-compensated shitheads and the often woefully undercompensated but enormously talented *artists*, the Michael Jordans of some other, less glamorous world.

I use the word "artist" because that's what all talented individuals are. Medicine practiced well is an art, as is engineering. Hell, doing a tax return well is an art form, as is baking a damn pie.

Consider my friend, Franz. He was raised in Communist East Germany before the wall came down. Franz didn't know who his parents were and even when his birthday was. As a young adult, he managed to escape to the United States where he literally bought the identity of an American boy who had died at the age of 10. Franz adopted the dead kid's last name and his Social Security number so he could stay in a country where talent can express itself in a whole lot of ways.

Today, Franz owns a small coffee shop where he serves sandwiches and pastries that he bakes himself. It's not a glorious career and it's probably not going to be all that lucrative, but let me tell you, if anyone ever turned owning a coffee shop into an art form, it's Franz.

Franz makes it a point to know every customer's name and what they drink. He knows what they do for a living and how many kids they have. He gives away as many coffees and as much food as he sells. If a new business comes into town, he'll send over 20 free cafe' lattes. A few hours later, he'll send over some of the pastries he makes at 4:30 in the morning, followed by some more lattes. He'll even deliver a coffee to your house if you're under the weather, and if there's a charity event in town, he'll wheel over his portable espresso machine and donate his time.

The result? A coffee shop that's become the social hub of the town, a place where people know each other and talk to each other and feel comfortable. What's more, there's always a line out the door and the cash register rings all day long like the phones at TicketMaster when the Stones come to town.

Ever wonder why so many places go out of business? Because the owners didn't turn running the business into an art form. They don't have the talent that Franz does.

I've got this theory about talent and artistry. I feel that to be good at something, you have to have read everything ... or read nothing. Only then is the mind unfettered by convention, unfettered by the work or thoughts of others. Only then can you do truly original, truly talented work.

I've often seen uneducated garage mechanics pick up a blowtorch and start creating incredible and totally original pieces of art with discarded metal. However, had they studied just a little bit, they might have been influenced by the work of others, or worse yet, felt that they weren't qualified to create *real* art.

By not reading anything, they're fresh. They can't imitate or copy or conform because they haven't seen anything else. Likewise, the guy who studies for years and years and sees everything can also tackle art with a fresh perspective because he's been influenced by everybody and can emerge from all that influence as fresh and innocent as the novice.

Picasso is an example of the latter. He studied conventional art, learned to paint objects as if his eye were merely a camera lens. However, as the years went by, his sensibilities left all that influence behind and he started creating artwork the likes of which had never been seen before.

I believe this lessen can transfer over to almost any occupation, any line of work. Obviously, a doctor or engineer or scientist has to study the rules, but once he knows them it takes a little imagination and a lot of courage to turn that talent into art. To quote Emerson again, "Whoso would be a man, must be a nonconformist."

I also think that everybody has some kind of talent, some little piece of divinity that is his or hers alone. Too often, though, this talent is hidden, undiscovered, or squelched by people with influence who denigrate that talent as not being marketable.

At the risk of sounding cheerleaderish, you have talent; you have artistry that deserves to be cultivated. It might require you to be yourself, to embrace nonconformity, to eschew imitation, but it's there. It might require a shot of confidence, bravery, or a good old-fashioned kick in the pants to bring it out, but you owe it to yourself to figure out what it is.

Most of all though, you owe it to the rest of us so we can enjoy it and benefit from it, you Michael Jordan–in-hiding, you.

Chapter 4

The Testosterone Man Defined

"Testosterone and its partner-in-arms, manhood, is like standing on a bluff overlooking the ocean on a sunny day and diving in, emerging from the spray of the surf into the cool breeze like King Neptune, only to be greeted by something beautiful with big tits lying in the sand."

I've begun to notice a disturbing trend among women I know. On one hand, the unmarried ones I know tolerate me, even *like* me. The pervert-turned-athlete-turned-scholar thing that I've got going doesn't bother them. They've come to expect and even appreciate my lusty nature, and they don't mind that I've read a bit here and there and can also unscrew the lid from the toughest peanut butter jar in the known universe.

A few of them also think that I'm not entirely repugnant; that I'm easy on the eyes, if the eyes happen to be a little myopic.

But to the married ones? I'm the flu. I'm a piece of spoiled fruit. The spider in the shower. Kobe Bryant at their daughter's graduation party. Twelve miles of bad road. An unpleasant odor. A boil on the butt. When the pest-control guy drives by, they see my face on the side of the truck instead of a cockroach.

In other words, they're not particularly fond of me.

Why do they, by and large, have a different opinion of me than the single women? Simple. The married women perceive me as a threat. My very presence in their house somehow destabilizes their marriage. And it's not that I've got some delusion that they'd rather bed me than the chipmunk they're married to; rather, I'm seen as being a bad influence on their husband.

I'm a man who hasn't been psychically neutered by women or our culture. I say exactly what I'm thinking. I tell bawdy stories. I make appreciative remarks about women's cleavage or tight buns. When I leave the room, I don't hug everybody and ask for the recipe and exclaim how the experience has changed my freakin' life. In short, I speak what I think is the truth.

When a lot of married men get around me, they're reminded of what life used to be like: bedroom romps with wanton girls who prance around wearing nothing but high heels; vacationing in Tahiti instead of with the kids at Disney World; and watching football all day long because that's what he feels like doing. I remind them of what it felt like when their tongues weren't scarred and mangled from continually biting them. Yep, I somehow remind them of freedom.

I'm the stray dog humping a poodle in their front yard while they watch from their comfortable homes with their noses pressed against the window. The women sense it and want to shield their hubbies from me like a mother shields a child from the carnage of a traffic accident. Too much of me and hubby might stray; worse yet, he might start acting like a man (*shudder*).

But the women shouldn't regard me as a threat. If anything, I should be perceived as a revitalizing tonic because I think I could help some hubbies reconnect with their manhood, the end result being a stronger, better relationship that has a fighting chance of making both parties happy and avoiding situations like the one in the following bit of dialog from, *American Beauty*:

Carolyn (Annette Bening): *Janie, your father and I were just discussing his day at work. Why don't you tell our daughter about it, honey?*

Lester (Kevin Spacey): *Janie, today I quit my job. I also told my boss to fuck himself, and then blackmailed him for almost sixty thousand dollars. Pass the asparagus.*

Carolyn: *Your father seems to think this kind of behavior is something to be proud of.*

Lester: *And your mother seems to prefer I go through life like a fucking prisoner while she keeps my dick in a mason jar under the sink.*

I think the problem is that some of these married women don't understand the type of unbridled manhood we extol here in Testosterone Nation. These women see manhood and its essence, Testosterone, as being *evil*. That's too bad because it's anything but evil.

This all points to a major contradiction in men's lives: Women, when they let their loins do the talking, prefer "manly" men, but when their hormones are disrupted and their emotions are swizzle-sticked—often by the institution of marriage itself—they want "safe" men, men who'll take them shopping every Sunday for eternity and dutifully drag dusty pieces of antique furniture into the back seat of the Volvo.

No wonder American men are so fucked up.

So maybe it's time to revisit the philosophy we created in the early months of T-Nation, time to redefine a little thing we describe as "being a T-Man."

Contrary to what the uninitiated might think, being a T-Man doesn't have that much to do with being physically powerful or imposing. Sure, T-Man is deeply interested in improving his body, but the alleys, halfway houses, and prisons are filled with powerful men. Instead, being a T-Man is a sublime blend of intellect, integrity, and the burning desire to *improve* himself physically and mentally.

He doesn't buy into the notion that all men are created equal, but he believes those who fall short should stop whining and get off their ass and *do* something about it. In fact, he's usually contemptuous toward failure or excuses of any kind. This sentiment is perhaps best captured by Sean Connery's character in *The Rock*:

"*Your best? Losers always whine about their best. Winners go home and fuck the prom queen.*"

And let's get specific about building his mind. Formal schooling and a degree are fine things, but learning occurs everywhere, not just in the classroom. Some of the brightest people I know didn't even finish high school, let alone college. And don't think I'm talking about the cliché known as "street smarts." Yeah, yeah, street smarts are fine, but I'm talking about rigorous self-education through books and the successes and failures of applied knowledge.

T-Man honors the aged and the disadvantaged, treating those who can do him no good equally to those who can. He's not petty or vindictive and he struggles to keep his ego in check.

He doesn't bow to authority and occasionally even breaks inane laws that were implemented because of some governing body's puritanical views or lack of scientific understanding.

T-Man probably couldn't be president. He wouldn't want to bad-mouth his opponent or opponents incessantly. Instead, he'd advertise his own strengths. And he'd lack the necessary ability to kiss a lot of ass. He might even be labeled "too smart." As such, the voters would deem him "out of touch." He probably leans more to a libertarian ideal, believing that government should help where it can but otherwise stay the hell out of his business.

T-Man acknowledges that which he believes about women: *They are indeed* sex objects, but sex objects that are treated respectfully, almost reverentially. In other words, T-Man doesn't lie about the fact that he'd like to bone everything female that moves but he doesn't manipulate, bully, or worse yet, force women to acquiesce to his desires. If being courteous and masculine doesn't get us what we want, we say "thanks" and go shopping elsewhere.

In no way does this way of thinking interfere with his belief that women are equal and that they be treated as such in pay, employment, status, and any other social construct. Of course, just because a woman is our boss doesn't mean we're not picturing her naked.

Men are what we are and denying that our urges exist is disingenuous.

Along the same lines, we treat beautiful women well, and ugly ones even better because ... well, because it's the right thing to do.

T-Man battles injustice and fights when necessary. Women shouldn't want to squelch this masculine impulse because when the bad guys come, they don't want a pants-pissing "soul mate" or "spiritual partner" to protect them; they want someone with a tank full of high-octane Testosterone around, one who embraces the following H.L. Mencken line:

"Every normal man must be tempted at times to spit upon his hands, hoist the black flag, and begin slitting throats."

Once in a while, T-Man finds himself in an office, social situation, or relationship, wondering how he got himself into this soul-sucking quagmire and all he can think about is tearing off his tie and marching triumphantly out of the office; throwing his drink into the face of the asshole who's droning on about his stock portfolio; or telling the harpy he's dating or living with that he'd like his balls back right now, thank you, and please pass the asparagus.

While all T-Men experience one or all of those aforementioned scenarios or desires, his decision on whether to actually follow through with the desire is based on reason and not emotion. Of course, if reason agrees with emotion, then it's time to get the hell out of Dodge.

Most of all, we revel in our manhood. It's the *best thing* we've got going. You know those stupid Yoplait commercials where the two women compare the taste of their yogurt to something pleasant in life? Well, Testosterone and its partner-in-arms, manhood, is like standing on a bluff overlooking the ocean on a sunny day and diving in, emerging from the spray of the surf into the cool breeze like King Neptune, only to be greeted by something beautiful with big tits lying in the sand.

Now why would any woman want to take that feeling away from you? Worse yet, why wouldn't any woman want a man like that at her side?

Chapter 5

The Last Stand of the Dinosaurs

"There's a right way and a wrong way to play this 'game.' You're playing it the wrong way, and the rest of us don't like it."

American sports fans are in their glory this time of year. They wake up each morning, smile at the sun, and declare that life is good.

We are, after all, in what sports-fan astrologers call the *cusp* of the football season. The baseball season is winding down, and the pennant races are heating up. Likewise, college football is in full swing, and the gridiron pros are just starting to see what kind of team they've managed to put together in the off-season.

Oh, yeah, when the American sports fan gets up in the morning to relieve himself during this time of year, he no doubt does it while humming the Notre Dame fight song. As he dons his fuzzy bathrobe and ventures outside in the crisp autumn air to harvest his precious sports section, he can't help but do a couple of Terrell Davis–type feints to shake off an entire backfield of imaginary defensive ends. As he picks up the tightly rolled-up newspaper, he simultaneously tosses an acorn into the air and smacks it into old man Patterson's yard, imagining that he's Big Mac and he's just hit number 71. *Oh, baby*!

Yep, life is pretty good for American sports fans right now.

America, and the world for that matter, is obsessed with sport. A few years back, NBA commissioner David Stern was traveling in China—not on business, but as a tourist. His journey had brought him deep into the heart of China, where non-Asians were a relative rarity. While exchanging pleasantries with a couple of locals, one of them asked Stern what he did for a living back in the US. Stern replied that he was a lawyer and worked for something called the National Basketball Association. One of the peasants replied:

"Oh, yes, I am a great fan of the Chicago Red Ox and Michael Jordan."

Sport is universal, although language apparently still has its glitches.

Figuring out why we love sport is probably a waste of time, somewhat akin to figuring out why humans like backrubs or why it feels good when we rub up against the washer when it's on the spin cycle. That's just the way it is. And believe me, I don't want to analyze this human trait, but it's probably also second nature for humans to seek out heroes who, because of some almost freakish ability, are able to do things most of us can't. Sport provides a forum for those heroes. We enjoy their athletic prowess—their heroism, if you will—and we live vicariously through their experiences.

The trouble is, too often the moral make-up of these heroes doesn't mesh very well with the hero status we confer on them. If you habitually read the "Sports in the Courts" section of the paper, you get a sobering dose of reality. Leon Lett of the Cowboys just received his fifth drug suspension. Fourteen UCLA football players were caught using handicapped-parking stickers. Football legend Jim Brown was acquitted of beating his wife, although he was found guilty of whuppin' her car to death. Bad guy Bill Romanowski of the Broncos cops to phentermine addiction and prescription fraud, but I don't think it explained why he used the face of an opposing player as a spittoon on *Monday Night Football.*

Likewise, we have Darryl Strawberry's on-again, off-again drug problems surfacing in the paper with a regularity that rivals the swallows returning to Capistrano every year. Dennis Rodman was a good player, but he could have been great if he had managed to discipline his mind a bit and stay out of Madonna's snatch. Mike Tyson has turned out to be a real piece of work, and we don't even need to talk about O.J. Simpson.

It's almost enough to make you want to hide the sports section from your impressionable son or daughter.

Of course, there are sports figures that seem to be pretty good guys. Sammy Sosa, so far, hasn't exposed himself, beat up anybody, or bet on baseball. He just smiles a lot and keeps on smackin' home runs. Mark McGwire, now available in the androstenedione-free version, is still hitting homers on a per-at-bat pace that exceeds anyone's in the history of the sport. Okay, so it turned out that Mark and Saammy were probably on steroids. Hindsight is 20/20. Football's aging superstar Dan Marino is trying to win a Super Bowl before retiring. Tennis star Andre Agassi, while hobnobbing with his ex-wife, mono-browed actress Brooke Shields, had all but disappeared from the rankings until he got rid of his boyish bullshit, got serious, and was crowned number one in the tennis world last week.

San Diego Padres outfielder Tony Gwynn quietly surpassed 3,000 hits this year, all while maintaining a lifetime batting average that's downright stratospheric. Although he could have been one of the sport's richest players, he decided that money was secondary, and he chose to remain with a small-market team throughout his entire career because he just plain-old liked living in San Diego. Baltimore Orioles infielder Cal Ripken is also marching toward his 3,000th hit, and his consecutive-game record is a testament to gutsy hard work.

Grant Hill of the Pistons is basketball's contribution to the good guy's team. He works with a number of charities in Detroit, and you get the distinct impression that his concern is genuine and not merely a PR move suggested by his agent. He's articulate and educated, and the lanky SOB even plays a pretty mean classical piano. His parents, both working professionals, were determined to bring him up without the encumbrance of a swelled head.

There are, of course, good and bad, although the ranks of the bad are a little too crowded. I guess that's what happens when you live in a society that gives so much leeway to sports heroes. They're largely excused from playing by the rules because they provide us with too much entertainment. If we made them bend to the rules the rest of us have to follow, we'd be depriving ourselves of the pleasure they provide. It ain't right, but it's the way it is.

Still, I'd like to tell you about my sports hero. His fans referred to him as "Pudge," but most casual baseball fans remember him as Carlton Fisk. Now, I know what the baseball fans among you are thinking. You're assuming that I'm a huge Boston Red Sox fan and that the homer he hit in the twelfth inning of the sixth game of the 1975 World Series against the Cincinnati Reds changed my life or something.

Okay, okay, so I watched the game, and that's about the last time I can remember crying in my life, but it's not why Pudge is my hero. In fact, it has nothing to do with his sports achievements. He was a capable player who had moments of heroism and exhibited remarkable longevity while playing a position that's the most debilitating in the game, but Pudge is my hero for another reason.

I'll always have a soft spot in my heart for him because of a game that was played early in the 1990 baseball season. Fisk was catching for the Chicago White Sox at the ripe old age of 43, and the Sox were playing the Yankees. Fisk was behind the plate when flashy 22-year-old outfielder "Neon" Deion Sanders came up to bat. Neon hit a soft fly ball to the outfield—an easy out. He trotted casually to first base and, before the ball was even caught (or missed), he took a right turn and headed toward the dugout. He must have heard footsteps, because he suddenly turned around, only to find a six-foot-two, red-faced Carlton Fisk—a player on the *opposing* team—screaming into his face:

"Run it out, you piece of crud!!! Go ahead, run it out!!!"

Neon was completely baffled as he walked toward the dugout. The game continued, and the next time Sanders came to bat, he turned to Pudge behind the plate and said:

"The days of slavery are over."

Fisk stood up and, as the veins in his neck and forehead started to swell and pulse, he replied:

"Let me tell you something, you little shit. There's a right way and a wrong way to play this game. You're playing it the wrong way, and the rest of us don't like it. Someday, you're going to get this game shoved right down your throat."

Well, both benches cleared.

Afterward, Fisk explained himself, saying that he did it ... "for truth, justice, and the American way, and to keep [baseball legend] Lou Gehrig from spinning in his grave."

Later on, *Washington Post* columnist Thomas Boswell wrote a tribute to Pudge, a portion of which said:

"I call it the last stand of the dinosaurs. We may never see the like of it in any pro sport. So relish it."

Man, I got another tear in my eye just reliving the event.

Now, I don't know if weight training is a sport, but I don't care. It's what I do, and if you're reading this, it's most likely what you do. Granted, it has moments of heroism (tell me that going to the gym four, five, or six days a week and beating yourself up isn't heroic in some sense), but it's not a spectator sport, and very few people would pay to watch us train.

Still, when I'm in the gym, it's my stadium, ballpark, and arena all rolled into one. And when I see "players" pulling a Neon Deion by reading the paper while they're doing leg presses or one-arm "concentration" curls, I feel like pulling a Pudge on them and screaming into their face:

"Hey, Dorian Yates, at least pretend like you give a shit about what you're doing, or take your limp dick home!"

Likewise, when I see somebody making small talk about the stock market or radial tires—*talking*, for Chrissake—during a set of half-assed squats or bench presses, I want to take the Olympic bar, squeeze it against their necks till the spittle starts to bubble out of the corner of their mouth, and tell them:

"There's a right way and a wrong way to play this game. You're playing it the wrong way, and the rest of us don't like it, shithead."

I have no idea what Carlton Fisk is doing nowadays, but I'd venture to say that he feels pretty good about himself, knowing that even if he didn't make it to baseball's Hall of Fame, he gave the game his all.

Let's all go to the gym and make Pudge proud.

Chapter 6

The Kid

"Men like Ted Williams are often regarded as surly, difficult, and all-around pains in the ass. However, men like Ted, whatever their occupation, make all of us want to be better at what we do. So, baseball fan or not, tip a glass to Ted Williams tonight."

"MY NAME IS TED FUCKING WILLIAMS AND I'M THE GREATEST HITTER IN BASEBALL!"

That's what Ted Williams would yell, at the top of his lungs, when he was taking batting practice. And then he'd belt a line drive into the stands.

"JESUS H. CHRIST HIMSELF COULDN'T GET ME OUT!"

And then he'd thwack another.

People would say he was psyching himself up for the game, but maybe they didn't know or understand Ted very well. More likely he was just expressing his thoughts at that particular moment, the thoughts of a guy who was so chockfull of Testosterone that it oozed out of him and permeated the air where it blocked out the smells of peanuts and Cracker Jack.

Hell, in his later years, when he spent his days playing tennis or fishing for tarpon in Florida, he would yell all the time, just because he was Ted Williams and if he felt like yelling, by God he was going to yell.

"TED WILLIAMS IS GONNA HAVE A DRINK!" he'd yell before pouring himself a tumbler of scotch.

"YOU SYPHILITIC SON OF A BITCH!" he'd scream when he hit a tennis ball a little too deep.

"HOW D'YA FEEL? HOW OLD ARE YOU? … JUST WORRIED ABOUT YOUR HEART HA HA HAW!" he'd yell at his tennis opponents.

"IT'S HORSESHIT!" he'd yell when asked how the fishing was.

People thought he shouted because he'd gone a little deaf from flying all those combat missions in Korea but close friends said that wasn't the case, that he shouted because there was just too much *juice* in the man.

Neighbors said that ol' Ted "don't do mucha' anything he don't want to do." On the other hand, ol' Ted pretty much did exactly what he wanted to do, anytime he *wanted* to do it. He never went anywhere that he had to wear a tie and he never went to parties because he'd have to spend time "LISTENING TO A BUNCH OF BULLSHIT."

Ted Williams died last Friday at the age of 83, and when a man like that passes, it diminishes us all. It's like almighty death stuck a siphon down into our collective pool of Testosterone and left us sputtering on fumes because, based on what I see everyday and read about in the paper, there ain't many men out there today who have testicles too much bigger than the period at the end of this sentence.

As such, I feel that a few words should be written about this politically incorrect dinosaur. He wasn't an intellectual. In many ways, he was deeply flawed. At times he was coarse and brutal, at other times heroic and compassionate, but you can bet your ass that he was a man and that entails a whole bunch of conflicting traits that those who aren't men—genetically or endocrinologically—can't fully comprehend.

Most of you have read about his baseball achievements: how he had a career average of .344; hit 521 home runs; earned two MVP awards; won the Triple Crown twice; was the last man to bat over .400; and was six-time American League batting champ. The list of baseball achievements goes on and on.

That's all impressive stuff, probably even to the non-baseball fan, but it doesn't do much to describe or explain the essence of the man.

TED WAS BORN in San Diego in 1918, and while I don't want to get into too much of that David Copperfield crap about his disadvantaged childhood, I will say that from early on Ted took his baseball seriously.

He carried his bat everywhere, even to school and classes. At night, he'd stand in front of the mirror in his underwear practicing his swing. And when he grew too tall too fast and was nothing but arms and legs, he started doing push-ups to build up his strength. Twenty-five, thirty-five, fifty, and then a hundred. And then he'd work up to a hundred doing them on his fingertips.

From early on, all he wanted in life was that when he walked down the street, people would say, "There goes Ted Williams, the greatest hitter who ever lived."

And so with that thought in mind, he worked toward his goal. The only thing that ever got in his way was himself. While he got along great with people he respected, he didn't suffer fools too gladly. He was combative toward convention, formality, dopes, a good number of sportswriters, and fans who had the gall to boo him.

Once, while in the minors, a fan made the mistake of booing him while he was at bat. Ted smacked the next pitch into the stands in an attempt to kill the bastard. Only trouble was, he hit the wrong guy. That kind of stuff, and his habit of sitting down in the outfield between batters and slapping his ass and yelling "Hi-Ho Silver!" as he ran down fly balls made his baseball superiors think twice about promoting him to the majors, but only for a microsecond. The Kid, as he became known, was just too damn good a hitter to keep down in the minors.

In 1939 he's called up by the Boston Red Sox. In his rookie year, he bats .327 with 31 homers and 145 RBI. He's the first to the ballpark and the last to leave. He spends an inordinate time boning his bats—literally rubbing the surface with a bone—and not just the handle like other players, but the whole bat, compressing the wood fiber to make the bat harder. No sonuvabitch baseball was going to stay in the yard if he had anything to say about it. Then he'd go to the post office and have his bats weighed, just to make sure they were the correct weight. And, just like he had always done, he'd stay up half the night in his hotel room swinging his bat in front of the mirror.

Once, when the team's on the road and the Kid's rooming with a pitcher named Charlie Wagner, Wagner wakes up after a loud crash and finds himself on the floor with the bed around him. Williams, in his zeal, had accidentally thwacked the bedpost while practicing his swing. Does he apologize? Nahh, the kid just steps back and admires his power.

But no matter how good he got, how many hits he got, he wasn't happy. Even after going 3 for 4, Ted would stew in his hotel room, telling himself that no HORSESHIT pitcher was going to keep him down.

On the next to last day of his third season in the big leagues, in September of 1941, Ted was batting .39955. According to baseball convention, they'd have to round that number up to .400, making Ted the first ballplayer to reach that hallowed ground since the 1920s. So his manager urged him to sit out the doubleheader the next day to protect his average.

Taking a seat was HORSESHIT to Ted, and so he played both games. He went 6 for 8 and finished the year with a .406 batting average. No one has reached .400 since. "IF I WAS BEING PAID $30,000 A YEAR," Williams said later, "THE LEAST I COULD DO WAS HIT .400."

But did the nation pay much attention? Nope, they were too busy singing about Joltin' Joe DiMaggio, who hit in 56 straight games and got the league's Most Valuable Player award, even though the Kid had better numbers. If only the Kid had smiled once in awhile, been a little, you know, congenial, maybe tipped his hat to the fans occasionally. BUT THAT'S HORSESHIT!

The next season, Ted's demons got hold of him again. Some punk in the stands started riding him hard, so when Ted got up to bat, he hit a line drive into the stands in an attempt to surgically remove the kid's head from his shoulders. He missed, so he took another swing. This time, though, the ball landed *fair*. Dumbstruck, Ted just stood there looking at the ball. He finally did run, but he was almost tagged out at second. His manager fined him $250 for loafing, but the truth was that the hit had just caught him by surprise.

Later that year, despite getting a deferment, Williams joined the Navy and spent the next three years learning how to fly fighter jets. The trouble was, no base commander was too keen on letting their star attraction be shipped overseas, so his orders were slow in coming. And just when Lieutenant Williams is to be shipped off to Hawaii, Japan caves in and surrenders.

So it's back to baseball and on opening day in 1946, despite having been away from the majors for three years, Ted hits a 400-foot home run. And he proceeds to hit one after another and tear up the league.

One manager, tired of having his team be the personal whipping boys of the Kid, decides to retaliate. Since Ted is a left-handed batter and pulls the majority of his balls to right field, the opposing manager, Lou Boudreau of Cleveland, decides to put all his players—with the exception of the left fielder—over to the right side of the field! Williams can't believe what he's seeing.

The Kid laughs but deep down he thinks it's HORSESHIT! But rather than taking the easy way out and plunking hits to left field, he attacks the shift. He hits again and again into the overloaded right side of the field. Other managers copy the scheme, and the Kid's batting average drops almost 30 points. The Boston press calls him selfish for not hitting to the other side.

Finally he relents and starts slapping pitches to left field, no doubt smirking as the lone outfielder scampers after the ball. At the end of the season he wins the MVP award again.

In 1950, during the All-Star Game, Ted refuses to recognize the outfield wall's right to stand before him and he crashes into it, knocking 13 pieces off his elbow. The surgeons tell him he's through, but two months later he's back and he goes four for four with a home run in his first game.

And then the Korean War start. Marine Lieutenant Williams is called to service in 1953 and proceeds to fly 37 missions and win three air medals. He narrowly escapes death when his plane is shot and catches fire.

A battle-worn Williams comes back to the majors in late '53. But baseball revitalizes the 35-year-old Kid, and in his first appearance at the plate in two years, during a pinch-hitting appearance in the bottom of the seventh, he hits a home run. At the end of his short season, he's batting .407 but doesn't win the batting title because he doesn't have enough at-bats to qualify.

Year after year, the hitting, the sheer excellence, continues. On each opening day, when the anthem is playing, he can feel the hairs on the back of his neck rising and he swears to himself, "This is the year … the best ever …"

In spring training in 1954, he busts his collarbone. The surgeons tell him he's through. But six weeks later, he comes back to play in a double-header and goes 8 for 9 with two home runs.

Later that year, he's booed by hometown fans for making an error, so while at the plate, he first spits toward the right-field fans, then toward the fans in left. When they continue to boo him after he's returned to the dugout, the Kid, in a fit of rage and disdain, comes running out and gives the fans a spit shower. He looks like one of those spasmodic lawn sprinklers!

The love-hate relationship he's had with the Boston fans and the press tips a little more to the hate side. They can't forgive him. After all, the sonuvabitch doesn't even tip his hat to the fans. Not *ever*.

FUCK 'EM! thinks Ted. But it gets to him. In 1958, after a called third strike, he throws his bat into the stands and accidentally conks an old lady on the head. He retreats to the dugout sobbing.

But Ted, regardless of all the shit raining down on him, seemed to thrive on being angry. They say there were plenty of women around who'd be willing to help him drive the demons away, but half-kidding he'd grab his crotch and cry, "WOMEN? ALL THEY WANT IS WHAT I GOT RIGHT HERE!"

He had a sub-par year in 1959 after having hurt his neck in the spring. For the first time, he's benched. Despite the wishes of a lot of his friends, Williams decides to come back for one more year. Everyone thinks he's washed up. After all, the son of a bitch is 42! But he comes back in 1960 and hits 29 home runs and bats .316.

In storybook fashion, he hits a home run in his last at bat. And as he runs into the dugout, he thinks about finally doffing his cap to the fans, but he thinks SCREW IT and doesn't.

With baseball behind him, Ted retires to Florida (although he did come back briefly to manage the Washington Senators and win the Manager of the Year award in 1969). He sets his goals anew and decides to become the greatest fisherman that ever lived.

Does he waste any time thinking about what baseball records could have been his had he not given up five years to the military? How he probably could have been the greatest home run hitter of all time? SHUT UP, YOU'RE SCARING THE FISH.

In 1961, while flying home from New Zealand (where he'd gone fishing), he spots a leggy model sitting across the aisle from him. He writes a note on a piece of paper and throws it at her. She looks at him with disdain and unfolds the note. It says, "WHO ARE YOU?" She writes her own note, crumples it up, and throws it back. It says, "Who are YOU?"

He writes back, "Mr. WILLIAMS. A FISHERMAN."

They start dating. He doesn't even tell her he's TED MOTH-ERFUCKING WILLIAMS until the third date. Later that year, they're married.

But Ted was married a lot of times. It takes a special kind of woman to handle that much Testosterone—SOMEONE WHO CAN STAND UP TO HIS HORSESHIT—so none of them lasted long. In fact, his love affair with fishing lasted longer than any of them.

Oh yeah, he loved tarpon and bonefish and salmon, and he treats fishing the same way he did baseball, getting the best equipment, tying his own flies, learning how the fish *think*. The other fishermen respect him, but people around town begin to think he's cheap, especially the restaurateurs: "No, he doesn't come in. He's too cheap. He'd go all over town, sonuvabitch, and he'd pay by check, hoping they wouldn't cash the check, that they'd put it on the wall."

But the Kid doesn't worry about horseshit like that.

One day, while accompanied by a reporter during yet anoth-er fishing excursion, he says, "AIN'T NO ONE ON HEAVEN OR EARTH EVER KNEW MORE ABOUT FISHING."

"Sure there is," answers the reporter.

"OH YEAH, WHO?' snorts the Kid.

"Well, God made the fish."

"YEAH, ALRIGHT. BUT YOU HAD TO GO PRETTY FAR BACK."

Up until the Kid died last week, people really did say, "There goes Ted Williams, the greatest hitter who ever lived," whenever he walked by. They didn't say that he was the greatest fisherman that ever lived, but if you asked the fish, they might have begrudged you the point.

Men like Ted Williams are often regarded as surly, difficult, and all-around pains in the ass. However, men like Ted, whatever their occupation, make all of us want to be better at what we do. So, baseball fan or not, tip a glass to Ted Williams tonight.

Bibliography

Ball Four, by Jim Bouton. Macmillan, New York, New York, 1970, 1981, 1990.
"Little Respect for the Splendid Splinter," by Richard Corliss, *Time*, July 15, 2002, page 72.
USA Today, Monday, July 8, 2002, Section C, Page 6.
"What Do You Think of Ted Williams Now?" by Richard Ben Cramer, *Esquire*, June, 1986, pp. 74-92.

Chapter 7

Now That's a Problem!

"Everyone's suing someone. Suing because their feelings were hurt; suing because fast food made them fat; suing because the rectal thermometer they used elicited homosexual feelings that had previously lain dormant."

There is a sound that haunts the people who live on the outskirts of Nairobi, Kenya.

It is not the roar of Numa the lion, nor is it the hiss of Histah the snake.

Instead, it is a man-made sound:

Thwip-thwip-thwip-thwip-THWUNK!

Thwip-thwip-thwip-thwip-THWUNK!

It is the sound of bags of shit flying through the air and hitting the corrugated metal roofs of their sheds.

That's right, bags of shit, or as they've become known in Kenya, "flying toilets." The problem is that in an area populated by roughly 2,000 people, there are only five conventional, sit-down, closed-door toilets, and they're pay toilets at that.

So, rather than wait in a line of what's often a hundred people, with or without newspapers in their hands, most simply go outside, shit on a piece of polythene paper, wrap it up, and chuck it as far as they can. Given the density of the sheds the people live in, the odds of one hitting your roof or landing right outside your door are pretty high.

The chance that one of these Third World FedEx packages will land on your head probably isn't quite as high, but that doesn't mean residents don't walk around with at least one cautious eye scanning the sky for shit projectiles. Maybe this is one of the reasons why Kenya produces so many amazingly fast runners.

Horrible poverty, poor sanitation, and flying bags of shit? Now *that's* a problem.

A couple of weeks ago, National Public Radio played some of the radio segments from around the world that had been awarded medals at the radio version of the Oscars. One of them was a first-person audio diary of a young girl with cystic fibrosis. In case you're not familiar with the disease, cystic fibrosis is fatal. Your lungs produce so much mucus that you can't breathe properly. Infection after infection sets in until your lungs become gossamer-thin. Eventually, they cease to function altogether, and you die.

This particular girl, armed with a tape recorder, made verbal entries into the machine over the course of two years. At the time the tape was finished she was 20 years old, which, in cystic fibrosis terms, is ancient.

She had seen most of her friends with the disease die long ago. She was quite cognizant of the fact that she could go at any time.

The audio diary was filled with segments where she'd gasp into the microphone from her hospital bed, explaining to the audience that would someday hear her tapes that the wheezing noise was the sound of her lungs trying to breathe.

She recently received a lung transplant, but now she has to deal with her body's endless attempts to reject the organs. Despite all of this, she doesn't really complain and, as she concluded her radio diary, she said that she didn't know if she'd live another day or another year. But she explained that either way, "I guess that's okay."

Cystic fibrosis and the knowledge that your days are numbered? Now that's a problem.

I've got a friend who's at the Mayo Clinic right now. He's suffering from inexplicable kidney failure. I've got another friend who has colon cancer. Another just got divorced.

Failed kidneys, colon cancer, and divorce? Now *those* are obviously problems.

Then there's the other end of the complaint spectrum.

The son of a friend just got cut from his college football team. He was a hotshot in high school, but college is a whole other universe. The son didn't have an inkling of what it took to excel in sport, nor did he have the requisite drive or will. Instead, he dropped out of school and blames the coach for not recognizing his greatness. He's destined to be one of those bitter sons of bitches who spends each day fantasizing about what could have been … if not for that bastard coach.

A friend of a friend bores the hell out of us whenever we see him because he's always complaining about how he can't afford a house in today's market and how there should be subsidized housing. "Tell me," I feel like saying to him, "where in the Constitution does it say everybody gets to have a house? It doesn't. You have to work for it, you putz."

Likewise, everywhere I look, someone's complaining about something. The editorial pages are filled with letters from indignant tightassess about the outrage of the week, which currently happens to be how "morally repugnant" it was for CBS to air the *The Victoria's Secret Fashion Show* a couple of weeks back. Man, these people, mostly women, probably turn out the lights and put on latex gloves before jacking off their husbands.

The week before, they were similarly outraged about rap lyrics, or the violence of video games.

The advice columns are filled with letters from losers who can't hold jobs or stay in relationships. They blame everyone but themselves.

Everyone's suing someone. Suing because their feelings were hurt; suing because fast food made them fat; suing because the rectal thermometer they used elicited homosexual feelings that had previously lain dormant.

Psychiatrists' offices are filled with people who blame their parents for every shortcoming they have. Sure, you visit laundry rooms and when no one's looking, steal thongs out of the laundry baskets of babes so you can sew together pungent, multi-colored quilts. Did it ever occur to you that it has nothing to do with your mother making you fold her Woolworth's underwear when you were 10, that maybe you're just a sick bastard?

Those aren't problems—well, maybe the underwear thing is, but pale in comparison to real complaints or problems.

And then there are the complaints we get. I don't think a day goes by that I don't get at least a half dozen emails complaining about how the letter writer can't lose that last bit of fat around his or her waist and how it's really a problem that's got them down because they're going to friggin' Tahiti next month and they're worried that the native islanders won't get down on their knees and worship them for the gods they are because they're 7 percent body fat instead of 6 percent; how they're 5'5" and only 250 pounds and they don't look quite as stocky and fire-pluggy as bodybuilder Lee Priest yet and how miserable they are because of it; how they can't stand the taste of cottage cheese and can't I please think of something else they can eat at night because, gosh, cottage cheese is so yucky.

Those are _not_ problems. You know what to do to lose weight. In a takeoff on Nike's slogan, *just fucking do it*. You know how to gain muscle. Hell, you've read about a thousand articles on it. *Just fucking do it.* If you can't, and you have no underlying medical problem, you're just weak-willed. Can't stand the taste of cottage cheese? For chrissake, *shove it down your throat*, you pussy!

Arggghhhh!

Man, I don't know how we got to be the most powerful country in the world because a good portion of the population is as weak as the urine flow of a man who suffered a botched penis-extension operation.

Likewise, we get complaints all the time from a small percentage of readers demanding to know why, if we're such experts, we don't all weigh 300 pounds and belch fire; why we only helped them put on 10 pounds instead of 20; why we're such big sellouts and charge for our supplements instead of functioning solely as some sort of big honkin' humanitarian weight-lifting site. Yep, instead of Toys for Tots, we'll be Traps for Tots, a non-profit organization dedicated to turning our nation's children into an army of no-necks.

I don't want to hear any more wuss complaints from these readers. Legitimate complaints about some policy of ours are fine. Suggestions are welcome. Questions are welcome. Asking for advice is fine. Letters to see how we're doing are fine. Naked pictures of women are more than fine. But complaints about something trivial or moronic? Woe-is-me whining?

Some of us need some perspective about what constitutes a problem and what doesn't. There are plenty of people who can't walk, can't get out of a hospital bed, can't find food, let alone get to the gym or worry about how they're going to dress up their cottage cheese to make it more palatable.

If we don't start putting things into perspective, we'll all be woefully unprepared when some real shit hits the fan—or should I say, hits the roof.

Now that would be a problem.

Chapter 8

Things You're Supposed to Do

"No wonder the divorce rate is so high in America, there's too much freakin' family togetherness and self-sacrifice. Both things are noble and wonderful ... until they turn into loathing."

You've waited all week for this. So what if the coffee's bitter and the scone tastes like the baker mistook the drywall paste for the flour? You just dropped the wife and the two brats off at church and the next glorious half-hour is all yours, yours to read the newspaper! Yours to look out the window and eyeball all the young girls dressed in their am-I-a-whore-or-am-I-an-angel? Sunday dresses! Yours to talk about March madness or spring training with anybody who'll listen!

Thirty minutes all to yourself! You're master of the universe! Could life be any better?

If you're Steve, the answer is yes, life could be better ... a lot better.

Steve manages a Kinko's copy center. He got married right after he graduated from junior college because, well, because that's what you're supposed to do. He then had two kids because that too is what you're supposed to do. The kids were the childbearing equivalent of a baseball doubleheader: back-to-back, 18 months of gestation. Eighteen months looking at a bloated, bitchy wife.

Hey, it's a beautiful day! Let's play two!

What in God's name was he thinking? He could hardly afford *one*!

He'd always wanted to become a professional poker player and not just after it became popular; he started playing cards before poker was cool. But with a wife and two kids, he did the responsible thing and got a job. At Kinko's. After all, that's what you're supposed to do.

He doesn't play cards at all anymore. He tried playing a little on-line poker, but when his wife found out he'd lost 50 bucks—50 bucks they needed for little Emily's swimming lessons—she hit the ceiling. Now he just watches poker on TV, but only if the kids have finished watching the video of *Finding Nemo* for what must be the 500th time. Fuckin' fish. If he ever sees Ellen Degeneres in person, he's going to strangle her just for the satisfaction.

Steve wears a white short-sleeve shirt and a tie to work. The short sleeves are so they don't get caught in the assorted copiers. The tie? Well, that's what you're supposed to wear, at least if you're respectable and all that. He tries not to look in the mirror too much.

While he used to lift at least four times a week, his gym membership is now an "unnecessary extravagance." At least that's how his wife sees it. Besides, it's "time away from the kids," and you're supposed to spend every minute of free time with the darling children. Otherwise, they'll grow up to be bums, criminals, or crack whores. It's absolutely true; Steve's wife read it in *Reader's Digest*.

He used to take incredible pride in his wife's body and took her to the beach whenever possible just to show her off, the idea of other men being envious of him for some reason, *whatever* reason, being enormously satisfying and even therapeutic. But her body has degenerated at an alarming rate, the end result of eating Happy Meals with the kids five or six days a week. She could get work as a body double for Kirstie Alley. Steve can't say anything about it because she'd rip his throat out, or worse yet, start berating him non-stop in that grating, high-pitched voice.

The ultimate irony is that if he left her, she'd sure as hell get her ass in shape quick so that she could snare some other poor schlub.

Of course, he doesn't know why he even cares about how she looks. It's not like they even have sex anymore, not with the possibility of the kids running into the room at any given moment. Hell, he can't even whack off anymore without a snot-nosed kid banging on the bathroom door and screaming at the top of its lungs.

So Steve really looks forward to his half-hour respite on Sundays, but lately, he can't convince himself that it's enough. He knew things were really bad when one day, while feeling particularly depressed about how his life had turned out, he consoled himself by thinking, "It's okay, I'll be dead soon."

If that wasn't bad enough, he found himself feeling envious of Christopher Moltisanti from *The Sopranos*. Yes, *Christofuh*, who after seeing his future in the guise of a wretched family that pulled up to the gas station in their rusted-out station wagon, agreed to let Adriana, his fiancée, get whacked.

Unfortunately, the world is full of Steves. While I've no beef with marriage or even children, a lot of guys get married and have families for all the wrong reasons. Despite the rigid framework of society we're all taught to believe in, some guys just weren't meant to be married and would have been a lot happier if they'd stayed single ... or stayed single until they were ready.

But unless you take stock in your life, it's oh-so-easy to get caught up in the "supposed to" undertow. And before you know it, you're being carried further and further away from the life you wanted. Some men manage to tread water for a long time; some just drown; and a blessed few swim parallel to the shore until they're free of the riptide. Others, the smart ones, don't venture out into the water until it's safe.

Steve's drowning and I don't know if he can be saved. He took on too many *supposed to's*—*supposed to's* that he wasn't forced into—and now he's got responsibilities. A far greater number of men swallow just one or two *supposed to's* and they might just emerge from the morass with their spirits intact ... if they've got the will and the guts.

I don't know why American men took it upon themselves to sacrifice so much to make everybody else happy. Sure, love and honor your parents, but don't become a freakin' orthodontist because that's what would make dad proud. Sure, love and honor your wife, but don't give up ever doing any activity that doesn't involve her. Sure, love and honor your kids, but don't cease to exist simply because they do.

No wonder the divorce rate is so high in America. There's too much freakin' family togetherness and self-sacrifice. Both things are noble and wonderful ... until they turn into loathing.

In a way, the fictional character most representative of the American male is Biff Loman from *Death of a Salesman*. Biff's dad wants him to sit behind a corporate desk. He believes Biff is destined for greatness, or his definition of greatness, but Biff knows he's not a leader of men. All Biff wants to do is stop agonizing over what his father wants him to be and work on a cattle ranch.

So I say to all you Steves and Biffs and potential Steves and Biffs, slow down; take stock of things. Think. Plan. Strive to achieve *your* definition of greatness, not someone else's. Cut down on the *supposed to's* and take some *want to's* out for a spin.

I'm fairly certain that getting a half-hour a week to enjoy yourself isn't the way life's supposed to be.

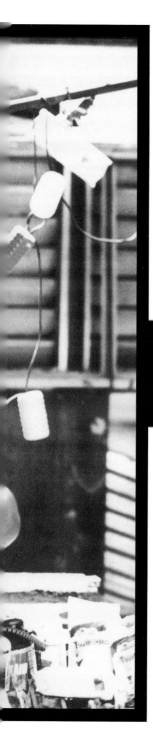

Boys to Men

SECTION

2

Chapter 9

The War Against Boys

"Yep, feminist types better come to grips with Testosterone. It's not just coursing through the veins of men, you know. You've got it, too, and if you seek to drive that particular demon out of you, be careful lest you drive out the best part of you. Testosterone is ambition, bravery, energy, and indignation over injustice."

I don't think women really like us. And when I say "us," I'm talking about the brotherhood of men. Oh sure, women will go out with us (usually after we offer them cash or valuable coupons) and even marry us, but that's largely because they don't have much of a choice.

As far as women and their choice of life partners go, they're like Eskimos eating at an Eskimo Chinese restaurant. They can order one from column A and one from column B, but it doesn't much matter because all that's on the menu is stir-fried blubber.

Well, I guess they do have another alternative, one that I'm often reminded of by Stella, the girl in the mailroom who looks and dresses remarkably like Russell Crowe in *Gladiator*. Stella makes a point of walking up to me at least once a week, sticking her face about an inch from mine, and telling me, with a Billy Idol sneer on her lips, "You and your kind ain't nothin' that can't be replaced with eight inches of flesh-colored plastic or a ripe garden vegetable, maybe something from the gourd family."

Lovely girl.

And really, when you think about it, it makes more sense for women to live together than it does for women to live with men. Lesbians probably don't roll over and fall asleep after having sex. They probably talk about their day, or engage in small talk about the latest Anne Heche movie or who knows what as they go into the kitchen and do the you-wash-I'll-dry thing with their assorted dildoes and strap-ons.

Women, apparently, *need* that conversation thing. And obviously, men don't. The one thing that even brave men dread hearing the most is, "Whatcha' thinking about, schnookums?" as their wives or girlfriends dismount from the hobby horse after sex and cuddle up next to them.

For some reason, women misinterpret our blank stares as evidence that some sort of thought process is going on and they want to know about it. They imagine that we're fantasizing about marriage, or fondly *remembering* our wedding day—the happiest day of our lives. Ha! You want to know what we're thinking about? *Nothing*!

Most of the time TV gives us something to stare at, and it usually wards off any questions about what we're thinking about. Of course, when we watch TV we're also thinking about nothing. If you looked into our minds, you'd see a vast white room, much like what Neo was introduced to by the Lawrence Fishburne character when he was first shown the Matrix. This white room, however, would be littered with old baseball mitts, some stroke mags, and a lot of empty pizza boxes.

And believe me, lady, you don't want to go there. You'd emerge batshit crazy, like when Spock accidentally looked at the Medusa in *Star Trek*.

This is why men spend as much time as possible staring at TV—to give the appearance that we're preoccupied—lest some female wants to talk about thoughts or feelings.

Truth be told, we're like dogs. We lie around in a semi-awake state until there's a call to action. This call to action might be the promise of some snackies in the kitchen, the urge to go the bathroom, or perhaps shifting our weight in an effort to dislodge a popcorn kernel that got wedged in our shorts (however, it should be noted that very few dogs wear shorts, or even eat popcorn, for that matter).

Yep, very basic needs. Of course, when something fun pops up, we're there, tongues hanging and tails wagging.

This communication problem is probably the least of the things that bother women the most about men. We're just too ...manly! When the time is right, we're physical beings. We're rowdy. We play games, and if there's nothing to do, we'll invent games—*that's how we express ourselves.*

Why, I remember one time when my partner and I had finished putting the latest issue of our mag to bed. We were exhausted, but when Tim suggested we take some of the crumpled-up coffee cups off the floor and play Home Run Derby using our penises to *fungo* them across the room while our secretary, Helen, fielded them, I was all for it. We kept at it for hours, only quitting when Tim's wife walked in and she was hit in the eye by a screaming line drive. But I digress.

Women latch onto us and assume that they'll be able to change us—a feat that would rival being able to alter time and space itself—but it never works.

At the root of the problem is that most women don't really understand masculinity; they don't understand Testosterone. So they've regrouped. They've contacted their feminist Colin Powells and come up with a new battle plan. The key to changing us is to get us *while we're young.*

Here are some examples of what's going on in our schools, according to a new book titled, *The War Against Boys*, by Christina Hoff Summers.

At University High School in Pacific Heights, California, boys have to sit quietly through "Women's Assemblies" where women are celebrated and men (boys) are blamed for all the misfortunes of the world.

Just north, in San Francisco, boys have to "enjoy" quilting while being forced to listen to girls vent their anger against males.

And lest you think that this is just another example of how all Californians are fruits and nuts, a female teacher in Boston decided to help pick up the low esteem of the males in her class by making T-shirts for them that read, "Boys Are Good." The 10 female teachers under her strongly objected. One of the 10 was wearing a button that read, "So many men, so little intelligence."

Perhaps worst of all is the fact that some schools are employing the Bem Androgyny Scale—named after a feminist psychologist—to measure how well masculine traits have been eradicated from boys.

How in the wide, wide world of XY chromosomes did being a man suddenly become *bad*?

Why are young men, who'd rather play, noisily I might add, expected to sit around quietly, talking about their feelings and working on relationships? And, if they don't adapt to this mode of thinking, if those little broncos aren't easy to "break," they're doped up with Ritalin.

Is it news to today's feminists that boys—men—are different from women? Hell, all you gotta do is go back to the original user's manual to figure out what boys are like:

The boy from 10 to 15, like the savage, is purely physical in his needs. I do not know that I ever met a boy that would not rather be John L. Sullivan than Darwin or Tolstoy. Therefore, I accept the fact, and seek to keep in view an ideal that is physical, but also clean, manly, heroic, already familiar, and leading with certainty to higher things.

Hrrumpph! No doubt a passage from some neo-Marxist, woman-hating, degenerate, subversive pile of hooey! Not so. That passage is from no less a woman-hating piece of literature than the original Boy Scout manual published in 1910.

So what's the result of this constant hormonal brow beating? Women now account for 56 percent of American college students. 11th grade boys now score at the level of 8th grade girls in writing. In many schools, boys account for three-fourths of the students in special-education classes. They're five times more likely to commit suicide and up to nine times more likely to be drugged with Ritalin.

In no way am I suggesting that the gates be opened and young men be allowed to vent out all their hormonal urges. Instead, education and feminist attitudes need to be adjusted to fit the male hormonal *milieu*. Boys and men don't need to be forced to act like women. Sure, they need to be taught to express their feelings, but through ways that come naturally to them, through sports, action, and yes, maybe even talking.

They need positive male role models. They need to be given tasks that challenge them, because there's nothing like a challenge to bring out the best of them. And frankly, making a quilt isn't the kind of challenge I had in mind.

Above all, women need to accept that males are different.

Why? Because when the goddam aliens come, when the Amazon women of Mars come to enslave all of you, it's men that will beat their metal-thong–wearing green asses all the way back to the red planet.

Eradicate Testosterone, and hell, every TV show would be a soap opera. Why, you'd have no *Sopranos*. Tony Soprano would be a dog groomer, and ratings would plummet faster than Pussy when he was pushed off the boat last season. And then what would we stare at?

Yep, feminist types better come to grips with Testosterone. It's not just coursing through the veins of men, you know. You've got it, too, and if you seek to drive that particular demon out of you, be careful lest you drive out the best part of you. Testosterone is ambition, bravery, energy, and indignation over injustice.

In fact, if I had a kid, I'd have some small Testosterone T-shirts made so the little nipper could wear them to school, to band practice, to glee club, and under his football jersey, just to let the anti-boy types know that he's proud to be a man.

Granted, he might be gang-tackled by the anti-boy forces and forced to sit when he pees, but when he came home, I'd negate that brainwashing by taking him outside so both of us could pee our names in the dusty road, with broad, artistic strokes and great flourish.

And maybe we'd then go inside and write a new Boy Scout oath, one more in-tune with the times, something like the original one:

A boy is trustworthy, loyal, helpful, friendly, courteous, kind, obedient, cheerful, thrifty, brave, clean and reverent. Wait a minute, the original one ain't so bad after all.

Chapter 10

My Speech to the Graduates

"Remember that living strictly by the rules doesn't make you a man. It makes you a robot. True, children don't always live by the rules, either, but there's a difference. An actualized man knows which rules to break, which broken rules will take him by the hand and lead him out of a passive, tame, domesticated existence."

Every one of you, having now graduated, faces a cross-roads. One path leads to mindless conformity; a soul-sucking passivity that allows you to coast along on life's swirls and eddies until you fall dead of prostate cancer. The other path, much less traveled, overgrown with vines and made hard to navigate by fallen trees, almost always leads to danger but occasionally to bliss, after which you'll fall dead of a heart attack.

God grant you the wisdom to choose correctly.

Okay, that wasn't too cheery, was it? Let me go about it a different way. I see that most of you are sitting there with a glazed look in your eyes. You don't really know how you got here, and you sure as hell don't know where you're going. No one even told you that you were a *man* yet, and here you are, expected to go out into the world.

It only seems like yesterday you were riding a skateboard, wearing your caps backward, and jacking off into your mom's scented toilet paper. And now you're graduating;

now you're supposed to be a man. Only you *still* do all those things you used to do, except that now you have to use some of that cheap Costco toilet paper with wood chips in it that gives your cock splinters. So are you ready to take your place in the world? Are you a man yet?

Other cultures take 13-year-old kids, give them a knife and a spear, and throw'em out in the jungle for a week. When they come back—if they're still alive—they're *men* and the tribe treats them as such. Here in the Western world, the closest thing we have to a rite of passage into manhood is sneaking into an R-rated movie. Not exactly the same thing. You didn't really walk out of the theater a changed person, unless, of course, the movie you snuck into was *The Crying Game*, or maybe *Boogie Nights*.

So I don't blame you for feeling a little befuddled. You don't really know how to act or how to feel in practically any situation, but really, it's best that way. By keeping you confused and keeping you in a child-like state, they were able to shape you to be a good little automaton.

Your school trained you to go with the flow, to follow rather than lead, and to never question authority. Now, you'll vote with the consensus, work with the team, and adjust your fashion and music choices based on what's "in." Presto! You've been turned into a drone.

You'll make a good mid-level employee to some son-of-a-bitch boss and a good husband to some woman who wants to take over where your mother left off. You'll live by the clock and the calendar, waiting all year long for those two weeks at the end of August when you can take that vacation to Europe you've always dreamed about, but at the last minute you'll decide to stay home and paint the house instead.

You may have other dreams, too. Maybe you want to be a champion skier and marry a fashion model. Could be you have plans on being a millionaire by age 30. And of course, you're going to leave the loser town you grew up in and live on the friggin' coast and surf every morning and evening.

But, if you're like most people, you'll wake up one morning and you'll be, I don't know, 35 or 40 and you won't have done any of that stuff. You'll be in the same old town, waking up to the alarm clock, looking frantically for the symbol of your slave-like existence, the watch, and hurrying to your job as one of 35 vice presidents at Bingamton Savings and Loan. You didn't marry a model, but a girl that really, really, reminds you of your mother, and come to think of it, nags you the same way. She'll soon start dressing like her, too, and the transition will be complete. You'd best be a good son.

You used to work out, but you gave that up long ago. Your wife thought it was a waste of time. Besides, she lies and tells you that your potbelly "looks cute." Sure, guys with potbellies have always gotten the chicks. Besides, with the birth of Jason and Crystal, your two kids with trendy names, you don't have time to work out. Most of your time is spent ferrying them back and forth between soccer practice and horseback-riding lessons.

Don't worry, though. You'll be dead soon.

Of course, you probably didn't hear any of this. Because of MTV and stupid-ass movies that are nothing but longer MTV videos, your attention span is on par with the half-life of the element Fermium, which is about one-billionth of a second.

Unless I had fireworks coming out of my ass or employed some other kind of special effects, your mind is bouncing around like a the ball on an epileptic soccer player's head. Instead of paying attention to me, you're sitting there wondering if Becky Schlossinger, the class Valedictorian, is wearing underwear beneath that stupid robe. Well, I hate to disappoint you, but she is, and it's not even nice underwear. They're grayish white panties, full coverage, too, and the elastic is all stretched out. Life, unfortunately, ain't a *Penthouse* letter. Get used to it.

But, in the remote chance that you are listening, I'd like to offer some advice. I'd like to make a case for taking that second, less traveled road. Now, my life may not be a role model for others, but I may have learned a few good things.

First of all, I think that living our lives by the *clock* is the bane of our existence. I think I realized this at an early age since I stopped wearing a watch when I was 10 years old. Okay, I realize that we need to know when to go to work and when to meet our workout partners at the gym, and when reruns of *Star Trek: Voyager* are on TV, but only by at least loosening time's grip on you can you really be free.

I always liked this paragraph from *The Last Unicorn*, an experimental work of fiction by Peter S. Beagle:

But the skull was laughing again; this time making a thoughtful, almost kindly noise. "Remember what I told you about time," it said. "When I was alive, I believed—as you do—that time was at least as real and solid as myself, and probably more so. I said 'one o'clock' as though I could see it, and 'Monday' as though I could find it on the map; and I let myself be hurried along from minute to minute, day to day, year to year, as though I were actually moving from one place to another. Like everyone else, I lived in a house bricked up with seconds and minutes, weekends and New Year's Days, and I never went outside until I died, because there was no other door. Now I know that I could have walked through the walls."

Heady stuff.

Most people have their Honey Graham cereal at exactly 7 a.m., shave and shower exactly at 7:30, and do absolutely anything and everything based on the clock on the wall. Maybe they have dinner with the Frisbees on Wednesday night and maybe they nail the wife on Saturday night. Monday, however, is very special as the wife and kids are at kazoo practice, so they lie naked on the bathroom floor and slowly run an oiled-up loofah all over their quivering bodies while listening to the soundtrack of C-SPAN.

Maybe people should deliberately shake things up once in a while. Work a different schedule, eat when they feel like it instead of by the clock. Nail the wife on Saturday afternoon, loudly, so the neighbors can hear. And most importantly, run that oiled up loofah all over their bodies when they feel like it. Maybe by doing that can they walk through a few walls.

I also recommend waiting a while to have a family, and if you don't want to wait, at least don't have any daughters because you've never known real heartache until you've seen your precious little girl flashing her hooters on a late night commercial for *Girls Gone Wild*. Likewise, I recommend that you wait a while before you even get married, because you've never known real heartache until you've seen your darling wife flashing her hooters on a late night commercial for *Wives Gone Wild*.

Trust me, I know.

Actually, I've got nothing against marriage, but I really think that most guys should wait to get married. Hell, it's hard enough for one person to grow up, let alone two at the same time.

I also want to tell you that pretty much everybody, to a certain degree, is full of shit. The sooner you learn that, the better. Politicians, of course, are historically full of shit, but so are almost all of the people you admire. Reverend Jesse Jackson, while counseling Bill Clinton on his evil ways, was busy impregnating some woman who wasn't his wife. The minister at your church just got slapped with a class-action lawsuit by a group of choirboys who got tired of hitting a high C whenever he fondled them.

Sports, held to be heroes by some people, are often drug addicts, adulterers, or rapists. Self-help gurus, whether they be spiritual self-help gurus or body-for-life self-help gurus, are often the most dysfunctional, spiritually and morally bankrupt people you'll ever meet.

That's okay, though. Don't let that discourage you. Even people who are full of shit might be able to teach you something. And maybe the part that's full of shit doesn't surface that often. In any event, just develop a sensitive bullshit antenna and learn to recognize it when you see it. That way, when you run into somebody who's genuine, you'll know it and you'll really have something worthwhile there.

And I wouldn't for a minute work in a place that didn't thrill me. I realize that's easy to say, but damn, you'll be dead before you know it and you've got to make sure that being alive is at least a little bit more fun than being dead.

Don't get conventional. Don't do stuff because it's expected of you or because that's what everybody else does. If you want to be a bodybuilder and live in Venice Beach, well hell, do it. If you want to live in Katmandu and lead foolish rich people up Mt. Everest to freeze and die, go ahead and do it. Just know when it's time to move on to something else, though.

Speak out against evil, but pick your battles wisely. I know lots of bastards who get pissed over anything and everything. Be critical, but don't get obsessive. As my father used to say, "Before you criticize someone, walk a mile in his or her shoes. That way, when you start to criticize them, you're a mile away! Plus you'll have some nice shoes."

Well, at least he had part of that right.

It's all right to get pissed when the local delicatessen discontinued your favorite sandwich—corned beef and Gouda cheese on a Kaiser roll—but organizing a march on their business, taking hostages, and demanding that they bring it back is overkill. Wouldn't your time be better served launching a letter-writing campaign against some politician who was trying to have your living room used as a repository for nuclear waste? Now that's someone to get pissed at—him, and maybe that idiot congresswoman who's trying to ban *The Sopranos.*

Remember that living strictly by the rules doesn't make you a man. It makes you a robot. True, children don't always live by the rules, either, but there's a difference. An actualized man knows which rules to break, which broken rules will take him by the hand and lead him out of a passive, tame, domesticated existence.

And, at the very least, try to keep an open mind. The last thing you want to end up being is some crotchety guy who screams at kids for running on his lawn, and who, for the life of him, can't figure out why those dang kids can listen to that that kind of music. Realize that 95 percent of your opinions were poured into you by your parents, your schools, and your friends. Realize too that there's a good chance that they were wrong. Keep learning. Keep reading. Try to keep the "game" even.

If, by half-time, the score of your game is Hormones' 42, Logical Thinking 7, then you need to try a zone defense, and while on offense make some short passes because there's a weakness in Hormone's secondary. In short, close up that score a bit so your hormones aren't always trouncing your logical thinking.

If you can do some of this stuff, your life will be a friggin' *poem*. A heroic poem, and you'll take that road less traveled, skipping over the underbrush and fallen trees like a damn elf—a masculine elf, mind you.

Chapter 11

My Speech to the Graduates, 2002

"And while you might find it hard to believe right now, you might someday find a small stick in your ass .... Believe me, that stick grows and grows until it pokes clear through your viscera and into your brain, thus impairing rational thinking."

For many of you, this is the closest thing you'll have to a rite of passage. No killing a lion for you, no tribal ceremonies, no readings of religious texts that have been handed down for thousands of years. Nope, all you had to do was *show up* in that cap and gown that makes you look like a drag queen with bad fashion sense.

Of course, a lot of you came just because you think the girl sitting next to you isn't wearing anything underneath her gown. That may or may not be true, but you'll never find out. Life is full of naked women that you'll never see. It's the single most vexing thing about life, so get used to it.

So *poof! Ala Kazam*, you're now a man. And I hate to be the one to tell you this, but you'll be expected to put away at least a few of your childish things.

I'd like to suggest that one of the things you put aside is your endless pursuit of *cool*. Here's what I mean by that: If next week, in *Cosmo* or *Maxim*, some dope was pictured wearing a urinal cake around his or her neck, half of you would stampede the nearest bowling-alley lavatory to fish out your new fashion statement.

And despite the tattoos on the small of your back, the piercings, the turned-around baseball caps, the loose pants that expose your Fred Flintstone underwear and put you one step away from an old guy running for the toilet with his pants down around his ankles, you're not rebels. You're *conformists*. When the next generation looks at your pictures, you'll look just as dopey to them as you think those kids in the fifties looked with their poodle skirts and letter sweaters.

I think I've known maybe five legitimately cool people in my life, and the one trait they all held in common was that they didn't give a shit if they were cool or not. See? True coolness is kind of a Zen thing. If you strive for it, it eludes you.

Another thing that many of you might not realize is that the next few years are really going to determine what kind of person you'll be. You might think your personality is already formed and set, but it really hasn't. You might think that the pivotal psychological point in your life was when you were a 12-year-old at Camp Chichimunga and the other kids stripped you naked, sat on you, and used your butt cheeks to make s'mores. But it really wasn't.

The next few years will determine if you're the kind of guy that gives up—which is roughly 99 percent of the population—or the kind that's got the force of will to do anything. I figure it happens by the time you're about 30. Although a few souls pull themselves out of the nose dive after that, most continue on their downward plunge and it's only at the last minute that they realize what's happened and they start screaming their lungs out.

If you don't presently have any big plans for your future, at the very least try to establish your own identity. Try not to copy someone else. For years I tried to be like my business partner. I walked like him, talked like him, and even shuffled around the office in those flannel pajamas with the feet attached to them like him, and when he wanted his farina sprinkled with gummy bears, I wanted my farina sprinkled with gummy bears.

But then I remembered what ol' George Bernard Shaw had said when some reporter asked him who among his dead friends he most missed. George said that the guy he most missed *was the guy he could have been.*

So I stopped wearing pajamas with the feet built in and stopped sprinkling gummy bears on my farina. I became my own person. I started wearing those nifty little Capri pants that the young Mary Tyler Moore popularized and that were picked up by The Gap again last year. And the gummy bears? Nahh. I take my farina straight—like a man.

And while we're at it, since when did being bad or evil become glamorous or cool? When I see some punk kid on a skateboard make some old people grab their rheumy-eyed poodles and dodder into the relative safety of a rose bush so they won't get run over, I feel like grabbing that young punk by his Abercrombie & Fitch mock soccer jersey and asking him, "Hey, product of our failed educational system, didn't you ever want to be the hero in the movie of your life instead of the human turd that causes the audience to clap when he falls into a vat of acid?"

But I've done my share of dancing with the devil, too. While I'm embarrassed to admit it now, there were even times when I went swimming 50 minutes after a heavy lunch rather than waiting the full hour my mom told me to wait. And then there was the time I only pretended to give money to that Salvation Army Santa Claus by saying, "Hey, isn't that the guy who used to play Screech on *Saved by the Bell* over there?" while holding my hand over his cup and making a "ching, ching, ching" noise with my mouth.

Yep, I've been to the dark side, all right, but thanks to a good woman, I came out of it without too much spiritual damage. And that brings me to another point. I can think of nothing more helpful than finding a supportive mate.

Try to put a little more thought into picking a life partner than you would in picking out a pair of socks, though. Say, for instance, the girl you're thinking about marrying squats down while naked and picks up a dollar bill between her legs, only to moments later deftly drop a perfect origami unicorn on your desk without ever having touched it with her hands. If that happens, chances are she's not as inexperienced with men as she'd led you to believe.

Or say she has calluses on her vagina and has to rub it with a pumice stone and then soak it in some Neet's Foot Oil every night before retiring. That's a real good sign that there have probably been enough men in her life to reenact the battle of Gettysburg.

So be careful. Pick your mates wisely.

Some of you have jobs waiting for you. Some, however, are still indecisive as to your plans, while still others are simply planning on moving back with their parents and pulling the Battle Bots out of the attic.

Put some thought into what you want to do with your degree. And don't necessarily confuse success with excellence or integrity. There's a proverb from the Bible that says, "It's easier for a camel to pass through the eye of a needle than it is for a rich man to get to Heaven." Of course, you can't take this statement literally, because with all that weird genetic engineering going on, it's probably easy to make a really small camel that could pass through the eye of a needle. On the other hand, some of those guys who work in the steel industry could probably make a really big needle that would allow several camels to pass through. But I digress.

In any event, the original meaning of the line was that rich guys often got rich by being bad guys. They may have walked over other people, taken advantage of them, and hoarded all the money for themselves.

Real success is in doing a job well and taking pleasure in it. It doesn't matter if you're part of Leonardo DiCaprio's posse and it's your job to make sure there are no dribbles on the toilet seat in his master bath, as long as you do a good and thorough job; as long as you take pride in keeping Leonardo from getting grossed out; as long as you don't lie to Leo about having scoured the seat with Ajax and Lysol, well then, you're a success.

Besides, you gotta take care of your soul. If you try to go through life being a straight shooter, but then pull back at the last minute by getting involved in some scam where you try to get old people to financially back a whaling expedition in Nebraska, your soul gets blue balls. It's just like the other type of blue balls, but your testicles don't ache and change color and whacking off won't help much.

Another thing I can't recommend strongly enough is finding a few good friends to ease the inevitable pains that life brings, as well in sharing in the equally inevitable joys it brings. In other words, you need a Dick to your Jane, a Goose to your Maverick.

But try not to kill Goose with your pride, like Maverick did when he augured into the drink. No other pilots will want to fly with you and that pesky Iceman might beat you out in the Top Gun competition.

And while you might find it hard to believe right now, you might someday find a small stick in your ass. I'm not talking about a real stick (unless you sat down naked onto the forest floor while attending an alternative-lifestyle wilderness retreat), I'm talking about a metaphorical stick; the kind you get in your ass when you become conventional and inexplicably start thinking that everybody has to have your exact values and opinions.

Believe me, that stick grows and grows until it pokes clear through your viscera and into your brain, thus impairing rational thinking.

But the most important thing I can tell you is to remember that in addition to trying to be yourself and having integrity and friends is to remember to throw some fun in there on a regular basis. In the words of the Bloodhound Gang, and as recited by author Tom Wolfe in a graduation speech he made a couple of weeks ago, "You and me baby, we ain't nothin' but mammals, so let's do it like they do on the Discovery Channel."

Chapter 12

Graduation Speech 2004

"Bet on a long shot once in awhile. Strive for something totally outrageous where the odds are strong you'll fall on your keister. Remember those fool figure skaters in the Olympics? "Safe" routines never score big points."

Students, faculty, and staff: Thank you for allowing me to speak today.

Before I begin, I'd like to explain the oratory format I've chosen this afternoon. While unorthodox, I've decided to make two speeches. The first one is targeted toward the majority—the 99 percent of you who are little more than sheep that will keep this country economically strong for years to come by dispensing Slurpies and fries and tearing ticket stubs in half at the local Cineplex.

I thank you for your lack of intelligence, ability, and ambition.

The other half of my speech is targeted toward the 1 percent of you who will truly reflect whatever integrity our society retains. You'll forgive me, of course, if I first address the 99 percent as their attention spans are woefully unprepared for anything that doesn't involve PlayStation, bitchin' music, blood, fast-moving objects, or fellatio, hardly any of which are part of my planned speech.

So, let me begin by quoting one of the troubadours of the sheep generation, Eminem:

Awww naww, big slim dogg

Eighty-pound balls, dick six-inch long

Back up, in the, heezy bay-bay

He's sha-day!

While I was raised just a few miles away from where the flaxen-haired, quasi-albino poet grew up, I have no freakin' idea what he was talking about, but I suspect he was referring to the other poet laureate of your generation, the venerable Snoop Dog.

No matter, because I'm well aware that you draw inspiration from inane song lyrics, much the same as prior generations drew inspiration from philosopher-giants like Elvis, The Big Bopper, or Katrina and the Waves. After all, reading real philosophy or literature—truly contemplating the meaning of existence—is hard work and makes your head throb like it did when you crawled into the dryer at the laundromat as an homage to Johnny Knoxville.

I guess it doesn't surprise me when I read that 50 years ago the average high school kid had a vocabulary of about 50,000 words whereas his modern-day contemporary has a vocabulary of about 10,000 words.

That's like, you know, *bad.*

I guess that's part of the reason a study released yesterday indicates that only one in six of you is ready to function adequately in society. Given that statistic, I'll try to give you some advice that will make the transition from slacker into a member of sheep society a little more effective and a little easier.

First of all, most of you are morons, so try to get comfortable with that notion. It's not really a bad thing. America *likes* morons. The less you know, the more people will accept you. Practice becoming "plain spoken."

Being smart labels you as different—an outsider. People who read or study are freaks and you should never hesitate to snicker at them or give them wedgies. Ogre knew this simple fact and you should too. If you're smart, you'll never be asked to join the bowling team, strip naked to the waist and paint your body with the colors of your local football team, or drink Bud until you pass out. And really, what's life without simple joys like those?

Don't read. I remember a Calvin and Hobbes comic strip from about 10 years ago where Hobbes, the tiger, had given Calvin a book to read. In the first panel Calvin says, "I finished the book you gave me. It really made me think and it changed the way I look at things." In the next and final panel, Calvin completes the thought by saying, "Don't give me another one."

That's why it's best not to read. Introducing new ideas into your head can be dangerous and threaten your complacent slacker existence.

Don't use big words, even if you know a few. And say things as if they were fact and the vast majority of people will believe you. Try this one on the next person you talk to:

"The Department of Homeland Security has just asked that all women shave their pubic areas because it gives the terrorists one less place to hide."

I just made that up ... or did I? It doesn't matter! Truth has very little value in today's society. What matters is appearance! Strength coach Charles Poliquin once told me about the time he addressed the Mighty Ducks hockey team about training principles.

Most of them started yawning or studying whatever stray organic matter they'd excavated from their ear or nose when, out of the blue, former Ducks player Paul Kariya, for whatever reason, asked Charles to do a front double-biceps shot. You have to understand that Charles is short and doesn't look all that formidable ... until he pulls out those guns. Charles flexed those 19-inch arms and suddenly he had their respect. He could have told them to drink kerosene or give themselves hockey-puck suppositories and they would have done it.

Furthermore, if you do anything wrong, never admit it. It's frustrating and maddening to those you wronged, but they'll get over it and you won't be expected to make amends for anything. However, if denying it doesn't work, feign being teary-eyed. America loves teary-eyed people. Most of the country is so devoid of sincerity that if someone even has the faint appearance of being compassionate or sensitive, they're duly impressed. Remember, appearance is all that counts.

Since we're talking about appearance, I'd like to say a few words to the female morons in the audience, especially the really attractive ones. You've hit the jackpot. By turning yourselves into robosluts, you're destined never to want for anything. You'll never have to work that hard, demonstrate any real abilities, nor even buy a drink for yourself. If you play your cards right, you can marry some poor well-to-do schlub who'll take care of you. You'll be human female equivalents to Butterscotch, the companion pony to super horse Smarty Jones. Smarty is worth a lot of money, so Butterscotch gets to enjoy the good life, too.

Better squirrel some of his money away, though, because once you start to get a little baggy and tired looking, you'll be dumped pronto, because it's not like you had any other positive traits, least of all being an engaging conversationalist. Nope, your lives will be as shallow as your thoughts, so you might as well get some good shopping in.

I see that most of you have started to blather on your cell phones, so I think I'll segue into the second part of my speech, the one for the outcasts.

Thanks for being patient. You people are the only excuse I have for not praying for nuclear annihilation. I probably don't have much to teach you, but what the hell, I'll give it a go.

I've learned the veneer of civilization is pretty thin and that underneath that veneer, we still think with cock and club.

That's okay. Being in touch with your primal side is good, as long you're able to temper and control it with smarts.

Being smart is the silver bullet that kills all the monsters, solves all the problems. Being plain spoken is bullshit. Being smart is not only about having information, but also having *knowledge*. There's a distinct difference. Having information is like having Charisma Carpenter's phone number. Having knowledge is like *having* Charisma Carpenter.

However, remember please that knowledge is only as good as what you do with it. There's a little poem—if you can even call it that—written by Stephen Crane around the turn of the 20th century that, if memory serves, goes something like this:

A man said to the Universe, "Sir, I exist."

"Yes," replied the Universe,

"But that has not created in me a sense of obligation."

I take it to mean that you can't put yourself in fate's hands. Rather than be a rudderless ship, you've got to use whatever talents you have and do something with your life. The universe has better things to do than take care of you.

Bet on a long shot once in a while. Strive for something totally outrageous where the odds are strong you'll fall on your keister. Remember those fool figure skaters in the Olympics? "Safe" routines never score big points.

Furthermore, try to become extra smart in a particular field, i.e., become an expert in something, even if it's the history of lawn furniture. It might not lead directly to monetary riches, but being really knowledgeable about something is like a life raft that will bring you pleasure and nurture your soul throughout your life.

Don't look for inconsequential battles, but don't shy away from them. Back when Bill Russell was playing basketball, he was getting beaten up under the boards game after game because he wouldn't throw an elbow in retaliation. His coach told him, "Do it one time. Throw an elbow in a nationally televised game and you'll never have to do it again."

Russell did just that and from that point on, he never got beat up underneath the boards again. So throw an elbow once in a while.

And while I busted the sheep about getting their wisdom or inspiration from the moronic lyrics of rappers or rock bands, it's okay to delve into what I categorize as "cereal-box philosophy" once in a while. Go ahead and assimilate a catchy phrase from some moronic song, but let's not go overboard, okay? Real understanding takes work and contemplation.

Find some good friends, but cut them the same slack they cut you. Who cares if they borrowed five bucks and forgot to pay you back, or that they grabbed the big piece of chicken? If a friend sticks up for you when you're not around, that's a friend worth keeping.

Along the same lines, remember what Lou Reed said, that there will always be "some evil mothers who think that life is full of dirt." Their sole purpose is to bring you down. Avoid these emotional vampires but don't bear them malice. You don't take it personally when a storm knocks a tree over and it falls on your Honda, do you? Similarly, these rotten bastards are just forces of nature.

Nurture your body because it's the vehicle that totes around that big, beautiful brain of yours. Why carry it around in a rusty old wheelbarrow when you can use a high-horsepower Benz?

Now go out, celebrate your graduation by letting your primal side take over for a while, and then go out there and make me proud.

Chapter 13

Revenge of the Nerds

"Being smart gives an individual the distinctly valuable trait of being able to conjure money out of thin air. Obviously, there are plenty of rarefied professions where "un-nerdy" types make wads of cash, like professional athletes or those leaf blowers with tits that they call female pop stars, but generally, those with brains have a better chance of earning some serious coin."

One of my buddies has a kid named Grant. Grant is six years old. When he was four, Grant told me all about suspension bridges and how they're constructed. He also explained some of the science behind volcanoes.

I sent him a toy submarine for his fifth birthday. Rather than use it in the bathtub, the tiny modern-day Archimedes took it to his kindergarten show-and-tell and did a presentation on water displacement.

Just last year, for his sixth birthday, Grant's mom and dad bought him a book on architecture. He read it and became so excited he couldn't sleep at night. He kept waking his parents up in the middle of the night to tell them about some of the architectural designs he was erecting in his head. They had to restrict his reading to daylight hours lest his powerful hyper-active imagination deprive them of sleep forevermore.

A few days later, he asked his dad to build him a desk for his room. But not just any desk: Grant presented him with a blueprint that had exact specifications, including finished drawings with expanded views that showed the exact placement of a globe, stapler, clock, and books.

Most recently, his teacher gave his first-grade class an assignment in which they were given 10 minutes to write a sentence using the word "maybe." Instead, Grant whipped up a couple of pages on the design and function of aircraft carriers. Trouble was, he neglected to use the word "maybe."

As a result, the teacher—obviously a moron—diagnosed Grant as having attention deficit disorder, or ADD. She also insisted that he repeat the first grade because, obviously, the boy just wasn't very bright. After all, he can't stay *focused*.

It doesn't take a genius to figure out that Grant might be a genius, but that word's probably a little overused nowadays. Let's say he's *gifted*. And it doesn't take that much imagination to assume maybe, just maybe, using the word "maybe" in a sentence wasn't too challenging for him. Taking 10 long minutes to write a measly sentence would be like using a supercomputer to figure out the tip on a five-buck lunch. Rather than use all that mental horsepower for something so mundane, so infantile, he wrote about something that was interesting to him.

As possible proof that the world isn't completely insane, subsequent testing was initiated. It revealed—big surprise—that Grant didn't have ADD. Not only that, but it proved that he was exceptionally bright. The school psychologist recommended that he be enrolled in a school for gifted students. Out of 350 students considered, only 30 were accepted, Grant among them.

Now here's the clincher: Parents of six of the 30 removed their kids from contention because they were afraid that society would regard their children as *nerds*.

I don't know how it happened, but somehow, being dumb is cool and being smart is, well, a bad thing.

While Grant's parents are planning on letting him attend the special school, they too, are afraid that he'll be stigmatized as a "Brainiac" and be a social outcast. Even Grant is somewhat uncertain about the merits of his gift. Sure, he's seen the repercussions on TV, and even in real life Smart kids get beaten up, made fun of, and have their lunch money confiscated. Sadly, Grant's taken to wearing a specially-made T-shirt that says, "Being Smart Is Okay." Good Lord, since when did we have to start apologizing for intelligence?

Other cultures revere brainpower. Smart kids are respected by peers and society. Here in America, no one likes the smartest kid in the class. Many people, regardless of political affiliation, don't regard our politicians as being intellectuals or even very bright. Okay, but what's surprising is how that alleged lack of cerebral horsepower is considered an asset. "So-and-so is a regular guy; he represents the common man." Jesus! The bowling alleys, bars, and crowds at tractor pulls are filled with the common man. Give me a socially inept, nerdy, *smart* guy any day of the week.

When it comes to initiating laws that pertain to cloning, global warming, the environment, the Internet, drugs—even supplement laws—I want leaders who not only can spell words like *gamete, carbon dioxide*, and *beta agonist*, but know what they mean, too!

I've got this feeling that a decent segment of Testosterone Nation readers are, or were once, "nerds," and by that I mean kids who were smart but didn't have the same physical gifts as some of the other kids. As a result, they were ultimately drawn to weight training because they saw it simply as a tool to achieve social acceptance.

Once they got older, of course, the pure pursuit of aesthetics largely superseded social acceptance. I don't think I need to tell these former nerds that being nerdy, being smart, is *good.*

A good brain can develop a good body, but a good body can't develop a good brain.

Their brains earned them their degrees, and their brains learned how to build bodies that matched their brains. So what if while growing up they preferred playing Dungeons and Dragons to hanging with the guys and chugging beer until they puked, or whatever it is that the "cool" guys do?

I'll tell you something else that's true about brains, and I'll even present it in mathematical terms for you fellow nerds out there:

$$Smart^2 = Money^3$$

That's right, being smart gives an individual the distinctly valuable trait of being able to conjure money out of thin air. Obviously, there are plenty of professions where un-nerdy types make wads of cash, like professional athletes or those leaf blowers with tits that they call female pop stars. But generally, those with brains have a better chance of earning some serious coin.

Nerdy types gave us computers, the I-Pod, PlayStation, DVDs, MRI machines, Positron Emission Scanners, and the *Matrix* movies. Nerdy types have developed just about everything else that's cool about modern life.

Maybe you know one of these brainy kids. They're the ones that might be a little bit thin and a little bit pasty and who are usually walking alone. Do him a favor. When he's about 14 or 15, bookmark a link to Testosterone Nation on his computer and give him a slap on the back—but not too hard. Chances are his body hasn't caught up to his brain just yet.

Of course, he—or she—might not even be interested in developing the body, and that's just fine. Still, he or she should see that there exists a species of nerd in the world that excels in mind *and* muscle.

And Grant? He's still kinda young and he's not my kid, of course. I will, however, continue to send him educational birthday and Christmas presents in an attempt to nurture that great little brain of his. He's got another birthday coming up, so maybe I'll get him a book on introductory engineering. That ought to keep his parents up at night.

Chapter 14

Boys to Men

"America has to stop loving merely the facade of toughness or masculinity. The virtues we hold dear — the virtues that truly reflect masculinity, traditional masculinity — come in different, often unexpected guises."

I spent part of the morning with a miniature Barbie doll stuck up my ass.

Let me explain. Let me explain *quickly*.

My shower isn't working so I had to take a bath, minus the Calgon, thank you. As I sat down, I felt a sharp pain in my keester, literally in my keester, if you catch my drift. I jumped up and looked at my reflection in the bathroom mirror and saw the problem: sticking out of my ass was a ball-gown bedecked Barbie.

That's when I remembered that I'd bought my daughter, Gucci, a set of 4 "Barbie Soaps." Each bar of soap is made of mulberry scented glycerin and comes with a tiny Barbie embedded within. The glycerin had largely worn away, but there was just enough slippery soap on her head to make her a viable substitution for Richard Gere's gerbil.

As I looked at my reflection in the mirror across from the tub, I thought, "That really doesn't look very manly. Come to think of it, that doesn't make me feel very manly."

These thoughts set off an internal dialog on the nature of manhood in America.

Is appearance related to masculinity?

What is the nature of manhood?

The answers don't come easily to me. Part of the reason is because things seem to have changed in the last few years. I once wrote that I didn't think the events of 9-11 had changed squat in America, least of all the attitudes of Americans towards each other.

Boy was I wrong.

Americans, particularly young male Americans, are permanently pissed. Oh, they've always been pissed about one thing or another—which isn't necessarily bad—but 9-11 made them feel more than a little frustrated, at least subconsciously, because they don't have a way to channel their aggression.

They want to show that they're courageous, but courage has become confused with violence or the promise of violence; manliness has become confused with aggressive posturing. They've fallen in love with machismo.

You know one of the reasons why the majority of men voted for George Bush? I think it's because he swaggers when he walks and he told the terrorists to "bring it on."

I'm sorry, but tough talk does not necessarily a man make. Personally, I don't think a guy—any guy—who was born with a silver spoon in his mouth can truly be a tough guy. Nope, I think you need to have been born with an old, rough-edged steel spoon in your mouth; I think you need to have tasted a little rust and a little blood to be a tough guy.

And looking or acting tough? Got nothing to do with anything.

The three toughest people I know or knew don't fit any stereotypical image. The first is my wife, who once, with her appendix about to burst, dutifully prepared for work (lying down on the floor while blow drying her hair because she could barely stand up), drove to her job at the hospital and attended to her first patient. When the second shift tech showed up to replace her, my wife staggered into the E.R. and collapsed. They wheeled her in and did an emergency appendectomy.

Why'd she do that? She didn't want to let the patients down, many who had waited weeks for an appointment.

The second tough guy I knew was named Dr. Michael Dullnig. He was a gay psychiatrist with AIDS...before there were anti-virals and many of the other drugs that now make the disease somewhat manageable. While he had managed to fight off the wasting effects of the disease with anabolic steroids, he developed CMV retinitis, which would have ultimately led to blindness. Almost worse was the maddening, constant, insufferable itching caused by the cornucopia of drugs he was using.

So this brave man cheerfully decided he wanted to die.

He made the decision about as easily as you or I might decide to leave a party that had gotten a little boring, and he didn't make it because he was scared or depressed. He just wanted to go check out the next life, dimension, or whatever lies waiting for us beyond this plane of existence. He wanted to go to the next party and see if it was a little livelier. He was genuinely curious.

But before he checked out of this life, he threw his own little real-life party, a party with champagne, music, and most of his friends in attendance. He danced, had some fun, posed for pictures, and then walked upstairs to his bedroom, stopping once on the staircase to smile broadly and raise a glass in a silent toast. He went to his bed, lied down, ate a yogurt laced with Nembutal, went to sleep, and never woke up.

No sadness, no tears, no regrets, no doubts. If that ain't tough, I don't know what is.

The third toughest person I knew was my father. He didn't do anything classically heroic, but he kept the same shit factory job for most of his life, working 6 or 7 days a week, 10 to 12 hours a day (for the overtime), and never called in sick no matter how rotten he felt. Did he hate it? Maybe, probably, most certainly, but that didn't matter. He had work to do and a family to support. He didn't agonize about what he coulda-shoulda done with his life.

I probably would have done things differently than all three of my examples, but having convictions and will is something I admire, pretty much regardless of the reasons or the consequences. Clearly, toughness–real toughness—can come in any guise, as can bravery.

But Americans, particularly young Americans, think toughness begins and ends with calling someone a shithead and threatening to "bust them up." They're little boys who never metaphorically graduated from wearing short pants. It's not all their fault, though. Unfortunately, unlike some cultures, we have no rites of passage into manhood. As such, young men blithely go on skirting responsibility, avoiding hard work and throwing frequent violent temper tantrums because they're still little boys.

Pundits and preachers and politicians claim that the solution to all this is a nation-wide return to "family values." I don't even know what the term means. When I think of family, I think of husbands and wives fighting, brats screaming and picking boogers out of their nose, grandma gumming her food, and tame Saturday night, roll-on roll-off sex followed by a nice nap in church the next morning. Since when did having a family place the mantle of virtue on some Neanderthal's sloping forehead?

I know, I know, they're talking about traditional family values, which means supporting a family and busting junior on the head when mom finds stroke mags underneath his mattress. Sorry. Family values are a little too estrogenic for me. Give me male values, traditional male values.

Walter R. Newell, in his book, "The Code of Man" advocates just such a return to traditional ideas of manhood. He writes that through the ages, courage and pride were about "the struggle to defend and extend justice and to overcome our baser instincts," but he laments the fact that somewhere along the way, traditional manhood gave way to false machismo and violent behavior.

How exactly do we reestablish these traditional male values? I'm not sure. It's a tall order. I know some cultures send their boys out into the jungle or the wild by themselves. When they come back–if they survive—they're pronounced men and treated as such. Americans? We send our young boys to Daytona Beach, or maybe the Bahamas! Or even—Junior will like this—snowboard camp! It's a reward for having the incredible tenacity and ability to make it through…high school, or even junior high school.

When they come back, they're not men; they're still arrogant, disrespectful punks, albeit with nice tans.

I'm not just being a coot. I thought this way when I was 20 and I think this way now, but current times have strengthened my convictions on this topic.

I've got an idea. Do you have a son? Do him and yourself a favor. Get some adult male friends–role models—together and throw the boy a ritual, a manhood ritual, when he reaches the age of 16. Tell the women to stay home. Then, have each friend stand up, tell him what it means to be a man, and give your son some small token of manhood or masculinity, whether it be a jackknife, a set of dog tags, or a special book.

They'll serve as talismans to both remind him of his new station in life and to ward off weakness. Tell your son that he's a man now and expected to act like one from now on. And if he screws up? Well, he's now got a whole tribe to answer to, any of which forever have the right to smack him in the back of the head when childish behavior creeps back in.

Seal the deal by eating some bloody steaks.

As part of the ritual, I'd take him to the gym the next day and introduce him to weightlifting. Weightlifting is where he channels his aggression. Weight lifting is how he builds self-confidence and pride and prepares himself for the physical challenges to come. After all, defending and extending justice is hard work. It takes a strong back.

Beyond all that, America has to stop loving merely the facade of toughness or masculinity. The virtues we hold dear–the virtues that truly reflect masculinity, traditional masculinity–come in different, often unexpected guises.

That being said, the embedded Barbie doll still isn't a very manly look.

Man Among Men

SECTION

3

Chapter 15

Men Were the Only Ones Wise Enough to Understand the Virtues of Fire

"Try being a guy at work nowadays . . . and you'll be slapped with a sexual harassment charge. I have a friend who was forced to quit because he told a coworker that she looked "hot." Never mind that the air conditioning was broken, she was moving some boxes and sweating profusely, and that her tank top revealed that she had more hair on her back than Ed Asner. She, in her deluded mind, thought he was coming on to her. She should be so lucky."

I went to a friend's house last week, presumably to partake in the one ritual where men reign supreme and where women have not yet dared to tread. Yes, since time immemorial; since our simian-like ancestors discovered that, "Hey, standing on two feet is a little harder on the back, but now I can see clear over to Stuey's cave," men have engaged in the practice of lighting a fire outdoors and holding some meat over it until it was indistinguishable from the charred wood beneath it.

Women, either instinctively or because they'd be beaten about the thighs and buttocks with birch branches if they did otherwise, stayed away. Men were the only ones wise enough to understand the virtues of fire. Failing to realize this law of nature was tantamount to walking into the lair of a saber-toothed tiger covered in tuna sauce with a small satchel of catnip affixed to your hoo-hah.

Yes, the much-hallowed barbecue has always been a males-only club, and it's remained that way, even in this day of Title IX, female soccer mania, Benson & Hedges "you've come a long way, baby" crapola. Venturing into some previously all-male territory is pretty much okay with us guys, though. Most of us don't mind all of this equality stuff, and even when babes put on boxing gloves, we think it's kinda cute—especially when they wear something tight and the sweat starts to creep through and it turns into a combination slugfest/wet T-shirt contest.

As long as we have our male-only barbecues, we're all right. We don't even mind if the women are *nearby*, say, in the kitchen, and it's even okay if they press their Maybelline 100 percent oil-free-makeup–covered noses to the window and mouth the words:

"Will the hot dogs be done soon?"

Of course, the females themselves may have some sort of secret kitchen ritual that we're unaware of, and what they may really be mouthing against the glass is:

"I just told my friends that your penis is smaller—much smaller—than that charred and smoking hot dog."

Either way, we give them a "thumbs up" or an "A-okay" and get back to the manly art of roasting animal flesh.

That's how it was last Saturday. The three of us males were standing there, participating in the time-honored ritual of watching the flames char the flesh. As the barbecue alpha-male turned the dogs over, we grunted our approval. Speech wasn't necessary, but had we attempted to articulate our feelings, this is what we would have said:

"The world was created in flames, my brothers, and as we roast the all-beef wieners that nature has bestowed upon us, we celebrate life and manhood. So it was, so it is, and so it shall be. Now, pass me another Budweiser."

But our solemnity quickly turned to shock. One of the women slid open the glass door wall and approached the sacred flames. We were flabbergasted. The three of us, with the possible exception of her all-too-forgiving husband, contemplated covering her ass with pineapple slices and turning her into a baked ham. She was, amazingly, totally unaware of her place in barbecue society.

And rather than stand there respectfully, which we might have tolerated, she began offering her advice on how the sacred meat should be prepared!

"Why is the flame so high?"

"Shouldn't the hot dogs be *over* the charcoal, instead of *in* it?"

"Why does the lump in the corner look like that tree squirrel I saw you guys trying to catch earlier?"

Out of respect for our friend, and with his solemn assurance that he would exact some measure of discipline from her later, we ignored her. We moved over to our Pier One Imports rattan thrones and sat downwind of the glorious black smoke while she continued to lean over the grill and scrutinize the meat.

We began to converse—in between coughing jags—about manly things in the hopes that she would go away. Favorite commercials, gas mileage, why some girls have pink smooth nipples that look like budding flowers in springtime while others have large brown bumpy nipples that look like the infield at Yankee Stadium. All these things we talked about and more, and yet she stayed. She even tried to turn the conversation toward herself. She cried:

"Help me! Help me! My hair's on fire!"

Me, me, me. She couldn't care less about the meat and the barbecue and the camaraderie of men. She just wanted to talk about herself:

"My God, I'm burning! Please get the hose!"

It was pathetic.

Oh, we ate our food, but the evening was tainted. It should've been great; the three of us men enjoying the culinary pleasures of our work and the black grit on our teeth and lips. But somehow, the encroachment had sullied our mood. And the female interloper was *still* oblivious to her crime against male barbecue hierarchy. Her with her head all coated in salve and wrapped in bandages! And she never even said she enjoyed the hot dogs!

As much as I like the company of women, there's something to be said for getting together with a group of men and reveling in sheer Testosterone. With men, you can be yourselves; you can talk about common experiences. Do you think that women can understand what it feels like to sink a cigarette butt in the toilet with a powerful stream of urine?

No way. Can women ever know what it's like to wake up in the morning and find that your erect member has created a makeshift tent out of the sheet, which has been taken up as a temporary venue for a traveling circus act of midgets and miniature ponies? I seriously doubt it.

Will a woman ever fathom that electric surge of Testosterone that shoots up through our loins when we see a girl with an impossibly short skirt open up her car door and lean really far forward in order to put her Nordstrom's bag in the back seat of her two-door sedan? Not unless she wears construction boots and works as a roadie for those Lilith Fair concerts.

The trouble is, there are very few places that guys can get together. Women have baby showers, book clubs, and friggin' Tupperware parties. They go shopping together. "Let's have coffee," they say, and they do. They even go to the bathroom together.

Guys, for some reason, are supposed to be as solitary as my left testicle (I lost the right one years ago in a freak accident involving a hooker with a really bad case of hiccups).

There aren't many places where guys are permitted to be guys, though. Try being a guy at work nowadays. Give anybody even a hint that you've got testicles hidden in your Dockers and you'll be slapped with a sexual harassment charge. I have a friend who was forced to quit because he told a coworker that she looked "hot." Never mind that the air conditioning was broken, she was moving some boxes and sweating profusely, and that her tank top revealed that she had more hair on her back than Ed Asner. She, in her deluded mind, thought he was coming on to her.

She should be so lucky.

Barbecues, of course, are one of the few places that guys can act normal and be with other guys and act like pigs. As much as I was screwing around earlier in this column, maybe there is something primordial about how guys gather around a barbecue.

The gym is like that, too. It's funny, but it's where I meet any new friends nowadays. Despite all the chest—or breast—thumping about equality, there's something inherently masculine about the gym.

Sure, the gyms are full of women, and they're more than welcome in my book. But somehow, the women in them seem to be acutely aware that guys have this stuff flowing through their gonads that makes them different from women. The women I like best are the ones who understand that difference and appreciate it.

After all, if men and women were exactly alike, life wouldn't be very much fun. Cross-dressing would be the norm, and if the image of Ed Asner in thong panties doesn't give you the shivers, I don't know what will.

Chapter 16

Well, Screw You, Tim and Charles!

"A good friend — a bud — wouldn't hesitate to tell you that your wife is a castrating little bitch if, indeed, she was. Wives would prefer that you were blissfully unaware of their insidious bitchiness, and they certainly don't need some male sidekick to fill their husband's ear with the truth."

Oh, I remember the old days when I used to have some friends. Guys I could call up for no damn reason. Guys who I'd play catch with. Guys who'd give me a place to crash after my woman threw me out for trying to nail her pedicurist.

It's true. I even shared some common interests with these friends. I know, I know, it's hard to believe that there are other guys out there who enjoy RealDolls and panty-bin diving, but there are, or at least there used to be.

Time passed, and my friends are pretty much all gone. I can now drop my pants and, using my dick as a crude version of a Chinese abacus, rapidly and efficiently calculate the number of close friends that I have left.

Sure, I have lots of *acquaintances*, but I'd never call them up if I had any problems. Nor would I ever ask them to drive me to the airport or do any of that other obligatory friend stuff. Nor would they understand if I made crude remarks about their girlfriends or wives, and that kind of stuff is important to me. If my friend's girlfriend has great tits, by God, I should be able to ask my friend to describe what they look like, in great detail. If her nipples are the size of saucers, I want to know about it! If the bumps on her nipples, when translated to Braille, say "Lick me, Conan," I *demand* to know about it!

Instead, when I talk to acquaintances, I slip into this polite dialogue that's so formal and so stilted that I have to slap myself in the face to remind me that I'm not running for some kind of public office.

The thing is, I'm not that unusual. Most of the adult men that I know lead pretty solitary lives. Most admit that their wives are their best friends, and that's lovely and makes me want to write a series of drippy Hallmark greeting cards, but it's also kind of sad.

The result is a society of men who are so dependent on their wives that many end up holding onto rotten, unfulfilling relationships out of fear that they'll have no one left to talk to should she leave. Honey may be a ball-shriveling shrew, but she's the only ball-shriveling shrew they have.

Most of us have to go back in time to junior high school to remember the last time we had buds. Of course, as soon as hormones kicked in, we were like a bunch of head-butting rams, vying for the attention of any female dumb enough to look at our pimply faces.

Were we happy for Joey when he started dating Pamela? Sure, as long as she wasn't hotter than our girlfriends. Were we happy for Douggie when he made the football team?

Sure, as long as he didn't make the starting team while we sat on the bench. And lastly, were we happy for that bastard Darren when he was voted president of the Star Trek club—*instead of me*—and got to meet Nichelle Nichols, the lovely Nubian actress who played Uhura on the original series, when the club went to the Star Trek convention? No f-ing way.

Things got competitive, didn't they? While we were all eyeing each other like a bunch of hungry, shipwrecked sailors who only had one tin of canned meat to last them through the week, the women we knew were being *supportive* of each other. If one of them ran for prom queen, her friends would help her do her hair, apply her make-up, and root for her as if they were rooting for themselves.

Would most guys be as supportive? I hardly think so. I ran for queen of the office prom last week, and neither of my supposed friends, Tim and Charles, gave a *damn* whether I won or lost. When deciding if my hair looked better in a bun or a jaunty bob, I had to depend on my own judgment. Nooo, instead of helping and being supportive and reveling in my potential victory, they were too busy being strangled by their jealousy. Well, *screw you*, Tim and Charles, I'm the reigning queen now!

Now, I'm sure most of you have had some friendships that either lasted or started after high school, but there's always a whole Everest-like pile of stigmas attached. If two men get together for any reason other than to hunt women, they've gotta be gay, right? And most straight men are deathly afraid of being labeled gay. As a matter of fact, I once saw two guys go to a store together—and the store didn't sell hardware, automotive parts, or sporting goods! Can you believe it?

There's another way that you can tell which way they swing, too. Do they convey their *feelings* about something? Bingo! The next train leaves for Gay City in five minutes, and I'll be sure to find a spot in the caboose for you, doe eyes! Do they ever pat each other on the back with less force than it would take to slap a baseball out of Yankee Stadium? Tootie fruities!

It's all pretty silly.

The scene from *Planes, Trains, and Automobiles* where Steve Martin had to share a motel-room bed with John Candy was funny because it was so true. Both men edged out to opposite sides of the bed to make sure that there was as much distance as possible between them, lest they accidentally touch.

Friendships between adult men are hard to come by because of distrust, too. If a man befriends another, then he obviously must want something. He may buy you a beer, but next week he's going to want you to help him move into his new fourth-story apartment:

"By the way, did I tell you that the building is real old and doesn't have a working elevator, and I've got the largest collection of old-time bank vaults in North America?"

And, in all likelihood, he'll be asking for your kidney the following week, the bastard.

Guys make casual friends at work, but it's rare that such friendships last beyond the workplace. Once one finds another job, they no longer share any common ground.

Think back to the last time you shared a table with a bunch of guys. Most spend the time looking around uncomfortably, only breaking the silence to share a joke or a clever one-liner. If one of them says that he's a little depressed because his dog was Osterized when the Frisbee he was throwing accidentally soared into the neighbor's leaf mulcher and Scoobie, in a fit of overexuberance, leapt after it, he's labeled as some sort of weepy wimp.

If, however, one of them mentions that he just found the cure for cancer, he's labeled a boastful braggart. Consequently, they keep such thoughts and feelings to themselves and, instead, relate to each other through lame jokes.

Put a group of women together, and they'll get along famously, talking about anything and everything. Of course, it would bore the snot out of any male, but at least women are able to have a good time.

Ever look at your wife or girlfriend's email? They talk about ... well, stuff—what's going on in their lives, what their plans are. They ask questions about what the other person is doing. Compare that with a man's email. Men use the Internet to send "top 10" lists, animated video files of Snoopy screwing Lucy, and Clinton jokes that have circled the planet more often than the Russian spacecraft Mir.

Now, I certainly don't want to hear a detailed list of what my friend is doing—I'd prefer to see the video clip of Snoopy—but I sure would like him to be able to tell me if something was bugging him.

If married men have friends, chances are that they're the husbands of their wives' friends. When my wife has her friend Laurel come over, I'm expected to chum around with her husband Howard who works at a store that sells arts and crafts. He's the manager of the Styrofoam aisle. When Howard starts telling me what a "dog eat dog" world the arts and crafts business is, my eyes glaze over like I've got shoe leather–thick cataracts.

Nahh, married guys aren't supposed to have friends. And they're definitely not supposed to have single or divorced friends. That would pose too much of a threat to their wives. Why, if you chum around with a single guy, he might know some single women, and that could lead to extramarital fornication. By hanging around with a single guy, you might remember what it was like to be free, to smell the good earth, to taste fruit, to feel the wind across your face, and to do a world-record free dive between that little Asian chick's honey-colored thighs.

Likewise, a good friend—*a bud*—wouldn't hesitate to tell you that your wife is a castrating little bitch if, indeed, she was. Wives would prefer that you were blissfully unaware of their insidious bitchiness, and they certainly don't need some male sidekick to fill their husband's ear with the truth.

There are other problems, too. By and large, male-male relationships are freer than some male-female relationships.

They're less possessive, there's less jealousy, and neither one has to fit into a preconceived role. Wives or mothering girl-friends don't like that.

I've known a lot of guys who act totally different from the way they act when they're with their wives when they're hanging out with me. When they're with their wives, they act as if their assholes have been stitched up with baling wire. The conversation alone will put you into a coma:

"Why, yes, I've found that applying mesh over the gutter prevents vegetation from clogging up the downspouts."

Shoot me, somebody, please! Or, better, shoot *him*. But once their wives go shopping, they're different—they're *fun*. I've known guys who, like dogs that have been penned up for a week in a four-foot-by-four-foot kennel, start barking and panting and chasing their tails around in a joyous circle until they collapse in contented exhaustion when they're let out by their wives or girlfriends.

They're like the Robert DeNiro character in the movie Awak-enings who, just after having been given an L-dopamine cocktail, comes out of a 20-year coma and suddenly takes childlike pleasure in getting his feet wet in a lake.

The prospect of a real male-male friendship is far too threat-ening for a lot of women, and they may even attempt to sab-otage the friendship by saying things like:

"He's not your real friend. Anybody who'd ask you to drive him to the airport is using you."

If stuff like that fails, they pull out the heavy artillery:

"You guys spend so much time together, why don't you just go to bed with him?"

Yikes! That line would cause most heterosexual men to immediately end a friendship, even if the friend in question had taken a grenade for him back in Nam.

It's no wonder that men don't have many close friends.

I'm not about to start preaching about how you should go over to that guy who once passed you the catsup at the diner and give him a noogie on the head before sitting down to share your feelings in the hopes of establishing a buddy-buddy relationship, because I'm not about to do that myself.

Still, if I don't, how will I ever know if he's a potential soul mate? How will I ever know if he's into the same things I am, like panty-bin diving or singing the national anthem at cockfights?

I guess I won't. I guess I'll have to find a girlfriend who's into those things.

Chapter 17

C'mon, Give Me a Hug

"Hugging isn't something I'm likely to take up, at least not without a whole lot of kicking and screaming. I'll always prefer the firm handshake, the slap on the back or, when women are concerned, a more sincere approach like a breast massage or a little kiss on the lips with some vigorous tongue action."

I dropped a friend off at the airport the other day. He lives in another town, so I really look forward to his visits and I'm always sad to see him go. Now, this is a very *close* friend, mind you. When it came time to say goodbye, rather than hug, we put our hands in our pockets, looked downward, and pawed the ground with our feet.

A couple of passersby, horse lovers no doubt, stopped to give us each a lump of sugar and scratch us behind the ears.

Finally, just to cut the tension and end the awkwardness, I did the manly version of a hug. I body slammed my friend into a coffee cart. It was a good one, too. Any self-respecting hockey ref would have given me two minutes in the penalty box.

He got up, shook the mocha java out of his ears, and socked me in the shoulder.

That was our goodbye. My eyes teared up a bit as I watched him walk toward his gate, a trail of coffee grounds falling out of his pants.

My wife and I had a get-together at my house a few weeks ago. We had invited some people over, mostly couples, to eat some burnt animal flesh, courtesy of our brand new barbecue, which, when not being used to char meat, is employed by Cal Poly to conduct fusion experiments.

When the evening ended, and everyone decided to leave en masse, we exchanged the usual pleasantries. "Oh, thank you for having us and we must do this again and you've just *got* to give me the recipe for that runny Jell-O stuff with the gummy bears floating in it that reminds me of that lovely scene at the end of *Titanic* when all the corpses were floating in the water!"

Everyone started the ritual mass hug, but when it was my turn to be hugged by the meat cinder–filled females, I explained, much to my wife's chagrin, that I don't hug anyone unless they're naked. The guests looked at me in the same way that the people outside a courthouse look at the serial baby killer who's being led to trial by burly sheriff's department personnel.

It's true. I don't hug women unless they're naked. I know we live in a huggy world nowadays, but hugging just ain't my thing. I only hug someone, as mentioned, if it's a prelude to doin' the nasty and I want to peek over her shoulder to check out her ass.

Scratch that. I'd probably hug someone—man or woman—if they pulled me out of quicksand, or maybe I'd hug another man if I was a center fielder for a professional baseball team and our pitcher had just thrown a perfect game in the World Series, but that's about it.

There are those who will say my inability to hug other men stems from homophobia. That's not the case. I just don't like locking in an embrace with some guy. Guys, for the most part, smell like cheese, or stale beer, or whatever they've ingested in the last 24 hours. Besides its lack of appeal, what's the point?

If a guy wants to show some affection for me, he'll lend me 20 bucks and show me naked pictures of his girlfriend.

And, admittedly, there are times when I've actually touched another man. Why, just last February, I was spotting my business parnter at the gym as he attempted to set a personal record in the squat. He failed miserably, and after I had run to the hardware store down the street to get a long two-by-four, jammed it into the crack of his ass, and levered him and the 400-pound bar upright, my arm briefly brushed against his back.

So there, that ought to prove I'm not homophobic.

You could probably trace this abhorrence of physical contact to my childhood. My family, being of Scandinavian descent, wasn't exactly all warm and fuzzy. In fact, the only time I remember having much physical contact at all with anyone in my family was when I was 13 and had caught fire while trying to start a campfire. Rather than wrap me up in a blanket and roll me around the forest floor, my brother drove to the camp store to get some marshmallows.

After my family had gathered around my flaming body to toast the marshmallows until they were the exact shade and color of Thandie Newton's ass and eaten their fill, they took turns standing over me and beating me with rakes and shovels.

Being Scandinavian, such close physical contact was extremely painful for all of them, but they bore the discomfort admirably.

This disdain of hugging hasn't ever really been a problem for me, but lately, hugging's become quite fashionable. Everyone on TV hugs. Men who live next-door to each other hug goodbye after one of them comes over to borrow a pair of garden shears. Guys in the gym hug after a particularly good set of squats.

In the past, I was able to avoid hugs by feigning a stroke and collapsing to the floor with just the right amount of spittle leaking out of the corner of my mouth, but you start to lose credibility when you have several strokes a day.

Vanity Fair just published an article on the phenomenon of hugging, and earlier this year, the *New York Times* even went so far as to theorize that Democratic presidential hopeful Bill Bradley had lost the primaries when he was unable to hug his second-grade music teacher after she'd hobbled up to the podium to make a speech on his behalf.

Me? I would have just slapped her on the back and given her a couple of tickets to the Ice Capades.

Hugging women or girls should be a different matter to me, but I guess what I dislike about it is its insincerity. You see guys hugging girls all the time, but you women out there should believe me when I tell you that they're just copping a feel. While I suppose it's possible that the guy in question has an iota of sincere feeling toward you, more than likely he just wants to squeeze your tits into his pecs and check out how much body fat you're carrying.

Hours later, he'll be lying in bed, the sheet propped up and looking to the casual observer that little Timmy was playing pup tent, trying to remember that sweet hug, the feeling of your proud breasts pressed firmly against his chest, and the tantalizing pressure of your pelvis brushing against his Dockers, your private parts separated by mere millimeters of fabric ...

Oh! Oh! Oooooooohhhhhhh!

Excuse me. I got myself excited.

Anyhow, I have no idea where this hugging thing started. It might be an offshoot of the old 70s anti-drug slogan, "Hugs, Not Drugs," or those cute little posters of drenched cats hanging woefully off clotheslines with the caption, "I need a hug today."

Or, hugging, specifically where men are concerned, might have started off as a kind of jousting. Years back, men used to engage in that old Indian arm wrestling game where two men, foot to foot, lock hands and try to yank each other off balance.

The man who made the other lose his footing, of course, was the winner, and the inclination, usually unacted on, was for the winner to pull the vanquished toward him in a near hug and mock him by whispering, "You're a loser, I make more money than you do, my dick is bigger, and I could have your wife, *just like that*, for the asking."

Of course, when all that aggression stuff became more and more unfashionable, maybe the little tug contest evolved until all that was left was the handshake and the near or full-fledged warm, fuzzy, non-aggressive hug (even though a lot of guys who *do* manage to force a hug on me still whisper that same line in my ear).

No, hugging isn't something I'm likely to take up, at least not without a whole lot of kicking and screaming. I'll always prefer the firm handshake, the slap on the back or, when women are concerned, a more sincere approach like a breast massage or a little kiss on the lips with some vigorous tongue action.

18

They're Just Blobs, Totally Dependent Blobs

"You'll be expected to do a lot of gushing about how cute the baby is, too. Never mind that the thing looks just like Roddy McDowell in Planet of the Apes . . . . Oh, and remind me to show you the sonogram!"

I have friends with babies. Or should I say, I *used* to have friends with babies. Once those wrinkled little blobs squirted out of their mothers' wombs like so many howling watermelon seeds, I made myself scarce. I found new friends.

It's not so much the babies that bothered me, but the way their parents would act once they'd experienced the "miracle of birth." Maybe it's just me, but somehow birth is no longer a miracle after the first, say, *billion* times it occurs. Besides, how special can it be when the 17-year-old down the street, who keeps confusing Tic-Tacs with her birth control pills, pops out the little bastards with frightening regularity?

For those of you who haven't had any friends with babies, here's how the whole sordid thing generally progresses: First, life is good. You and your friends think nothing of dropping everything and heading to Cabo San Lucas for a margarita-drinking, bodysurfing, hell-raising binge that would tax the recuperative powers of Scott and Zelda Fitzgerald. Weekends, and working days, too, are made for Michelob, mosh pits, mountain climbing, jet skiing, pick-up basketball games, and just about anything else you can cram into the brief spaces of time between work and more work.

Then, one of your friends, for some reason, feels the urge to procreate. The fun stops, as quickly as if your doctor had called you up and said that your Wassermann test for syphilis came back positive. Your friends start taking classes on how to give birth. Hell, give me one of those African Ubangi women who, when it's time to give birth, momentarily stops working, goes into the tall reeds, squirts out the brat, bites off the umbilical with her teeth, and goes back to work. Classes? They doan need no steenking classes!

Mary Sue, who used to think nothing of doing four or six or eight tequila shooters, whipping her top off and gyrating in such a way that it would send a moose into cardiac arrest when she heard a Red Hot Chili Peppers tune, is now a veritable nun. She doesn't drink, she doesn't stay out late at night and, Lord knows, she eats all of her vegetables. She reads *Better Homes & Gardens*. And no one but her hubby will ever see her breasts again because, suddenly, they're functional organs and they're for the bay-bee! You wouldn't want to see them anyhow because you want to remember them as the pert little puppies that they once were, rather than what they're about to become: wrinkled, droopy, teeth-marked vessels resembling the deflated sheepskin wine flasks that Basque herdsmen drape over their shoulders.

Her mate, Joe, who used to occasionally carry nude photos of his ex-stripper girlfriend in his back pocket, now carries around ultrasound pictures of the fetus, mistaking the umbilical cord for a really long horse-cock of a penis and beaming proudly. You won't know what the hell you're looking at when he shows them to you, but try to act interested, for God's sake.

Soon, Joe and Mary Sue will drop out of sight entirely as they prepare for the baby. That new stereo system he wanted? The new Audi sports car? He's forgotten about all of it! He spends his free time at Costco, buying up bassinets, car seats, potty trainers, and all the other assorted crap that babies allegedly require. Then one day he'll call you out of the blue and start nonchalantly discussing various aspects of his wife's vagina:

"She's starting to dilate!"

You'll be invited over soon after the blessed event to watch the video of the birth. You thought the scene in *Alien* when the creature burst out of the guy's chest cavity was gross? Ha! Wait till you see a woman giving birth! The only difference is that, in *Alien*, the thing had the decency to scamper off and hide under a drainpipe. This thing just lies there and screams. It might make you swear off sex forever.

It's even worse after the birth thing. Mary Sue, who used to wear tube tops and barely higher-than-thigh-high blue-jean shorts, now wears gray sweats with asymmetrical puke stains on either shoulder. You'll no doubt be given the ultimate honor of being asked to hold the baby, so you better say goodbye to that nice DKNY sports jacket because baby spit is the most caustic stuff known to man, and the slightest bit of it can pemetrate the outer layers of a Kevlar vest.

You'll be expected to do a lot of gushing about how cute the baby is, too. Never mind that the thing looks just like Roddy McDowell in *Planet of the Apes*.

You might even get to join the couple for dinner periodically, but gone are the days of eating at your favorite sushi place or bistro. It's Chuck E. Cheese's for you, boy, or maybe the International House of Pancakes, or some other place where the shrill little banshees known as children are tolerated. You won't eat anything anyhow, because watching a baby eat would make the late Chris Farley lose his appetite. Maybe having cherry sauce, juice, and mashed potatoes smeared all over a face and chest is cool if a naked Kim Basinger is on your kitchen floor and you're recreating a scene from *9 1/2 Weeks*, but it's dreadfully disgusting if a baby is involved.

The discussions you and your friends used to have about politics, working out, anything remotely interesting? Fuggedaboudit! You'll now discuss the baby. He or she's a genius, you know. Why, just the other day, she took a brown crayon and made what looked like a shit Rorschach test on the bedroom wall. If you can't see that this is indicative of her highly evolved artistic ability, why, you're just not using your head. And by the way, did you know that she's such a good eater? Yes! Yes! She eats all of her mushed-up carrots, and she prefers the carrots over the peas, you know, and she now weighs *24 1/2* pounds, which puts her in the upper 80th percentile of children her age, and we are just so fucking proud!

Want to reminisce about that great time you had on that houseboat you rented one summer? Go ahead and try, but Joey is on the ground making choo-choo noises for the bay-bee! And he's talking baby talk! He sounds like your 80-year-old grandfather after he drinks a fifth of Jim Beam and can't find his teeth:

"Ooogaly-oogaly-oogaly."

You better start putting in some overtime at the job, too, because you've automatically entered into a kind of unspoken covenant where you're obliged to cough up some dough for a gift every birthday and Christmas until the brat reaches the age of 18. It seems kind of rude that they didn't discuss it with you beforehand to make sure that you could handle this kind of financial load, but that's just the way it is.

It's all pretty sad.

You've probably figured out for yourself that I'm not too keen on the idea of having children myself. For a while, I was caught up in that bullshit about achieving some sort of immortality because I'll have passed on my genes, but I've gotten over it. With my luck, my kid would wind up being one of those guys who sits shirtless in the stands at NFL games in sub-zero temperatures with his overgrown belly painted like a Broncos helmet. Either that, or he'd end up following in his dad's footsteps and writing potty-mouth columns for a webzine. Still, I miss some of those friends that I abandoned. Maybe if I dress up Grandpa in a diaper, I'll have something in common with them again. After all, he's wrinkled, soils his drawers, and makes unintelligible noises ...

One of my friends recently fathered a daughter. Now, Rick is about as Testosterone they get. There isn't an ounce of bullshit or excess sentimentality in the son-of-a-bitch. I think he'll make a good father, though.

Here's how he describes his daughter and kids in general:

"These kids are blobs; they're just blobs, totally dependent blobs."

Still, he takes pride in teaching her things:

"I taught her to accept a pacifier. And there's something to be said for teaching a woman to accept something that will satiate her orally. Of course, she's not too intelligent, because she just stuck the pacifier in her ear, but some women need to get it from anywhere."

All right, all right, I don't want any indignation on the part of any of you more easily offended readers. He was kidding, and that's why I think that I'll be able to tolerate him and the whole fatherhood thing. He didn't go nuts; he didn't romanticize the whole bullshit thing, and he has no aspirations or delusions of grandeur about his kid. She's just a baby, and he'll accept her however she grows up, smart or stupid, talented or klutzy, pretty or butt-ugly. And there's something to be said for that. I just hope she doesn't play soccer.

Rick is one in a million, though. Frankly, most parents tend to over-sentimentalize the whole thing. Personally, I think I'll stick with dogs, but did I tell you that I'm due to pick up a darling little puppy in a few weeks? I'm going to get the pick of the litter, and our friends are even throwing us a nice little doggy shower, and I just want everything to be perfect for our little bundle of joy (he's going to be a show dog, you know), and I can't wait to see his itty-bitty little face and his cute, itty-bitty tail, and I'll take him for walks, and I'll hug 'im, and pet 'im, and tell 'im all about the rabbits, George, and if I feed him just right, he'll be in the top 80th percentile of all little puppy-wuppies!

Oh, and remind me to show you the sonogram!

Chapter 19

The Age of Dumb Guys

"Well, that's where most of our society is now. We're the Skipper, Gilligan, and Thurston Howell, and we spend most of our time eating the fruit that drops from the trees and wondering how to catch a glimpse of Ginger and Mary Ann as they loofah their taut, naked bodies with natural sea sponges. It's all we can do to keep from looking up with our mouths open when it rains and drowning ourselves like big turkeys."

Hey, want to know how to insult someone nowadays? Call him an *Einstein*.

Sure, compare someone to perhaps the greatest scientific brain of the century, and the guy's liable to apply a little physics to your skull: "While I realize that energy can neither be created or destroyed, it can be transferred via my fist to your skull and give you a terrible boo-boo."

Welcome to the age of dumb guys. Welcome to an age where intelligence is a liability.

Somewhere along the way, being smart started being uncool. My friend Chris used to teach high school as recently as last year, and he tells me that kids no longer want to study and make decent grades because it will make them less popular.

Read a couple of books, get a few good grades, and *wham*, you're hanging out with the rejected souls who wear pocket protectors and make up the bulk of the Chess Club and the Star Trek Club.

Now, smart guys have never truly been loved or even respected in America. According to Russell Jacoby, author of *The End of Utopia: Politics and Culture in the Age of Apathy*, "There is a home-grown Yankee do-it-yourself attitude that is suspicious of someone who seems to know too much. We love education but we don't love educated people."

Ain't that the truth.

Somehow, though, it's gotten worse. Maybe it's because the smart guy isn't usually too in touch with current fashions, choosing instead to wear functional clothes rather than flashy stuff that keeps giving him wedgies. Maybe it's because smart guys don't dance too well, and if you ask one what they think about Eminem, he'll tell you about how dental caries thrive on sugar and that he, personally, doesn't partake of candies.

Sure, maybe they deserve to be smacked occasionally, but I'll generally take a smart guy over a dumb guy any day of the week.

I first realized something was terribly, terribly wrong with how we perceive book learnin' about 10 years ago. I was at a bar with some guys, and the conversation was droning on and on about various mind-numbingly dull subjects—radial tires, life insurance—when the conversation somehow switched over to hobbies. Since I'd had a couple of beers, my guard was a bit down and I momentarily showed a bit too much of my underbelly by telling them that I like reading, particularly the books that had won either the Pulitzer Prize or the National Book Award.

One of the guys, who knew me pretty well, but from whom I'd been able to hide this terrible, terrible secret from in the past, sneered at me and said, "Man, get a life."

Sure, sitting around swilling beers with this lugnut was some-how more gratifying than doing a workout for my brain. Now, I'm certainly not the smartest guy around—not by a long shot—but I can communicate fairly well, articulate the occasional complex idea, and even manage to regularly an-swer the first question on *Who Wants to be a Millionaire?*

Okay, I was lying about that last part. I can usually answer the first *two* questions on *Who Wants to be a Millionaire?* (I was downplaying my smarts so you wouldn't write me off as an egg-head.) Personally, I think that show is pretty emblematic of the times. I remember, as a kid, watching *College Bowl* or the old *Jeopardy!* show (pre-Alex Trebek) and man, those questions were muthuhs! Still, I used to be able to guess the occasional answer, or, in the case of *Jeopardy!*, the occasional question.

Today's big game show, the aforementioned *Millionaire*, is but a pale shadow of those other, more cerebral quiz shows. Whereas a typical question on *College Bowl* might have been something like, "Name the secretaries of state that served under Hoover, FDR, Truman, and Eisenhower," the typical question on the *Millionaire* show could be a real brain teaser like, "What colors are in an Oreo cookie?"

That cookie question was actually part of the show. I suppose the guy who answered that will be labeled an egghead and shunned by some: "Yeah, bright boy knows it *all*. Whaddaya say we pull those flood pants up even *higher* and give him a wedgie that stands a good chance of causing a brain hemorrhage?"

Maybe I'm being too hard on our culture. Maybe there are other ways of being smart, other than book-smart. For in-stance, psychologist Howard Gardner has labeled seven dif-ferent categories of intelligence:

1) Bodily/kinesthetic—like gifted athletes or even surgeons
2) Spatial—chess players, architects
3) Logical/mathematical—scientists
4) Musical—performers, composers
5) Linguistic—editors, authors, journalists
6) Intrapersonal—shrinks, counselors
7) Interpersonal—political leaders, religious leaders, diplomats

For instance, a guy could be a real prodigy in category 3, but a total numbskull in category 7. That means he'd grow up never having had many friends or even so much as had sex with anything other than the pleasingly slick vinyl couch cushion in his parent's living room. Maybe it doesn't matter, because when he grows up, starts a software company or invents a cure for some terrible disease, he'll make lots of money and suddenly, no one will care how nerdy he is. He'll suddenly be guardedly hip.

Likewise, somebody who's gifted in category 1 could be a huge sports star like Michael Jordan. He may also be gifted in other areas, but chances are he never bothered to cultivate those other talents because, alas, most of them just took too much work.

Take me for example. I'm gifted in the ways of love, which wasn't even mentioned by Gardner. I just have a knack for doing things that mesmerize the opposite sex—flowers, sweet talkin', and doing considerate things like rolling up my socks before lovemaking. I even carry my own lighting effects in case I get lucky. Three hundred pounds of lights and strobes and a generator. Lug it all around the city in a grocery cart. Even used to have a fog generator, but I gave it up when I once accidentally kicked the "high" button. Thing put out so much fog, I couldn't find the girl and ended up tripping on a footstool and breaking my pelvis.

But I digress.

I tend to believe in Gardner's theory, but I want to caution that all those traits, all those specific areas of intelligence are innate. Without care and nurturing, those innate traits start to wither and fall off the tree like so many frost-damaged grapes. Eventually, the brain starts turning into Campbell's split-pea soup and the only way you know it's functioning at all is by the occasional microscopic piece of ham that comes riding up on a bubble as it simmers.

This eventually manifests itself in a disdain for learning, where the guy who studies and works hard to potentiate his abilities is frowned on by the rest of society. He's a nerd! Why isn't he going through his dance steps like the rest of us? They never consider that if the professor on *Gilligan's Island* hadn't used his brain and initiative, he never would have gotten that bunch of looneys off the island! Well, come to think of it, he didn't, but he sure did build some cool stuff from coconuts.

That's where most of our society is now. We're the Skipper, Gilligan, and Thurston Howell III, and we spend most of our time eating fruit that drops from trees and wondering how to catch a glimpse of Ginger and Mary Ann as they loofah their taut, naked bodies with natural sea sponges. It's all we can do to keep from looking up with our mouths open when it rains and drowning ourselves like big turkeys.

So we've ended up with a country where making change for a buck requires a calculator, where people blindly follow dumb rules that don't pertain to the situation because making exceptions based on logic requires too much thinking. The whole place thinks like the waitress in *Five Easy Pieces*. As I remember it, Jack Nicholson tries to order a couple of pieces of toast, but the waitress informs him that they don't serve toast. So Nicholson, irate, orders a tuna fish sandwich "on toast" and tells her, and I paraphrase, to "hold the f-ing lettuce, tomato, tuna, and mayonnaise and serve me the damn toast."

In the gym, you see this lack of thinking manifest itself, at the most extreme, in the guy who keeps putting three 45-pound plates on one side of the bar and can't figure out what magical force is causing the bar to catapult itself across the gym and impale the liver of Sven, the guy whose job it is to wipe the sweat off the benches. At its most benign, you've got guys who do the same workouts all the time and pay as much attention to their eating habits as a fly on a shitpail and wonder why they never grow.

I have another theory. Part of me believes that the people who are physically gifted are often mentally gifted, too. Now, I know that's hard to believe, but bear with me. Physical gifts are, arguably, a product of good genetics, healthy genes. When one part of the genome is healthy, there's a good chance that the rest of it is, too. So it's quite easy to see how someone who was blessed with a healthy body might also get a healthy mind.

The trouble is, since the bearer of these good genes is physically attractive, society starts putting pressure on him. He's popular! Girls open their legs for him with the regularity of the pressure-sensitive door at the supermarket. Guys want to be his friend. He gets invited to parties. Coaches want him to play sports and teachers wink at him as they give him a passing grade on a test for which he didn't study.

Given these pressures, the quest for truth and enlightenment is kicked aside like the pairs of panties that litter the floor of his bedroom. The brain never really gets cultivated. Weeds started popping up all over the place and you get an infestation of locusts. Hence, you have a bunch of good-natured Labrador retriever–type human beings who prance around with their tongues hanging out, waiting for the next nice person to give them yet another free bone.

In looking back at this essay, I see that I've rambled on quite a bit. The trouble is, I don't have any answers. Sure, I'd like to see teachers get paid more, and maybe that would help, but I don't think that even shoving truckloads of money at teachers is going to give them the ability to inspire students more than TV, Nintendo, sports, and sex.

Maybe it would be good enough if just a few of us would strive for a happy medium. Maybe it would be good enough if just a few of us didn't think that intelligence is a liability.

After all, there was only one professor on that desert isle. Of course, nowadays, whenever he's around the rest of the castaways, he pretends to be just like them, laughing like a hyena when one of them makes armpit noises, but when he goes back to his hut, he cracks open the books and scans the Internet for at least a few sites that don't contain the words "hot" or "throbbing."

Chapter 20

Street Fightin' Man

"Sure, honor is on your side, but is the legal system? Nope. Try anything and you could well lose everything you have, including your freedom. Don't do anything, and you possibly lose your honor. . . . Ah, hell with it, maybe I am a beast, but I'm a beast people would want around if they were being mugged in a dark alley, because out of thousands of passers by, I'm one of the few who might help them without worrying too much about the repercussions."

M an, it always looks so easy in the movies. Some punk will cause some trouble, and Arnold will throttle the guy.

"Ja, I said I vould kill you lost, Solly, but I lied."

Pop! Crack! Smack! There goes Solly off the side of a cliff.

Same thing with any of the action heroes. If Stallone, Steven Seagal, or Dirty Harry sees anyone being picked on, the perpetrators are treated to either a fist in the face, a kick to the head, or a shot in the leg. It's all so simple up there on the screen.

Trouble is, real life ain't so easy, especially if you're a Testosterone type of guy. If you try to stick up for anyone or anything by being physical, you're thrown in the pokey. Worse yet, you could accidentally hurt the guy and turn him into a vegetable; and not even a vegetable that people actually *like*; but maybe a Brussels sprout or turnip or something. And then they'd sue you, and the courts give lots of money to vegetables, regardless of whether they're Brussels sprouts, turnips, or eggplants. Of course, all you'd have to do nowadays is *touch* somebody to get sued.

Now I know that everybody from our mothers to Michael Jackson on down wants us to "beat it" when faced by trouble. I don't blame mom because she wants sonny-boy to be safe, no matter what the cost. I don't blame Michael Jackson, either, because as soon as he says to his tormentor, in that high, breathy voice, "I'm a lover, not a fighter," he's going to be admitted to the hospital where emergency techs will labor long and hard to remove a sequined white glove from his acid-washed, cosmetically whitened butt.

Running is safe, usually smart, but what happens when you get home? How do you look at yourself in the mirror, knowing you ran away from a fight?

I'm not talking about a fight with some pudknocker at the bar who disparaged your hockey team; I'm talking about situations where some Cro-Magnon who just learned to walk upright this morning insults your wife or girlfriend, or carves his initials into your car with his keys as he walks by it.

Sure, honor is on your side, but is the legal system? Nope. Try anything and you could well lose everything you have, including your freedom. Don't do anything, and you possibly lose your honor.

Now I'm an amiable guy. I don't look for fights, but sometimes fights come looking for me in the guise of a bully. I remember standing in the hallway the other day, talking to Ruby, the staff manicurist, when my partner Tim Patterson walks by and for no reason at all, gives me a big-time wedgie and starts guffawing like a drunken frat boy. Do I act like a mouse and take it, or do I retaliate? If I do nothing, will Ruby still respect me and do my nails for free?

So I say to Tim:

"You're a poo-poo head!"

And he says, "No, you're a poo-poo head!

"Oh yeah?"

"Yeah!"

"Oh yeah?"

"Yeah!"

This continues until it gets dark and our wives call the office to tell us we're late for dinner.

We see men facing this kind of dilemma all the time, even in the sports world. Take a look at the second game of the 2000 World Series. Mike Piazza's up to bat, and Roger Clemens zips in a 96-mph fastball. Piazza makes contact, but too far down on the handle and the bat splinters into a dozen pieces. The barrel of the bat ends up bouncing in front of the mound and Clemens manages to grab it before it shish kabobs the Rocket's payload, if you catch my drift.

Big-baby Clemens, acting as if Piazza *intentionally* splintered the bat and sent it flying toward the mound, flings the barrel of the bat back at Piazza. Now, in case you're not a baseball fan, this isn't part of the game. Generally, the rules prohibit you from shooting, maiming, or hurling any object, least of all a splintered baseball bat, at an opposing player.

Obviously, it's a big-time confrontational act, and Piazza's not only being watched by his teammates and the 50 thousand fans in the stadium, but millions of TV viewers around the world. What should he do?

If he goes and lays a few haymakers against the Rocket's noggin, he's thrown out of the game and deemed selfish for hurting his team's chances of winning the game. However, if he ignores it, he's deemed gutless. See? Dilemma city.

I remember walking down the streets of New York City at night a few years ago with bodybuilder Lisa Lorio and my wife. I was walking with Lisa's dad, and the two girls were about 30 steps in front of us. Three guys, seated on the ubiquitous New York City stoop, began whistling at the girls and making crude remarks (oh yeah, that's a *real* effective approach in getting the chicks).

Given that Lisa's dad is from the South, the *old* South, and the guys on the stoop weren't white, his ire started bubbling up like the vat of moonshine he no doubt had brewing behind his house. He looked at me with disgust and drawled, "Ain'tcha gonna beat the hell outta them?"

Now, this is clearly a case where a fight wasn't warranted. For one thing, Lisa's dad's urgings were mostly based on racial prejudice. Furthermore, it's not like we were even walking with the girls. As far as the three bozos on the stoop were concerned, the girls were alone.

And, lastly, the girls were dressed, well, kinda nice: tight pants, tight tops, high heels, all the stuff that cries out to men like the Sirens of Greek mythology, calling them to come smash their nuts on the rocks.

But I often think about what I would have done, what I *should* have done, had we been walking alongside the girls. When a guy—regardless of race—makes a comment to a woman that's clearly your date or your wife, it's a challenge to you. The girls are merely incidental. Still, had I acted, several things could have happened. I could have been like an action figure and avenged their honor, which would have assured me some "hero" sex, which is, I've heard, the best sex there is.

From what I've heard from firefighters and policeman, the girl, or girls, do all the work during hero sex, and they don't even care if they orgasm! And afterward, they usually take you out for ice cream and a pony ride, and maybe give you a gift certificate to a sporting-goods store.

Hell, maybe I would have gotten hero sex from *both* of them. More than likely, though, I would have had the snot beaten out of me, possibly *shot* out of me, and I could quite possibly have endangered the girls' lives.

In that case, avoiding conflict would have been the best course of action, but God, it would have eaten me up alive later when I got home to face that cursed mirror, especially knowing that I had kissed off a potential bout of tag-team sex.

As the editor-in-chief of an Internet magazine, I'm occasionally faced with another "fight or flight" type of dilemma. It probably comes as no surprise to you that we've got some enemies in the biz; people who, because of jealousy, general psychosis, or warped business ethics, continually harangue us on the message boards, even going so far as trying to sabotage some of our efforts.

Probably a week doesn't go by where I don't fantasize about doing a Dirty Harry number on these guys. But I know it will never happen, never *can* happen. The current structure of our society doesn't allow for it. They'll either have me thrown in jail, as mentioned, or sue me for everything that I have, which would leave my wife really, really, pissed.

Maybe I'm a throwback to a less-civilized time, but I can't help but thinking that this is one situation when the "old way" was better than the modern way. Years ago, if anybody made a crude remark to your woman, you'd pop him one, and everybody would applaud and buy you drinks. Same thing for anybody that tried to screw with your business or livelihood.

Not so anymore. It's considered bad form. Besides, a couple of cars with disco lights on their roofs will come to take you away, while the idiot who caused all the trouble gets to go home and watch TV.

I think people might have been a bit more respectful of others when they knew that their actions often had repercussions—namely, a hairy fist in the snout, or a punch to the ol' breadbasket.

Maybe the much-ballyhooed decline of manners and civility in our culture is just the byproduct of the current legal structure. Rudeness simply stems from knowing that rude actions don't have any consequences. Hell, you can pretty much do any crappy thing you want, say any crappy thing you want, as long as you don't touch anyone.

It's too bad, because I think that there wouldn't be quite so many bratty kids around if adults were allowed to occasionally pluck one off a skateboard and beat some manners into him.

Even the United States is faced by rudeness—international rudeness—all the time. Try to retaliate against some foreign dictator for having attacked Americans and the country is considered a bully. When some hostile country takes U.S. citizens as hostages, do we retaliate? Nah, we negotiate, because even we don't know how to act nowadays. It's Mike Piazza on a big scale: Retaliate against a third-world country and you're a bully; don't do anything and you're called gutless.

I sometimes think of how the Russians have handled that kind of thing in the past. Several years back, a terrorist group took some Russian embassy members hostage. Did they negotiate? Nope. They sent the terrorists a message that, in essence, said, "Harm one hair on the heads of our comrades and we'll go to your house, your in-law's house, your cousin's house, and the house of everybody you know and wipe them all out."

The hostages were released the next day.

Sigh. Kinda reminds me of the end of the Clint Eastwood movie, *Unforgiven,* where Will Munny leaves the bar and shouts out to the townspeople, "All right now, I'm comin' out. Any man I see out there, I'm gonna shoot him. Any sumbitch takes a shot at me, I'm not only gonna kill him, I'm gonna kill his wife. All his friends. Burn his damn house down."

I figure the Russians must have written the script for the movie.

Similarly, when Israeli athletes were killed at the Munich Olympics, the Israelis hunted down and disposed of most of the perps.

I can almost imagine the howls of indignation out there right now among the politically correct. They no doubt think I'm a fascist, a high-Testosterone beast not fit to roam the countryside. I'm not a beast, just a modern man trying to reconcile his emotions, hormones, and old-fashioned sense of justice with modern trends and modern definitions of what constitutes a "civilized" man.

Ah, hell with it, maybe I am a beast, but I'm a beast people would want around if they were being mugged in a dark alley, because out of thousands of passersby, I'm one of the few who might help them without worrying too much about the repercussions.

And I guess I'll just have to live with the occasional rude son of a bitch or Cro-Magnon thug and save my battles for those life-and-death situations. Still, I can't help wishing that life were at least a little like the movies and that justice wasn't so complicated and hard to come by. I also can't help wishing for some of that hero sex, along with that pony ride.

Man vs. Woman

SECTION

4

Chapter 21

The Worst Thing You Can Call a Man...

"Maybe we should just admit that men, in general, are cursed — particularly those of us who pay so much attention to physical appearance. My only hope...no, our only hope is that more women start weight training, too, so that they can look similarly juicy well into their late thirties or beyond. Of course, all of the 20-year old guys (you bastards) will nab them, too, and then we'll be stuck sitting in front of Victoria's Secret, making lewd comments and hoping that one of them will take pity on us."

So I'm at a shopping center in San Diego the other day, sitting in front of Victoria's Secret. I do that a lot. It's just that Vicky's is near my house, and there's a great little fountain out front where it's convenient to sit and have a cup of coffee. Anyhow, it's just me and my hound, relaxing, drinking some Starbuck's (me, not the hound, because the caffeine makes him edgy, and then he can't fall asleep until Ted Koppel comes on), and watching people ... well, girls, really.

Once in a while, just for grins, I'll see a cute one leave the store with a package that's no doubt stuffed with lacy underwear, and I'll make my voice a little gravelly and ask her:

"Hey, lemme see whatcha bought, okay? You look like a thong lady to me. C'mon, pull those suckers out."

Okay, I don't really ask them that, but God knows I've come close a few times.

Anyhow, I'm sitting there enjoying the sun, and I see this really hot number, maybe 18, 19 years old, sit down opposite me. She's wearing one of those tube-top numbers that Satan invented to test the mettle of good men everywhere. I see the little vixen occasionally glance up at me, flutter her Maybelline eyelashes, and then turn away rapidly when we make eye contact. This goes on for a few minutes, and I start thinking:

Hold on, here—I smell a *Penthouse* letter in the works.

Quickly, my memory searches through the inventory of my underwear drawer and struggles to remember which ones I'm wearing today. Are they the navy blue Jockeys that make my butt all perky, or the white, threadbare ones that are as revealing as the dress that Jennifer Lopez wore to the Grammys? It's okay, I'm safe. I retired the white ones from regular rotation last week, and they'll live out their last days as a middle-relief pitcher, being called on only in the event that the starters are in the laundry hamper.

And then, wonder of wonders, this silky blonde creature gets up and *walks toward me.* She gets close enough so that I can see the tiny blonde hairs on her belly as they reflect the sunlight and, for a moment, I forget to breathe. In my mind, we're already prancing naked through fields of wheat. (Never mind that, even in my imagination, things go horribly wrong as I stub my toe on a wheat thresher and, while hopping around in pain, I knock her into a compost heap.) I look up at her green feline eyes, and just before the spittle starts to form at the corner of my mouth, she speaks to me. She says:

"Sir, could I please pet your dog?"

She wasn't looking at me—she was ogling my hound! And, she ... she called me the absolute worst thing that any young woman can call a guy ... sir! Arrrghhh! She's just fired missiles at the raging, nuclear-spawned Penissaurus that's struggling to free itself from my pants and lay waste to Tokyo! She's held up a crucifix to the Dracula that lies in the coffin of my zipper.

The ultimate effect? *"Down goes Frazier! Down goes Frazier!"* Like Ali, she's whupped him, and he's lost his once-proud stature and is now linguini.

To her, I'm a fossil, someone who might pal around with her dad. Never mind that I probably listen to some of the same music she does, or go to the same clubs, or wouldn't be caught dead wearing a suit.

Unlike Leonardo DiCaprio or Ricky Martin, my face isn't as smooth as a castrato's butt. Besides, I lack the accouterments of youth, like the backward baseball cap, the nose ring, and the crotch that begins at the knees of my jeans. Regardless of the May/December romances that are common in films, she ain't buying any of it. She's Denise Richards but, unlike James Bond, I ain't gonna get any action from this little physicist.

Some of you younger guys aren't old enough to have been called "sir" yet, but wait, just wait. You'll be walking along, feeling studly, trying to decide whether to beat the hell out of the next guy who gives you shit, or impregnate the next group of cheerleaders you see when, after buying a copy of *American Breast Enthusiast* from the local drugstore, some chick behind the checkout counter, in between chomps of her gum, will say, "Thank you, sir, please come again," talking to you as if you were a grownup or something, someone who's not in her age group.

You'll be momentarily puzzled, but you'll shrug it off as some sort of anomaly, until it starts to happen again and again. Welcome to the sobering world of adulthood, my son.

Some cultures tell time by the stages of the moon. Others, like the aborigines, don't even bother to recognize time. Me? *Playboy* magazine is my chronometer. I'm cognizant of the passage of years through the Playmate of the Month.

There was a time when the centerfold of the month was, to me, a sophisticated, older woman. Worldly. Impossible to obtain.

Then, as I got a little older, she became one of my peers. Wild, adventurous, but still impossible to obtain, at least until my skin cleared up a bit.

And then, seemingly the next day, I checked the birth date of the latest centerfold, and she was born in 1986. That's enough to make the hair on your neck stand erect. She's a girl who would, no doubt, call me "sir" out of respect because I'm a stale pork chop—at least, compared to her. And she's still impossible to obtain...unless I've got lots of cash, of course.

Okay, so we live in a youth-obsessed culture. And while yesterday's American boys and young men looked forward to the day when they'd be addressed as "sir", it sure ain't the case today. It's not necessarily maturity or advancing age that's a bitch because, with weight training and diet and supplements, our bodies can pretty much look as studly as they ever did. No, the real bitch about getting older is that nookie becomes more and more scarce.

Many of the women that we're physically attracted to generally don't regard anybody in their mid- to late 30s or beyond as being part of the game. It's a question of perception. Making it with someone that old would be like making it with their homeroom teacher, or Eddie, the clubfooted janitor. Of course, they'll never know that Eddie, despite having a stumpy leg, knows what vintage of wine to serve while mopping a toilet floor and is also the heir apparent to the company that makes those little urinal soap cakes.

It's your loss, baby.

You younger women out there—you tasty morsels—should realize that we haven't been dragging this granite-like piece of man-meat across the floor of terra firma for 30 or 40 years for nothin'—it's learned a few things. Oh, it may be battle-scarred, but it's a wise penis. It can sing, it can dance, and it's even done some backup work for Barry White. It can catch a Frisbee, bat a ball, or pluck out a romantic song on an angel's harp.

Sometimes it's a serious penis, and sometimes it's a whimsical penis. It's complex. It's a puzzle wrapped in an enigma, but beyond all that, it exists only to make you happy.

Now, how can anything that wants to make you happy be bad?

Such is the case with virtually any man over 30 (you younger guys will get there soon enough—just keep practicing, and remember to rub it with neats-foot oil every night).

Maybe we should just admit that men, in general, are cursed—particularly those of us who pay so much attention to physical appearance. My only hope—no, *our* only hope—is that more women start weight training, too, so that they can look similarly juicy well into their late 30s or beyond. Of course, all of the 20-year-old guys (you bastards) will nab them, too, and then we'll be stuck sitting in front of Victoria's Secret, making lewd comments and hoping that one of them will take pity on us.

Just call us "mister"—"Dude" even. Anything but "sir".

Chapter 22

Young Love vs. Old Love

"Sure, female behavioral engrams were already set in the womb and early childhood and as such, a few shots of Vitamin T (Testosterone) wouldn't change them all that much, but at least they'd know what it feels like to be just a tad aggressive about life in general, and to have a little ache in their loins all the time that isn't the result of pelvic inflammatory disease."

Testosterone replacement is a myth. It's complete nonsense. Men don't need it. In fact, as men get older, they become better lovers with fewer impotence problems.

An early April Fools' Day joke? I wish. Unfortunately, the above is pretty much what Dr. Lorraine Boule, from Sheffield University in northern England, told the assembled members of the British Psychological Conference last week.

"Older men," she added, "sustain erections for longer, are longer coming to orgasm, and satisfy women better. Sexual activity does diminish with age, but the quality should get better."

Dr. Boule, I should add, is also a psychologist.

I honestly don't know where to begin. I guess I should first remind you that psychologists aren't the same as psychiatrists, the latter having earned medical degrees and thus a bit of credibility when it comes to making statements about medical issues.

Psychologists, even the ones with their Ph.D.s, are the people who convince women that they have repressed memories of being systematically ravished by the Mormon Tabernacle Choir, who, for some reason, did this ravishing while being dressed as big bunnies. The courts usually award these women millions of dollars, which they then use to go live on some exotic desert island where they pay natives to serve them Mai Tais. Unfortunately, the drinks are served in little bunny-shaped mugs, which cause them to relive the original repressed memory and sue the hotel.

Yep, that's what psychologists do, so I'm not exactly going to pay too much attention to Ms. Boule. Besides, I'm one of them-there *men* she's talking about, and while I might not yet fit into the age group she specified, I have made love to a woman, experienced an orgasm or two, and read a bit about Testosterone. As such, I present myself as somewhat of an expert on the subject.

First, let's tackle the issue of erections. While Ms. Boule asserts that older men are able to sustain erections for longer, the only possible explanation for this is that they've learned to prop the sucker up with two popsicle sticks and some duct tape, which, in certain circles, is known as "poor man's Viagra."

As any man with a dick who's past 30 knows, erections do not increase in duration with age. While an average 18-year-old can go through high school commencement and most of a 4-year-college program riding the same boner, the average 35-year-old can usually coax the thing down occasionally by thinking of world destruction or looking at a picture of his grandmother doing barbell squats while wearing a thong—which he carries for just such an occasion—prior to going into a business meeting. And while 60-year-olds still get erections, they're certainly not hard enough to drive nails—maybe stir some tapioca, but that's about it.

Taking longer to come to orgasm isn't necessarily a great thing, either, unless, like certain subspecies of baboon, you mount a female and ejaculate within 0.7 seconds. Imagine the strain it puts on a relationship if, after your girlfriend has gone to the trouble of dressing up in the outfit you bought her that makes her look like the Little Debbie delicious-snack-cakes fame and propped her ass high up on the saddle you keep in the bedroom, you're done before she gets a chance to moan into the hitching post.

By the time she's just starting to realize that there's something poking around back there, you've already showered and gone downstairs to watch a rerun of the Tonya Harding/Paula Jones boxing match. Meanwhile, she's trying to figure out how to gracefully dismount without having the Wabash River of man juice you left on her back roll off and stain the berber carpet.

In cases like that, taking longer to come to orgasm is certainly desirable, but many older men take so long that they have to pack a lunch or at least some snacks lest their blood sugar drop and they go into a coma. Sometimes it takes so long that they become physically exhausted and have to have a nurses' aide come in to manually push and pull their buttocks back and forth until they finally climax. Personally, I wouldn't think that type of thing is very romantic.

202 Atomic Dog - The Testosterone Principles

Besides, Ms. Boule is looking at this through a woman's perspective. While a man who takes longer to come may be a better lover, do we really care that much if she comes each and every time? Hell, we didn't even know about female orgasms until the 70s and now we're supposed to spend all our time worrying about whether she got off or not.

What I want to know is how *women* can become better lovers, Dr. Boule. Maybe I should address a group of dentists and suggest that women who have no teeth are better lovers, and the idea of crowns and dental care in general is nonsense.

Okay, maybe Ms. Boule and her anti-Testosterone allies wouldn't buy any of the assertions I've made, but there's plenty of cold, hard science to back up the notion that Testosterone replacement is legit and often necessary. It's pretty clear that T levels—and thus sexual interest and performance—drop with age. For one thing, age often brings about testicular failure in which overall Leydig cell (the things that manufacture Testosterone) function and mass is diminished.

To make things worse, the level of Sex Hormone Binding Globulin increases with age, which leads to increased binding of free Testosterone and a resultant drop in the levels of free T. In fact, levels of free T, generally regarded as the portion of T that's responsible for doing all the magical things that T does, can be markedly diminished without affecting the measured amount of total Testosterone. That means you could still have a "normal" level of total Testosterone in your blood but not function optimally because free T is low.

There's also a loss of the circadian rhythms of T in the older male. While the T levels of young men spike in the morning, older men experience no such spike. This explains why younger men awake with an erection and are anxious for sex while older men are instead anxious to get the morning paper and a bowl of Malto Meal.

In fact, if Ms. Boule had simply done a search of Medline, she would have seen that there are scores of studies that show that libido is characteristically diminished in the elderly, as is the amount and quality of sexual activity.

While the female psychologist asserts that sex gets better as a man gets older, I doubt very much that an old man taking his semi-erect penis out of his pants and screaming, "Oh my God, it's orange! It's orange!" after failing to remember that he spilled Metamucil on it earlier that day, is capable of what any of us would consider "better" sex.

And old age isn't the only thing men have to worry about as far as having diminished levels of Testosterone. The general public is only just being made aware of all the hormone-disrupting chemicals found in our drinking water. Fish everywhere are being feminized, as evidenced by many fish showing an increased interest in daytime TV and handbags that match their shoes.

In fact, the average sperm count of men in Scotland is dropping by about 2 percent each year. The U.S. government's Environmental Protection Agency shows that, proportionately, a human male only produces about a third as much sperm as a hamster. This is why, at least recently, you sometimes see ovulating women leaving nightclubs with well-dressed hamsters.

And even if you don't pay attention to all the science, all the men who have ever given themselves a shot of Testosterone or taken a supplement that increases T know that it often leads to an increased desire for sex, heightened sensations during sex, increased performance during sex, and a shorter "downtime" before being able to have sex again. High levels of T also have a host of other less important effects, like allowing the male to hit the overhead light with his ejaculate and make it sizzle like a frying pan full of bacon.

Beyond all that, having high-normal levels of T is the best high there is. T is the straw that stirs the drink of life. I sometimes wish that women who don't understand the preoccupation of men with sex or who don't understand men in general would take a shot or two of Testosterone so that they'd have at least a tiny inkling of the way a man feels or thinks.

Sure, female behavioral engrams were already set in the womb and early childhood and as such, a few shots of vitamin T wouldn't change them all that much, but at least they'd know what it feels like to be just a tad aggressive about life in general, and to have a little ache in their loins all the time that isn't the result of pelvic inflammatory disease.

In addition to being baffled and amazed by Dr. Boule's inane assertions about Testosterone and the how Testosterone replacement is unnecessary, I'm also blown away by her apparent lapse in memory. It wasn't more than 20 years ago that women experiencing fluctuations in hormones during menopause and perimenopause were ignored by doctors, told that their lack of energy and loss of libido was "all in their heads."

As such, it strikes me as ironic that a prominent female psychologist is now telling men that drops in libido and erectile function don't exist, and that they should just ride that limp dick into the sunset.

Sorry lady, I'll definitely ride into the sunset someday, but it'll be with my gunbelt filled with pre-loaded cartridges of Testosterone and some loamy-loined babe sharing my saddle and hanging on for dear life.

Chapter 23

Take a Shot

"I was about as goofy looking a teenager as you can imagine. Thick glasses. Six-foot two inches and about 155 pounds with hair that was sort of a blonder version of David Spade's mop. Obviously, not most teenage girls' idea of a heart throb. We took the girls to the playground around dusk, and my friend Kevin, a bad boy, gave me a moldy old joint as a secret seduction weapon . . . then, using the most sophisticated tone possible, I said, "See this, baby? This'll take you places. "

P*retty women out walking with gorillas down my street*

From my window I'm starin' while my coffee goes cold

— "Is She Really Going Out with Him?" by Joe Jackson

I've got at least a half-dozen friends who haven't had a date in six months. All of them work out, are buff in varying degrees, and don't normally have pieces of food clinging to their teeth or tufts of jungle-thick nose hair sticking out of their nostrils. In other words, they're presentable. A few of them would even qualify as "good catches" for some female.

The trouble is, as they explain it, that they "can't meet anybody." Never mind that they spend several hours a week in what's pretty much the greatest singles club in existence—the gym. But from their perspective, they might as well be George Kennedy or Paul Newman in *Cool Hand Luke*, members of a prison chain gang who can do no more than ogle the little halter-topped vixen who's sudsing up her car with both a soapy sponge and her ample breasts.

Sure, there's a cupcake over there on the mat doing boner-inducing stretches that they previously thought were only possible by members of Cirque du Soleil, but they'll never approach her because their "chains"—their fear of rejection, or shyness, or whatever—won't let them.

Wusses.

It's ironic, or rather, sad. They spend all this time chiseling their pecs and rounding out their glutes—you know, trying to look good nekkid—but they don't have anybody to get nekkid with. It reminds me of my first dance in seventh grade. All the boys sat on one side of the gym, and all the girls sat on the other. Sure, weird Joey Leskanic — the kid who collected boogers in his hair — was flailing away by himself in the middle of the gym to the strains of *Brick House* by the Commodores, but other than that, there was very little activity of any kind.

Obviously, some guys do meet the girls. And once in a while, you see a perfect match, some top-notch, world class, wünderbabe with a male equivalent, but that seems to be pretty rare.

More often, you see some perfect loser, some just-learned-to-walk-erect-this-morning, knuckle-dragging, tobacco juice–drooling, monosyllabic cretin with a Flowbee haircut strutting down the street with a piece of ass that's so beautiful, it ought to have angel wings and pluck a harp with one beautiful, alabaster butt cheek.

Witness supermodel Claudia Schiffer and pull-a-rabbit-out-of-his-pants magician David Copperfield. Thank God that unholy union is over, but their relationship caused most males endless consternation. We all know similar examples. You feel like going up to the woman, as acerbic sportscaster Howard Cosell used to do, and say in that unmistakable, halting voice, "La-dy, you could do much bet-ter!"

Most of us keep those opinions to ourselves and instead tear our hair out and take our anger and frustration out on Toby by pounding him mercilessly against the porcelain.

What secret do these gorillas have? Sure, a lot of times it's money. I've known my share of rich guys, and they were able to buy Playboy-bunny ass, if not the Holy Grail of ass—beer commercial–actress ass.

But most of the guys wearing genetically gifted women on their arms aren't rich. Sure, a few of the Grade A babes go for the bad boy thing, but some of us wouldn't feel comfortable adopting the bad boy image. Especially if it means trading in your Polo shirts and Dockers for a mesh tank top and some pre-greased jeans. Besides, if you're wooing a girl who likes bad boys, you've got to play the part, 24-7. I don't know about you, but I'd get tired of running with scissors, or swimming after a big meal, or whatever it is that bad boys do.

Personally, I think a lot of these gorillas are with these women because they just *took a shot*. They either don't realize that they're gorillas, or they just don't give a shit. They'll walk up to any woman, lay out their best or worst line, and if they fail, they'll shrug their shoulders, burp, and hit on the next one that comes along.

Sooner or later, they score. Gooooooooooooaaaaaaaaaaaall lllllllllll!

They find a woman whose beauty has frightened away most men. She's tired of sitting around at night having her rear end detailed by a team of professionals. She wants to get out there and drive that rear end around the block a few times—maybe take the top down a notch and feel the breeze whistle through her butt cheeks—so she might as well go out with a gorilla. Hell, no one else is asking.

Back when I was 15, my friend called me up and told me that two of his female cousins were coming over. They were second or third cousins, so he didn't have any second thoughts about making a move on one of them. But he needed someone to tend to the other cousin. That someone was me.

Now I was about as goofy-looking a teenager as you can imagine. Thick glasses. Six-foot-two inches and about 155 pounds with hair that was sort of a blonder version of David Spade's mop. Obviously, not most teenage girls' idea of a heartthrob. We took the girls to the playground around dusk, and my friend Kevin, a bad boy, gave me a moldy old joint as a secret seduction weapon.

And as much as I tried to elicit some sort of verbal or emotional response from my "date," she was about as receptive as week-old roadkill. Finally, I pulled out the heavy ammo. I put my right arm around her shoulders, stuck out my left hand, and slowly unwrapped my fingers to reveal the joint.

Then, using the most sophisticated tone possible, I said, "See this, baby? This'll take you places."

No lie. I actually said that. And at the moment I said it, I could feel a nuclear tide of embarrassment flooding my face, the type of embarrassment that stays with you for, oh, I don't know, 20 years or so.

But as I look back on that night, I'm kinda proud of myself. Despite the failure of my slick line to make her pull off her top, reveal her lumpy, daffodil-covered Woolworth's bargain-bin bra and roll around with me on the infield dirt, at least I *took a shot*. I got off the sidelines and said, "Coach, give me that damn piece of pigskin." Never mind that I ran the wrong way and scored a touchback for the other team, I *tried*.

And this is the type of advice I want to give to my lonely, single friends. It doesn't matter if you're shy, embarrassed, or if you stammer. It doesn't even matter if you're a little bit funny looking. You have to try. Otherwise, you'll end up all alone with pee-stained underwear, sucking on a frozen TV dinner.

It's like sticking your hand in the toilet after you dropped your wallet in there; you have to force yourself.

You don't even have to have any pickup lines. Just say the first thing that comes into your mind: "Excuse me, but I just found out my uric acid levels are perfect." "My cousin works at the 7-Eleven and I can get you a discount on ham sandwiches and stuff." "I went to school with the guy who cleans Keanu Reeve's pool."

You can even try the honesty approach, popularized by the George Costanza character on *Seinfeld:* "My name's George. I'm unemployed and I live with my parents."

It doesn't matter! At least you'll have started a conversation! What's the worst that can happen? Sure, she could point at you and start making that high-pitched screaming noise that the plant people in the remake of *Invasion of the Body Snatchers* made whenever they spotted a human, but so what?

On the other hand, you may find yourself in a genuine conversation with a wünderbabe! You may even find yourself getting a date with one! And wonder of wonders, you might end up having the owner of one of those winged, alabaster butts on your arm!

Just think of yourself as a fisherman who keeps casting a piece of chicken skin into an icy pond. A lot of fish will ignore it, but every once in a while, a beautiful little bluegill with tits the size of howitzers will latch on. You won't catch one unless you drop bait!

Trust me. Be a man and get yourself a woman who's deserving of your studliness. Just don't try the "This'll take you places, baby" line. It doesn't work very well.

Chapter 24

Aroo! Aroo!

"If I were single and really out on the prowl, I'd limit my hunting to the gym. It's hard to hide serious flaws (cellulite, a vestigial penis, etc.) when you're wearing shorts and a sports bra. Why, many was the time, in my single days, when I would meet some seemingly attractive woman at a night club, take her home, and peel off her tube top and skintight Lycra slacks, only to be engulfed in mounds of flesh that, suddenly freed, had come gushing out like dough out of a Pop 'N Fresh muffin canister that Mom had just whacked against the kitchen counter."

My wife left me yesterday. Okay, so it's only for three days while she's out of town to take care of some business, but for the first time in a long time, I'm single (sort of, anyhow). And when any man is left alone for more than, say, three or four minutes, he starts to think about the "I" word, or the "A" word. You know, *infidelity*, or having an *affair*, or whatever you call banging some slut with wild abandon in the back seat of your Chevy Suburban while your wife's stuck in the checkout line at the local Piggly Wiggly.

Of course, it just doesn't happen that way. For one thing, most of us kind of like our wives, and we wouldn't want to hurt their feelings, especially since all that shit with John Wayne Bobbitt came down. I, for one, would find it disconcerting to drive by a field and see my penis being chewed on by some ground squirrels, and that would be a distinct possibility since my wife lettered in penis hurling back in high school (she won the Tri-City championships by hurling a penis 53 feet, 2 inches—and if it hadn't landed on its side, it would have been 53 feet, 9 inches).

But even if you did decide that you wanted to partake of some forbidden fruit, there's no way you'd ever even meet a girl that quickly, let alone get through all that "Hi, you come here often? Oh, you have pretty eyes," and "Hey, I had a cousin who lived in Minnesota, too," courting bullshit before you got to nail her.

Furthermore, many women, at least in my experience, are somewhat reluctant to meet a man in a grocery store parking lot and crawl behind some bushes or into a dumpster to have sex with a perfect stranger, even if he did lay a really good rap on her or even give her some coupons.

But let's say you accomplished all that. You met someone who made your penis do a mambo in your pants, managed to strike up a conversation that sounded remotely sincere, and she didn't mind lying down naked in a pile of leaves in the middle of the day while you bent over her and groaned like a dump truck with a bad muffler. Chances are, right about then your wife would be wheeling the grocery cart out of the store, hoping that you'll be there to help throw the 200-pound economy bag of cat litter into the trunk.

Okay, forget the infidelity thing. Single guys are all looking for action, too. They're in the same boat as married guys, the one that's floating in the toilet bowl in the old Tidy Bowl commercials, and someone has just flushed. I've got single friends who have looks and money but can't even meet anyone, let alone find an honest-to-gosh female who'll agree to have sex with them.

Personally, if I were single and really out on the prowl, I'd limit my hunting to the gym. There are several advantages to this. For one thing, you know what you're getting. It's hard to hide serious flaws (cellulite, a vestigial penis, etc.) when you're wearing shorts and a sports bra. Why, many was the time, in my single days, when I would meet some seemingly attractive woman at a night club, take her home, and peel off her tube top and skintight Lycra slacks, only to be engulfed in mounds of flesh that, suddenly freed, had come gushing out like dough from a Pillsbury Dinner canister your mom has just whacked against the kitchen counter.

Another advantage is the fact that you're both in the gym, which probably means that you're both superficial types whose only gray matter consists of some unlaundered underwear in the hamper. In other words, you're intellectually compatible.

Of course, you have to know what you're doing in order to "hunt" in the gym. You might not know it, but you can tell a lot about a woman based on what time she works out.

For instance, don't hunt in the morning. Generally, only married or unattractive women work out in the morning. The good-looking single ones were out late the night before and, if they're even up that early, they're probably still squeegeeing the seminal fluid off their chests.

Midafternoon is also probably a bad time. If an attractive girl is working out at 2 p.m., chances are she's a prostitute or a topless dancer who just woke up.

No, the best time is 5 to 7 p.m. This is when the prime flesh comes out. These are office girls, all single, who are probably there for the same reason that you are. You can often get one of them to come lie on you and stretch if you lie very still and pretend that you're a floor mat.

Of course, finding women is the easiest part. Actually initiating a conversation is often much more difficult. Many men have too much self-respect to start spewing all of that introductory "getting to know you" drivel. Oh, they try, but then they start listening to themselves and the phrase "Boy, do I sound like an asshole" starts going through their brain over and over again like some sort of low–self-esteem mantra.

It makes you long for the days depicted in the movie *Quest for Fire* where, if a girl bent over to pick up a berry, you gave her the bone.

I've got a solution, though. It would take years to implement, but it could be done. I propose that we come up with a universal pickup line, one whose implications were understood by all. And, in order to save time and avoid embarrassment, there would be a universal response that would allow two people to sit down and get all the obligatory bullshit out of the way.

For instance, if a man notices a girl riding a stationary bike whose taut, tawny ass, covered only by a single-molecule-thick veneer of spandex, has caused him to get so stiff that his dick snuck out the side of his shorts and he has to pretend that he's walking around with an Olympic bar in his hands, he should be able to walk up to her and say, "May I take a shot at nailing you?"

And, if the girl was impressed by his Olympic bar and, consequently, had to tape her Met-Rx shaker bottle to the insides of her thighs to catch the overflow of secretions, she could say, "Please do, kind sir."

This way, there would be no misunderstanding as to the man's intentions. He could say almost anything that he wanted without sounding like too much of a jackass. Furthermore, the woman could end the conversation as soon as she became convinced that the guy wasn't a complete loser, one who'd make her have to change her name and move to another town if she let him boink her.

And we could play with the actual words. Maybe asking, in plain English, is too civilized for what I'm proposing. Maybe this calls for some sort of neologism. What if the man shouted "Aroo! Aroo!" at the target of his lust, while the woman's appropriate response, assuming that she was receptive, would be "wubba wubba"?

That sure would make things a whole lot easier.

Ahh, who am I kidding? It'll never happen. Our brains have simply taken over our sexual inclinations. Besides, females already have a time-honored response that they use to indicate their sexual readiness. For those of you who haven't heard it lately, it's "Get lost, loser."

Still, even a married guy like me can dream of hearing a little "wubba wubba" once in a while.

Chapter 25

The Art of Romance

"Once the panties hit the floor, you can change the music to anything you want. A lot of women don't realize it, but without some sort of rhythmic music playing, we lack any kind of penile control. Nope, the beat of the music acts as a kind of a metronome and without it, we'd be thrusting about blindly, inadvertently poking air, the sofa cushion, or the eye of her darling little Pekinese."

I sat down in the waiting room of the doctor's office yesterday and I picked up the magazine that was lying face-down on the seat next to me. It was *Redbook*. For those of you who don't have any women in your life over the age of 40, *Redbook* is sort of a post-menopausal *Cosmopolitan*. Lately, though, they're trying to target a slightly younger demographic.

Witness this tip on setting a sexy, "romantic" mood:

"Food is sexy when shared. Serve dinner on one plate and use just one set of utensils. Then sit right next to your man and take turns feeding each other. (This makes even macaroni and cheese romantic!)"

I gotta tell you, if a woman sat down next to me and started sharing my food, I'd be inclined to react much the same as any self-respecting carnivore. In other words, I'd chew her arm off, bury the bone, and then take a huge, steaming dump on the spot where I had buried it.

Sorry, but nobody's touching my food while I'm eating it.

I've never really given all that much credence to the "Men Are from Mars, Women Are from Venus" way of thinking, but after reading stuff like the *Redbook* tip, I tend to believe the argument, except that I'd take the dichotomy between men and women a little further. In other words, if women are really from Venus, men are from some little orbiting piece of ice on the other side of the galaxy where the inhabitants communicate through a series of burps and sneezes and use one of their multiple penises to pole-vault themselves over the frozen terrain.

If you doubt me, take a look at *Redbook's* next *romantic* tip:

"Write a sexy message on his plate using a cake frosting dispenser filled with sauce (plain old tomato sauce works perfectly) or a condiment (try mustard, mayonnaise, or ketchup for colorful scribble)."

Now, I have to admit I have tried a variation of this trick. I once "wrote" a message on a girl's belly in man juice that was in fact a Chinese ideogram that roughly translated to, "There's Kleenex in the first drawer of the night stand."

Was it romantic? I'm sorry to say that I'm not really sure what the word means. Looking in the dictionary didn't help, either. Try it. Look up either "romance" or "romantic," read the multiple definitions, and tell me if you know what the hell they're talking about.

Of course, I know that it's supposed to have something to do with what women think love is all about, but beyond that, you got me.

For instance, buying flowers is supposed to be romantic. Writing friggin' love poems is supposed to be romantic. And for some reason, so is watching a sunset.

On the other hand, I know that buying a girl a toaster oven as a gift is not romantic. Neither is trimming your toenails at your anniversary dinner and seeing if you can make the clippings carom off the meatloaf and into the gravy bowl. This much I know.

Last week, my friend's squeeze called him up and wanted to know what the most romantic thing he had ever done was. No doubt she wanted to know so she could recreate the blessed event, but my friend was at a loss to come up with an answer. She probably wanted to hear something like, "I once hired a Hansom cab to pull me and my date around the streets of New York at sunset while drinking expensive champagne out of the bottle."

Truth is, he really did do that once, and his only memory of the event, romantic or otherwise, was that it had gotten him *way* past second base and he probably would have gotten *his* cab pulled all over town if the damn horse hadn't kept hitting all those potholes.

I, however, through years and years of being ruled by my balls, know how to fake romance. Is faking it unethical or sleazy? I don't think so, given that the idea of romance is kind of a paradox anyhow.

Consider that the whole point of being romantic is so that the girl will think that you're more interested in gazing into

224 Atomic Dog - The Testosterone Principles

her eyes than you are in gazing into her saucer-sized nipples. Ironically, if you do this—gaze dreamily into her eyes—you'll most likely be rewarded with sex. Wacky, isn't it? Act like you're not interested in sex and you'll be rewarded with it!

Anyhow, faking romance has kept me in fur for many years.

For instance, I know that it puts a woman into a romantic mood if you play music, but not just any music will do. Playing anything by Metallica, the Butthole Surfers, or Limp Bizkit will incite most women to leave you, go out and tattoo a colorful marijuana leaf just below their bikini line, and then sleep with the first rock star they run into.

Rap music won't generally cut it either, unless your date is named Moesha or Showana. Nope, women like the soft stuff where the word "love" is used more frequently than it is at a tennis match where Venus Williams is playing Stephen Hawking. Be careful, though, because it's a known fact that if a man listens to this type of music for too long, he can suffer irreparable harm. Overexposure to this type of music may make a man go insane, become temporarily impotent, or become a fan of women's soccer.

However, once the panties hit the floor, you can change the music to anything you want. A lot of women don't realize it, but without some sort of rhythmic music playing, we lack any kind of penile control. Nope, the beat of the music acts as a kind of a metronome and without it, we'd be thrusting about blindly, inadvertently poking air, the sofa cushion, or the eye of her darling little Pekingese.

And I know that you're supposed to take them out for some fancy-schmancy dinner on the anniversary of the day that you first met, along with the day of your first date, the day of your first trip to the motor-vehicle department, and so on and so forth, ad nauseum. I always do the fancy-dinner thing. Hell, I even carry her tray, and if that ain't romantic, I don't know what is.

I don't think I'm all that different from most men. I think a lot of guys are missing the organ or gland where the notion of romance lives. In the words of Dennis Miller, "Hey, I'm sorry, but some of us see a beautiful sunset and think, 'You know, I'll betcha' my accountant is boning me up the ass."

Amen.

Anyhow, for those of you who are romantically handicapped like me, I feel it's my civic duty to warn you that Christmas, next to Valentine's Day, is the mother of all romantic holidays.

If you ever want to see your woman naked again, you must not only be cognizant of this fact, but you must *play the game.* There are certain things that, no matter how revolting, no matter how denigrating, you simply must resign yourself to do.

For a few weeks each December, you must spend at least 20 minutes a week admiring the Christmas tree with her, and here's the hard part: *The TV must be off!*

And, as excruciating as it may be, you must, at least once, pop the Kenny G Christmas CD into the stereo. If it's simply too hard to endure, jam some fruitcake into your ears. Likewise, you're going to have to cuddle in front of the fire a couple of times and, if at all humanly possible, you should refrain from following your male instinct of shoving stuff into the fire to see how it burns. This is acceptable behavior while outdoors, but tossing plastic cups, old tennis shoes, discarded automobile tires or dead animals into the fireplace is likely to ruin the mood for her.

There are certain things that do not, however, fall into the realm of reasonable girl expectations. She may want you to decorate cookies (*shudder*), but warn her that this act may have long-term consequences. Putting faces on snowmen and gingerbread men may actually cause pituitary implosion. The emergency rooms are filled with cases around Christmas time year after year.

Gift giving is also an exact science, rife with potential romantic pitfalls. Through trial and error, I've discovered that the following gifts are not romantic. Any one of them may result in having sex withheld from you:

Appliances
Sports memorabilia
Pornography
Anything see-through
Bolt cutters
Groceries
Motor oil
Nasal hair trimmers (electric or manual)
A six-pack
Cured meats
Anything made by Dr. Scholl
Crotchless panties
Catcher's mitts

Do yourself a favor and take heed of the preceding list. All told, these gifts, given by me to assorted women throughout past Christmases, have resulted in me being celibate for roughly 14 years altogether.

Man, talk about ghosts of Christmas past! I had a pale, angry, one-eyed creature haunting my pants for many holiday seasons as a result of my ignorance of romance. Its nocturnal cries and moans made for many a restless night. In fact, until I learned some of the nuances of the strange, subtle art of romance, all it took to make me go limp was the sight of a Christmas tree or the whisper of a Christmas carol!

That's all behind me now. I've done my homework. I may not understand romance, but I know how to fake it. It's like being a first or second-year student of a foreign language. I don't understand a lot of the words or the grammar, but I can ask the locals where the bathroom is.

As a result, my Yule log is pleasantly ablaze through the holiday season and, in fact, throughout the year. Now, where's that Kenny G CD?

Chapter 26

Single Guys vs. Married Guys

"As soon as you get married, the Goddess becomes a mere mortal. Out come the sweat pants. Out goes the make up. All that exotic underwear that she used to turn you into a slobbering lap dog with an erection about yay big? It lies moldering in a little used drawer. Once in awhile, you furtively tip toe into the bedroom to excavate a pair of those exotic, memory-filled panties, place them against your face and sniff and snort like a pig looking for truffles, but instead of getting a scent of her perfumed Hoo-hah, you just get a semi-lethal dose of Lemon Pledge and have to make an appointment to see an asthma specialist."

My friend Chad and I were about halfway through a training session. I'd just finished my fifth set of deadlifts, followed quickly by our first set of Zercher squats. My mind should have been on the workout, but it wasn't. Instead, I was thinking about something far more important than my next set.

I walked over to the power rack, but as I started to cradle the bar in the crooks of my elbows, I paused, turned around, and said to Chad, "Did you know that sometimes love doesn't come in a minute; sometimes it doesn't come at all; I only know that when I'm in it, love isn't silly ... love isn't silly at all."

Maybe you're surprised that I have those kind of thoughts, but the truth is, if I ain't thinking about working out, I'm thinking about romance; romance, love, panties, all that stuff.

Anyhow, instead of giving me that steely hard glaze that usually reminds me of Curly in *City Slickers*, his furrowed brow started to unfurrow and his eyes seemed to soften, as he was no doubt remembering some long-lost love from his days on the farm, some sweet thing lying in a pile of hay with her legs up in the air and her gingham dress hiked high above her head and her Barbie doll carefully placed aside, its eyes covered with a piece of hay so it couldn't see the despicable things Chad was doing to her.

For a moment, I thought I saw tears welling up in his eyes. I walked forward to let him wipe them on the one dry spot left on my T-shirt, but as I approached him he gave me a kidney punch, knocked me to the floor, and stepped on my throat.

"Hey! Funny boy. Can the stupid McCartney tune and do your set."

I guess I misread his facial expressions. Apparently, he wasn't exactly in a sentimental mood. Okay, I can grok that. Men, depending on whether they're in love or not, are either sentimental (at least a little) or pretty much sexual preda-tors. For instance, a single guy like Chad spends most of his time thinking about what he'd like to do to that fitness model over by the leg-curl machine, the one he says makes his member swell and grow so that it's like the Yao Ming of penises—towering, yet slender; slender, yet strong; strong, yet able to score with impunity.

Married guys would like to show our Yao to that girl, too, but their married penises, sadly, are like Yao only in that they're yellow, yellow from their owners having snacked on too many cheddar-cheesy Goldfish crackers and not wash-ing their hands before going one-on-one with them in the bathroom while reading a stroke mag and fantasizing about playing some away games.

Yep, a lot of married guys dream about being single again, while single guys, once they've grown tired of the singles scene, often think it would be nice to be married. Man is totally schizophrenic in this regard, and therein lies his greatest curse and the only truly valid reason for thinking about killing himself.

But why do men get married in the first place? Is being married better than being single? It's a tough call.

I figure most guys get married for a couple of reasons. Sure, there's the sex thing, and at first, it seems really appealing. For instance, let's say you like Yoo-Hoo chocolate beverage. Then, by sheer circumstance, your uncle gets a job as East Coast sales manager for Yoo-Hoo. Suddenly, he gives you cases of it. You've got all the Yoo-Hoo you could ever want right there in your house. Who wouldn't want that?

You start drinking Yoo-Hoo two, three times a day. You think of weird places to enjoy Yoo-Hoo and innovative ways to drink it: on the kitchen table, in the garage, upside down. You even take out the video camera and tape yourself enjoying Yoo-Hoo while slapping its bottom and asking, "Who's your daddy? C'mon, tell me. Who's your daddy?"

You're only limited by your imagination.

It's great! But as the weeks go by, you start to get tired of drinking Yoo-Hoo and nothing but Yoo-Hoo. Pretty soon, you don't even want to touch Yoo-Hoo again. You start longing for something else tasty. Pretty soon, you're sneaking out of the house to sample some Tahitian Berry Snapple.

Trouble is, Yoo-Hoo finds out about it, and either cuts off your penis, sues you for divorce and takes everything you have, or hits you with her SUV as you're walking out of the hotel with your Snapple and runs over you not once, not twice, but three times, the *bitch*.

That's marriage.

And there are other problems, too. You know that girl you've been dating? The one that's a silken-haired, smooth-skinned, frilly-frock wearing *angel* who always looks like she walked out of a Maybelline cosmetics ad? Well, as soon as you get married, the Goddess becomes a mere mortal. Out come the sweat pants. Out goes the makeup. All that exotic underwear that she used to turn you into a slobbering lap dog with an erection about *yay big?* It lies moldering in a little-used drawer. Once in a while, you furtively tiptoe into the bedroom to excavate a pair of those exotic, memory-filled panties, place them against your face and sniff and snort like a pig looking for truffles, but instead of getting a scent of her perfumed Hoo-hah, you just get a semi-lethal dose of Lemon Pledge and have to make an appointment to see an asthma specialist.

In the morning, when your Testosterone levels are their highest and you want to usher in the day with what country boy Chad calls "a little sugar," you see the light streaming through the bedroom window and you notice, for the first time, that without makeup, the girl you married looks kind of like Andy Rooney from *60 Minutes*, albeit with pert little alabaster breasts that are much nicer than Andy's. So you roll over and pretend you're asleep while the words, "The Horror, the Horror," keep flashing through your mind.

Not only that, but after you get married, you start seeing weird things in the bathroom. Your angel uses hemorrhoid cream, and there's Tampax in the wastebasket. And the worst thing, the ultimate horror? You walk into the toilet that she just vacated and you're hit with the horrible realization that your sweet elfin baby has taken a dump that smells like one a Sumo wrestler might take after a night on the town in Tijuana.

There's this line from a 17th century poem by Jonathan Swift that, while simple, captures that particular epiphany perfectly:

Nor wonder how I lost my Wits;

Oh! Caelia, Caelia, Caelia shits.

We don't like to think of these perfect creatures as having these, these … *bodily functions*, and the mere contemplation of such is enough to short-circuit simple brains.

But there are, of course, good reasons to get married, reasons that make a lot more sense than limitless sex. Men often like to have someone around to share life-affirming experiences. Say they're watching something entertaining on television. If it excites them, they want to be able to shout out, "Hey, c'mere! Come look at this! The Skipper thinks that's *Gilligan* in a gorilla suit. He doesn't know it's a real gorilla!" Having someone to enjoy moments like that makes them all the more special.

Similarly, if you wad up your paper towel after eating some Buffalo wings and toss it in the trash basket from 20 feet out, you need someone to witness and appreciate your athletic skill. Wives do nicely in that situation.

So marriage ain't all that bad.

Wanting children is also a perfectly sane reason to get married. Men want children to achieve some sort of immortality. Of course, raising some slack-jawed kid whose career path is cleaning the grease traps at Mickey D's isn't how I want to achieve immortality. I'd prefer to achieve it by living a hell of a long time.

Scientists say that Testosterone levels go down in men after they're married and especially when those same married men have children. Anthropologists speculate that it's nature's way of keeping men monogamous.

That doesn't seem to hold water nowadays. Hell, with the advent of women's fitness, liposuction, breast implants, thong underwear, low-rider jeans, latex, Lycra, *Maxim*, MTV, the *Sports Illustrated* Swimsuit Issue, those beer-commercial twins, bikinis, Victoria's Secret catalogs, *The Man Show*, push-up bras, Hooters restaurants, Internet porn, *Baywatch* reruns, the lingerie ads in the Sunday paper, the little skanks with pierced belly buttons and bare tummies who magically appear in the grocery stores and the coffee shops and even the Kinko's down the street, and all the other sexual demons that cry out to us, even a married man's supposedly low Testosterone isn't going to keep his penis from rising up, shaking the sleep from its eye, and thrashing about in his Dockers like an angry weasel trapped in a gunny sack.

All of that is what makes life for a married man so ridiculously unfair. There's so much sexual temptation out there that life becomes almost a living hell. It's as if married men are all recovering alcoholics and in some weird *Twi-light Zone*-ish twist of circumstances, they've woken up in a world that's a giant Costco with nothing but aisles and aisles of reasonably priced liquor.

But then again, if you're single, chances are you're going home alone most of the time anyhow. And, like your married counterpart, you spend a good deal of time locked up in the bathroom with the *Sports Illustrated* Swimsuit Issue, some Goldfish crackers, and a sore yellow penis.

Death, take us now … please.

Chapter 27

Testosterone Vampirellas

"The U.S. is filled with their victims; spiritless, sallow skinned sons of bitches who plod along until death takes them — only they don't notice they're dead since they've been living their lives in oblivion anyhow. They spend their weekends doing what their wives want them to do and they drive sensible Swedish cars. At night they're made to sit through Ally McBeal or Biography, "because they're doing Audrey Hepburn!""

I've got a friend who was a hotshot college football player. Jerry blew his knee out so he's since had to settle for activities that won't send his kneecap spinning across the field like it was part of an Ultimate Frisbee competition.

He's married now, to the former head of the cheerleading squad, no less.

Their courtship was torrid, and if I plied him with enough Jack Daniels, he'd sometimes tell me about some of the stuff his wife did while they were dating. For instance, she once gave him a blowjob in a graveyard. Man, talk about whistling on your bone in the yard … or is it whistling in the bone yard? Whatever.

And once, she even jerked him off underneath the tablecloth during a fancy dinner with all four parents in attendance.

His wife always wore great underwear, too. They must have come from France or something because he'd never seen stuff like this before. Either that, or they were designed by elves—horny elves. They were always silk, extremely ornate,

usually crotchless, and in general were such marvels of cur-
vaceous engineering that they would keep a man in a per-
petual state of hardness.

That was 10 years ago.

As soon as they got married, there was no more head in the
graveyard, other than the ones that were buried there. Hell,
the only way Jerry could get what approximated oral sex was
to disguise his dick as some sort of exotic fruit. As soon as
she noticed that the weird-looking thing lying in the fruit
bowl wasn't a hairy plantain, she'd try to dump it in the garbage disposal and Jerry would have to 'fess up.

Long gone was the fancy underwear, too. It'd been replaced
by granny panties and the white utilitarian JC Penney jobs
that you used to see the cleaning woman wearing when she
bent over to scrub the floor.

Last week, he saw a pair of the French underwear that he used
to love. They were in the "rag bag." What was once an object
of lust and magical sex was now a faded dust rag that smelled
faintly of household cleaners. He almost started crying.

And if you walked into their house, you'd hardly know a
man even lived there. Every room was filled with porcelain
knick-knacks and little frilly pillows that were hand-stitched
and had crap like "Home Sweet Home" stitched onto them.
The bedroom is the worst of all. The bed is covered with
a flowered quilt and a horde of those horrendous Cabbage
Patch dolls, which, to me at least, look a little too much like
the malevolent Chucky from *Child's Play*.

You take one look and wonder if even Pamela Lee could coax a boner out of your body in these surroundings.

Sure, my friend has his own room, a "study," but it's decorated just like the rest of the house. He tried putting some of his old football trophies on the bookcase, but she didn't like the way they looked. So she replaced them with some pieces from her ceramic tortoise collection.

Jerry used to like watching sports on weekends, but his wife thinks that's a waste of time. Instead, they go "antiquing" through musty-smelling shops that are always owned by people who are as old, leathery, and stained as the furniture she oohs and ahhs over.

Amazingly, I hear from female friends that Jerry's wife always complains about him. Says he isn't the same man that she married, and she even hints that there's some problems in the bedroom department.

Now Jerry's wife isn't a bad sort; I actually like her and she's still pretty attractive. Trouble is, she's totally ignorant that she's solely responsible for Jerry's current hermaphroditic status. He's no longer a man because, like some sort of hormonal vampire, she's sucked all the Testosterone out of the poor bastard.

I know a lot of people who've met a similar fate. They thought they were marrying Testosterone Vixens, but they were really marrying Testosterone Vampires, or more accurately, Testosterone *Vampirellas*.

The U.S. is filled with their victims; spiritless, sallow-skinned sons of bitches who plod along until death takes them—only they don't notice they're dead since they've been living their lives in oblivion anyhow. They spend their weekends doing what their wives want them to do and they drive sensible Swedish cars. At night they're made to sit through *Ally McBeal or Biography*, "because they're doing Audrey Hepburn!"

These Testosterone Vampirellas admire the beast in the jungle, but when they capture it and then domesticate it, they dimly wonder what it was about the beast that first attracted them. They saw King Kong, were turned on by his power and animal nature, and they gassed him, shackled him, and shipped him off to New York as a circus attraction. Then they were careful not to pop off too many light bulbs in his face. Otherwise, he'll revert back to his true nature and end up knocking over a lot of expensive knick-knacks.

However, if they slowly deprive Kong of all his animal pleasures and scold him whenever yearnings for these pleasures start to surface, they'll eventually be able to tie ribbons in his hair and teach him to piss sitting down, lest he splatter the hell out of the place. If he instinctively takes a look at some other ape in a tight pair of low slung jeans, he'll quickly avert his eyes and look as guilty as the dog that jumped on the table and ate the roast. True, Kong's nutsack will eventually look like a deflated Swiss ball, but he'll be much more manageable.

In my humble opinion, these women should have gotten themselves roommates instead of husbands. Either that, or pet poodles.

The bookstores are filled with books about how women have been browbeaten and spiritually suffocated by men, but I think men, in many ways, are a lot worse off than women. Women are supposed to talk about their feelings and man-bashing is a rapidly growing sport, surpassing even women's soccer or the WNBA. Women have an outlet for their frustrations. Men, however, don't talk about how their spirits have been squelched.

If, somehow, men everywhere suddenly were cajoled into expressing their feelings about their lost manhood, they'd probably start busting up the place as if it were a room at the Sheraton and they were the original members of *The Who*. They don't have any experience verbalizing their frustration so they'd get physical. Either that, or they keep it to themselves and watch their dicks turn into vestigial organs.

Most aren't involved in sports anymore, and their only friendships—the only "approved" friendships—consist of their wives' friends' husbands, who oftentimes are as stimulating as the Dustin Hoffman character in *Rain Man*.

These aren't your guys; they aren't your *goombahs*. They're just acquaintances, and you're as guarded among them as the guy who was hiding Anne Frank in his attic when his wife invited a bunch of Nazis over for brunch.

So a lot of these men lead secret lives, looking at porn on the Internet, going to strip clubs during lunch, and in short, doing things that society or their wives don't approve of. These men are trying to grab back their Testosterone, but the fact that they have to hide these things paradoxically drains them of even more Testosterone.

242 Atomic Dog - The Testosterone Principles

Why do these men stand for this? Because no one tells them it's *okay* to be a man. Society wants you to be prim and proper. The voice of society that we hear through the news on television and through magazines and our President and congressmen and senators is a voice of civility—castrated civility. It's all so proper. Ban *Sopranos*. Close down the strip clubs. Get rid of boxing. Get rid of girlie mags because the children might see them. Make football less violent.

Who are these men who are behind this sort of crap? I think I know who the women are behind these sentiments, but I gotta believe that the dicks and balls of the men in cahoots with these women are somewhere in the back of the freezer, back there with that last slice of wedding cake.

Well, I wasn't exactly appointed to speak on behalf of men, but shit, somebody's gotta do it. Here's what I say. It's okay to be "piggy," to express your masculine nature. It's okay to like sports, to look at porn, to get mad, to lift weights, to play stupid Nintendo games that everyone says you should have "outgrown" years ago.

It's okay to look at other women, to have hobbies that are a waste of time, to be uncommunicative if you feel like it, to yell once in a while, to do stuff for yourself instead of the damn kids, and to slide around your house in your underwear like Tom Cruise. It's okay to have mud on your shoes every so often, to burp, to say, "Screw it, I'll paint the house later, I'm going to shoot some hoops," to ask that your mate ditch those granny panties and dress like a floozy for once, or to grab your balls and do a manly dance.

If you're like my friend Jerry, put some garlic around your neck, carry a cross with you, and reclaim your Testosterone. If your wife has made your house look like a bad homosexual decorator's nightmare, reclaim a piece of it for yourself and express your individuality, your manhood. Take a room and put up your trophies. Slap a babe calendar on the wall, and light up a smelly old cigar. Hell, even Superman had his Fortress of Solitude.

And if the bedroom you share with your wife is like a huge, pink, frilly, Testosterone-sucking vortex, carry a red light bulb in your pocket, screw it into the socket, and the red glow will make you think you're screwing Satan's mistress herself and it'll act like an aphrodisiacal talisman, restoring your boner to a 10 on the Mohs scale, which is as hard as something can get.

Marriage or relationships can be a great thing, but only when women accept that men are not women with dicks. If a woman can't accept that, can't accept that it's a sin to domesticate a wild thing, to dress a lion up in clothes and a hat and make him do cute tricks, she should get herself that roommate or poodle dog instead.

A lot of women—*Testosterone women*—do realize the difference and they're happy because there's a wild thing lying in bed next to them. And, as anyone knows, it's a lot more fun to sleep with a wild thing.

Men should just remember that in King Kong, it was *beauty* that killed the beast. Otherwise, you may find yourself lying in a pool of blood at the foot of the Empire State Building, your empty nutsack flapping in the wind.

Chapter 28

Home Alone

"I think too many guys hide that aspect of their personality from their girlfriends ... these are the guys who go nuts when their wife leaves town. They act like dogs that have been chained to a tree in the backyard all their lives that suddenly break loose. Momentarily set free, they'll start dancing around the house in their underwear, peeing in trees, and eyeing the neighbor lady ..."

My wife's leaving town again. For a week. Whoo-weeee! She's going back east to help her parents move into their new house. I'll miss her, but I'm also a bit excited because, for a short time, I'm going to be a bona fide bachelor again.

And I've got big hand-rubbing plans. Soon as I drop her off at the airport, I'm going to rush right home, strip down to my skivvies, turn that stereo up real high, and start Tom Cruisin' it around the house.

We don't have any wood floors, though, so I gotta be careful. The last time I cranked up the Seger tunes and did the *Risky Business* thing, my feet snagged on the carpet and I went flying through the picture window and ruptured my spleen.

I'm gonna eat every meal over the kitchen sink, too, because it's the only way guys are really, truly, comfortable eating. I've often thought that there should be a chain of restaurants around the country that consist of nothing but platters of meat placed next to individual sinks. You'd just walk in and look for an empty sink. We wouldn't have to feel self-conscious about burping, either, because the background music would be carefully calibrated to drown out the noise.

Maybe they'd even play songs where the chorus sounded like men burping, so it would masquerade the belches.

Who let the dogs out?

Burp, burp? burp, burp, burrrrppppp!

When you're done, some kid walks by and flips on the garbage disposal and that's it!

Anyhow, while I'm home alone, I'll eat nothing but turkey legs and tear off big, awkward pieces with my teeth. I'll look like an iguana trying to choke down an overweight peccary.

Maybe I'll even invite some friends over for dinner and we'll each grab a sink around the house (I don't like Joey too much, so he can use the one in the downstairs toilet). None of this putting on pants and eating at the table for us. And vegetables? Ha! Kale, my ass!

We'll wipe the grease on our bare chests and growl at the moon, after which we might find a crayon and draw a petroglyph or two on the wall to commemorate our "kill." Good thing I learned how to draw a turkey in kindergarten by tracing around my fingers.

Later we'll start a fire in the family room and each take turns pantomiming the hunt, which involved, much like it did for our primitive ancestors, bringing home a turkey from the Piggly Wiggly.

After the guys leave, I might take a nappie to digest my gluttonous meal, I'll probably spend half the night watching the Spice Channel, and I won't have to worry about her coming down the stairs catching me, if you get my drift. I'll just carpet the floor and the walls with thirsty Bounty towels. It'll probably dry by morning, but with a few swings of a pick ax, I should be able to break it up. Incidentally, if I'm not mistaken, that's how drywall is made.

At night, if I have to get up and go to the bathroom, I'm just gonna open up the window and see if I can make that set of wind chimes over in the neighbor's tree ring like they were Janis Joplin's tambourine.

On day two, it'll get even better. I won't get dressed at all. I've got this flannel bath coat, and if I concentrate, I can almost make myself believe that it's a smoking jacket. Sure, I'm Hef, and the twins are in the glass-walled shower, sudsing each other clean with that Irish Springs soap that I like so much. You know, it's manly, but gosh darn if they don't like it, too!

Maybe I'll even invite some real girls over, like Hef would do. Of course, I don't really know many girls, except for the ones at the office, and I can't get within 100 feet of any of them because of that court thing.

I could invite Mrs. Krupnik over from next door. She's in her late 40s, and I've never seen her without hair curlers and a big mumu-esque house coat on, but I'm hoping that maybe she's like one of those librarians. You know the type, shy, glasses, no make-up, hair in a bun and baggy clothes, but as soon as you give them some white Zinfandel, down comes the hair, off come the glasses, and tossed into the corner is that baggy sweater, revealing a rack that could support the Encyclopedia Britannica.

Yeah, Mrs. Krupnik, you're *mine.*

If that doesn't work, maybe I'll call over some strippers to give me a private show. Of course, last time I tried that, I got confused while thumbing through the Yellow Pages and some guys came over and started stripping the paint off my house. I tried to talk them into, you know, gyrating their hips a little bit, just so I wouldn't feel totally ripped off, but one of them freaked and pointed a power sander at me as he slowly backed up into his truck and locked the doors.

Similarly, another time I looked up an escort service, but again I wasn't paying too much attention. About an hour later, a guy from the Ford dealership comes over. Rather than let him know I screwed up, I bought a little brown Escort, one with power steering and Scotchgarded upholstery. It's not much to look at, but you can't beat the mileage.

Ah, who am I kidding? I won't do any of that stuff. I'll just write, read, and edit articles like usual. I'll go to the gym, along with walking the hound, and I'll probably end up eating out most of the time rather than eating over the sink. Maybe I'll hit a strip club, but that's something I might do when the wife's around. She doesn't mind. After all, she knew I was a pig when she married me; hell, if you ask me, that was the main attraction.

In fact, whenever she has to fill out a missing person's report to the police (I get lost a lot), she describes me as if she were Tuco in *The Good, the Bad and the Ugly:* "He's tall, blonde, smokes a ceegar, and he's a peeg."

I've always been rather porcine—at least when it comes to sexuality—but I've never hid it, except maybe when Reverend Tonkin comes over for dinner.

I think too many guys hide that aspect of their personality from their girlfriends, and if you ask me, that's asking for trouble. They act like perfect little gentlemen. They act *different*. And if and when they eventually get married, their wives think they've married Little Lord Fauntleroy or something. And only when these guys get away from their wives do we see their repressed nature come exploding out.

These are the guys who go nuts when their wife leaves town. They act like dogs that have been chained to a tree in the backyard all their lives that suddenly break loose. Momentarily set free, they'll start dancing around the house in their underwear, peeing in trees, and eyeing the neighbor lady ... uh, bad example. But you get my point.

It's my belief that you shouldn't hide your true nature. The only way to maintain a relationship—one that won't leave you doing a Meatloaf and praying for the end of time—is sexual, hormonal, *honesty*.

Don't pretend you're only mildly interested in that Victoria's Secret catalog. The only thing potentially of more interest in that stack of mail is news that you've *really* won the Publishers Clearing House sweepstakes, and even then you'd have to think about which item you'd want to grab first.

If you see a girl at the gym who you think is hot, ask your wife to check her out in the shower and describe her to you. Hell, as your friend, it's her damn duty! Size and color of nipples; firmness and overall demeanor of breast (perky or sullen?); tautness of the buttocks; you want to know it all!

As a pig, this is information you *need* to know.

And when she asks you, "Honey, what are you thinking about?", don't lie about it by saying something like: "I'm thinking about being trapped in an avalanche, under tons of snow, with no hope of survival, and how I wouldn't mind because I've been able to spend the last few years of my life with someone like you, and how that's more pleasure than any man on earth has ever known or deserved, so even if I die now, it won't matter, because my love for you will transcend death."

Nahhh, you tell her that you're thinking about frolicking naked through fields of wheat with the star of that *Dark Angel* show on Fox.

There's nothing wrong with being romantic and all that, if you genuinely feel it, but don't spend your entire life with a woman pretending to be something you're not. The inevitable result of this type of charade is that sooner or later, your true nature will come out, and she'll regard you with the same horror usually reserved for pedophiles. She'll write letters to Dear Abby, without even bothering to use an alias, about how suddenly, you've turned into a sexual monster, actually *looking* at other women!

Abby will recommend counseling and castration.

Now I'm no friggin' marriage counselor, nor am I in the league of those babes on the Playboy channel that give sexual advice, but in my humble estimation, you need to let your true nature present itself from the get-go. Without doing that, you're in for a life of regret. Your lecherous thoughts are perfectly normal. Hell, they're your birthright. Don't let some woman make you believe there's something wrong with you and that you need to change.

Obviously, there has to be some discretion. For instance, don't take her to a Jenna Jameson film festival on your first date, and don't ever ask her to describe any of her family members naked. Especially her brother or dad. That's asking for real trouble.

Break her in slowly, but definitely do break her in. Don't end up being one of those guys that acts like Al Gore around his wife and then turns into a towel-snapping frat boy like George W. when his wife so much as leaves the room for a moment to go to the bathroom. If you act natural, neither personality extreme will ever show its face, and believe me, we'll all be the better for it: you, your mate, and the rest of us who have to witness that stuff.

And if you like dancing around the house in your underwear to Bob Seger tunes, don't wait until she leaves town; do it in front of her, but only if you look good. It might lead to some hot sex. Of course, if you're fat with pencil-thin legs, and you've got hair like a wire brush sticking out of your ears, don't do it. It might put her off sex forever. Next thing you know, she'll start, making up excuses like, "I'm going back east to help my parents move."

Chapter 29

Home Alone II

"Sure, I always took my shots when I was single, but it was never a pretty sight. I'd say "Hi," and before I knew it, I'd be telling her how my uric acid's a little higher than I'd like it to be, and how the miconazole I'm using to fight my fungal infection isn't working very well . . . . My approach usually fizzled, unless the girl had only one eye, a shaved head, and carried a squeegee to wipe the spittle off her chin. And even then the little Popeyed vixen would sometimes play hard to get."

My wife's out of town again. She's making her annual trip to Michigan to visit the folks. And, for a few days at least, I'm a bachelor again ... well, sort of.

Time to break out my Hawaiian shirts, my Dockers, my Disney World souvenir baseball cap, and my special fish-net underwear—you know, all the stuff that drives women really wild.

Ah, who am I kidding? Even if I was to go *rogue male*, I've never really been one of those smooth bastards when it comes to women. You know the type, the actor on par with Olivier who can walk up to a woman and act like he's really interested in what she's saying and flatter the hell out of her for just about any reason:

You're kidding ... you actually used a coupon that had expired to buy that can of peas? You're like that Xena chick on TV! They ought to make a movie about you! Especially with eyes like you have. They're like ... like jewels ... jewels shimmering in a mountain stream ....

Five minutes later, her skirt's around her ears and her heels are propped up against the ceiling of his BMW—one of those econo versions that he can barely afford on his salary as the manager of the concession stand at the movie theater, but yet gives the impression to the automobile-naive female that he's an up-and-comer, a promising young executive.

Nahh, that was never me. Sure, I always took my shots when I was single, but it was never a pretty sight. I'd say "Hi," and before I knew it, I'd be telling her how my uric acid's a little higher than I'd like it to be, and how the miconazole I'm using to fight my fungal infection isn't working very well.

My approach usually fizzled, unless the girl had only one eye, a shaved head, and carried a squeegee to wipe the spittle off her chin. And even then the little popeyed vixen would sometimes play hard to get.

Of course, my lack of conversational panache wasn't my only problem. They've done studies on why women like particular types of men. Most of the time, they go for cute-little-boy faces, guys who don't look very threatening and who'd be unlikely to beat them for losing the remote control. However, when they're ovulating, women apparently go for extremely masculine types. It seems they'd rather procreate with some guy who's got a lot of Testosterone, but when it comes to the long haul, they'd prefer some lovey-dovey type who doesn't mind being covered with baby puke from morning til night.

Me? I'm pretty masculine-looking. I've got one of those faces that would look right at home in a spaghetti western, with Clint Eastwood as the handsome, nameless stranger and special guest star TC as the weather-beaten, face-looks-like-the-rear-mud-flap-of-a-two-ton-semi gold miner.

Regardless, it seemed that every time a woman was ovulating, I was in the shower, or getting a haircut or something, so I was never able to take advantage of my supposed advantage.

Besides all that, I'm married, and supposedly, according to my wife, I took some sort of half-baked vow about not ever sleeping with other women. Sure, like I'm supposed to believe *that*. Why a man would have to be drugged or crazy to make a stupid promise like that!

It's also true that a lot of women, for some reason, don't like to hear that the man they're talking to, or thinking about sleeping with, is married. As an example, every Friday morning, after writing my column, I go have breakfast at a little outdoor café with my dog Toney. There's this cute little waitress there I've been lustfully eyeballing for months. We usually talk about Toney—whom she loves—but that's about it. So last Friday, while she was rubbing T-dog's head, she asked me if I was married.

Well, my vocal cords just shut down. I tried to answer, but the words wouldn't come out. I started coughing like a baby gila monster that had swallowed a particularly fat kangaroo rat: *Hhhhaacccck! Hhhhaaarrrcccck!* As hard as I tried, I couldn't clear my throat: *Ha-tooooommm! Ha-tooooommmm!*

I would have felt better telling her I had erectile dysfunction or something. Instead, I made the international sign for choking, which is to fall onto the ground, roll into a puddle, and turn cobalt blue.

She never got an answer, and neither did I follow through on what *might* have been a come-on.

It's that damn marriage thing. I can't help thinking I'm far from being alone when I admit to at least a small dagger-in-the-heart–like pang of remorse every time I have to give my marital status to some beautiful nurse, insurance agent, or waitress. Whenever I say it, I simultaneously imagine my poor dick being put in one of those stocks with which they used to publicly punish offenders; you know, the ones that had holes in it for the feet and hands? Yep, the head of my penis is in the middle of one of those stocks, and each ball is locked up in a hole, and all the single dicks and balls walk by jeering at me.

I also feel a pang of remorse when I find out that some beautiful piece of ass is married, too. For instance, a part of me always dies—a big part, about seven inches long and ribbed like a rattler—when I hear that Pamela Lee or some supermodel is getting hitched. Sure, it's big-time delusional (like I had a chance with her, anyhow), but it's human nature… scratch that, it's guy nature. But a lot of famous babes are cognizant of this part of guy nature, too.

Case in point: Last Tuesday night, I made my annual pilgrimage to see Anna Kournikova play tennis, and the buzz around the court was not on how crummy Anna was playing, but whether or not she had recently married Red Wings center Sergei Federov in a secret ceremony.

She wouldn't say, realizing that an admission of guilt would result in a psychic tweak of her male fans' testicles. She *wants* us to think that we have a chance with her. She wants us to fantasize that after winning the match, she'd excitedly scan the audience for our face, and then, after seeing us, would run gazelle-like over to the side of the court, scamper over the wall, and fight her way through the fans to throw her damp, nubile body into our arms and firmly against our manhood while she covers us with kisses as the other men wail and gnash their teeth in envy.

Yeah, Anna's my squeeze, suckers!!

In fact, I got so carried away with that particular fantasy that I found myself passionately hugging and kissing the short, fat, squirming Italian grandmother from Brooklyn who was sitting next to me. Apparently, she'd been given tickets to the tennis tournament by her grandson, Johnny "The Butcher" Conigliaro, who has since vowed to "pull my guts out" with his bare hands and "strain them through a tennis racket."

Women. They're the bane of us all, you know, one way or another.

While walking by the Presbyterian church in my neighborhood last Saturday, I saw scores of people arriving for a wedding. Being the romantic slob at heart that I am, I stopped to check it out. After most of the guests had taken their seats inside the church, the bride and the bridesmaids gathered outside for some photos before making their grand entrance. I don't know if any of you remember the Swedish Bikini Team that used to be featured in the beer ads for Old

Milwaukee, but that's what these women looked like. Either that, or Hef's seven blonde girlfriends. Each was taller and more beautiful than the previous one, and they were wearing tight, backless, black evening gowns—none of those poofy-sleeved Little Miss Muffet, sat on her tuffet, eating her curds and whey dresses.

But, there, amidst all that beauty, was one pale, short, pudgy-armed girl, looking as out of place in that group of women as a Tasmanian devil in the finals of the Greater Westchester Poodle Championships. She must have been the groom's cousin from Nova Scotia, where she eviscerates cattle for the local slaughterhouse.

To me, the whole group of bridesmaids, including the troll-like one, served as some sort of metaphor aimed at the groom. It's as if the fat one was there to represent what the marriage could become: fat, dumpy, *there*. All the time. And the beautiful ones were there to taunt him, as if to say, *"Look! This is what you're giving up, you putz!"*

I tell ya, I don't know who in their right mind would get married nowadays … of course, you know, now that I think of it, my wife looks kind of like one of those blonde bridesmaids. I bet if she wore that black dress she has from Nordstrom's and put on those heels she got from Frederick's of Hollywood, she'd look just like that one on the left.

Man, I sure miss her.

Chapter 30

Attack of the Blue Whales

"Wal-Mart, presumably due to complaints from fat women in blue tights who were championed by some religious groups, yanked some other "pornographic" titles from the magazine stands of its stores. The titles of this smut? Maxim, FHM, and Stuff, which are known in the business as "lad mags." . . . Cosmopolitan, however, survived their Puritan purge. In Wal-Mart land, the lad mags represent pornography, while explicit instructions about how to make swallowing cum more palatable do not . . . . Ladies and Gentleman of the jury, what in the wide, wide world of cooz is going on here?"

I left the office early the other day to run some errands and my co-worker Cy asked me if I wouldn't mind stopping at the local Wal-Mart to pick him up some panty shields, the kind with the "stay-put wings." (He likes to use them in lieu of weightlifting gloves because, according to Cy, "they're comfortable, doubly absorbent, and pleasantly fragrant, just like the ads say.")

After finishing my errands, I stopped by the Wal-Mart and picked up a dozen boxes for Cy, but I wasn't in any particular hurry to get back to the office because the boss was in one of his cleanliness moods where he makes everyone get on their hands and knees to look for dust bunnies.

So I stopped by the magazine rack to kill some time. I skimmed through *Newsweek, Esquire, Rolling Stone*, and some of the usual titles you'd find on any magazine rack. But then I stumbled on something that caught me off guard. There, in the midst of Wal-Mart, one of the last bastions of middle-class morality and good ol' American values, was a magazine that was about as pornographic as anything I've ever read.

262 Atomic Dog - The Testosterone Principles

It had pages and pages of scantily clad bodies, both female and male, but it was the actual text that was more shocking. I mean, if I wrote stuff like this, I'd get even more letters accusing me of being a misogynist pig than I normally do.

For the sake of example only, here are some excerpts:

My girlfriend gets a glazed donut and sticks my penis through the hole. She nibbles around it, stopping to suck me once in awhile. The sugar beads from her mouth tingle on my tip.

When he's catching some zzz's on the plane, reach under his blanket, unzip his pants, and give him a mile-high wake-up call.

Start with his shoulders and smooth the slick stuff all the way down to his shorts—and below—for a grease job he'll never forget.

O gentle reader, as these words bounced off the back of my retinas, I could feel the blood flow shifting south, quickly flooding the dams and farmlands of my nether regions and raging mightily into the reservoir of my manhood. I looked down, saw the bulge in my pants, and quickly turned to the left to make sure no one was looking, but in doing so, my tumescence knocked over a display of miniature personalized license plates, the kind that kids attach to the back of their bikes. A shower of Claras, Connies, Constances, and Cathies fell to the floor and made a sound like hail on a tin roof.

I quickly picked up the license plates, hung my baseball cap on the front of my pants, and resumed reading.

Swirl your mouth around the tip of my penis, and then, without warning, take all of me in your mouth.

When I'm about to reach the brink, tell me to pull out. Then bring me to release in your mouth.

The bottom of the scrotum is the most sensitive part of my body. Stroke it. Cuddle it. Love it.

I was now in a non-discriminatory, lycanthropic trance, and I sidled up to a gum-smacking, acne-dotted Wal-Mart clerk, noting how her sweat-stained smock complemented her fireplug-like figure. I stole a brief glance at her badge and said, in the smoothest, whiskey-drinkin' tone I could muster, "Agnes, could you tell me where the condoms are, the really, really big ones?"

Agnes pushed up her already smudgy Gloria Vanderbilt glasses with her palm and pointed to Aisle 5. Whatever chance we had at romance was interrupted by the tinny, over-head speaker asking for a price check on Dr. Scholl's bunion pads. Agnes shuffled away, a trail of price stickers—and my heart—affixed to her left orthopedic shoe. We were not to couple then, or ever.

The name of this pornographic magazine that had put me in such a randy state? *Cosmopolitan.* No lie. And I'm told this is pretty representative of the stuff you'd find in any random copy of *Cosmo.*

What I find surprising is that just this past week, Wal-Mart, presumably due to complaints from fat women in blue tights who were championed by some religious groups, yanked some other "pornographic" titles from the magazine stands of its stores. The titles of this smut? *Maxim, FHM,* and *Stuff,* which are known in the business as "lad mags."

If you've ever read or looked through any of these mags, you'd know that they specialize in pictures of pretty women in lingerie and bikinis, tame stuff by almost anyone's standards. Oftentimes, you'll find racier stuff in the Maidenform ads that grace the pages of the Sunday edition of *The New York Times.*

Cosmopolitan, however, survived their Puritan purge. In Wal-Mart land, the lad mags represent pornography, while explicit instructions about how to make swallowing cum more palatable do not.

Ladies and gentleman of the jury, what in the wide, wide world of cooz is going on here?

Could it be that the typical mid-American Wal-Mart shopper—who this action was clearly meant to appease—is illiterate? Sure, soft-core porno pictures are one thing, but readin'? Hell, that's work. Ain't nobody actually gonna read these things. Consider that the brainiest stuff you'll find in their book department is *Chicken Soup for the Soul.*

But if that's the case, why are the shelves of Wal-Mart filled with other visual examples of "porn," either explicit or implied? There are the aforementioned condoms, see-through panties, and even a new line of "lingerie" Barbie dolls where she dresses exactly like the girls in the lad mags. Add to that the CDs by gangsta rappers, complete with the prerequisite lyrics about ho' slappin' and you wonder why all the fuss over some photos of girls in short-shorts.

I gotta think the CDs slipped through because the typical Wal-Mart shopper isn't even aware of rap, never having listened to any music that wasn't played on a six or 12-string guitar by somone wearing pointy cowboy boots. But the rest of it represents what I call the T-and-A Paradox. Those things that appeal to man's sexual instincts are evil. Those things that appeal to women, like *Cosmo's* soft-porn; daytime soap operas and the non-stop bedhopping practiced by their stars; and romance novels, most of which center on rape and reconciliation, are just fine. But the fat ladies in blue spandex tights, the blue whales, would never admit what they're reading is porn. Never! But they do object to visual glorification of female flesh.

When I lived in Denver, droves of these women came out to protest a high school fundraising stunt where girls in bathing suits would wash your car. Apparently, this would lead to … hell, I don't know. My mind is either so evil or so pure, I can't even imagine what the problem would be.

Similarly, another group of blue whales protested the opening of a gentleman's club that was setting up shop across the street from a children's dance studio. Either they were worried about their little girls leaving the dance studio, seeing some topless dancers arriving for work, and putting two and two together to arrive at the conclusion that was what they were practicing for—to become professional nonnie shakers—or they were simply fighting against the "seedy element" that habitually hangs out at strip clubs. You know who hangs out at strip clubs? Me and Tommy Lasorda. That's about as seedy as it gets. Run, you blue whales, run!

This kind of thing happens all the time. It often just takes one or two complaints to start the ball rolling, and corporations, who depend heavily on the purses of the blue whales, will do whatever it takes to appease them. Meanwhile, as far as magazines are concerned, *Cosmo* will likely endure, jammed up there on the stands next to *Better Homes & Gardens* and *People* while mags like *Maxim* and the *Sports Illustrated* Swimsuit Issue will be relegated to a space behind the counter where they can't be seen by innocent women and children.

Nope, the blue whales won't be happy until they've turned us all into middle-aged women. Pass the panty shields, please.

Chapter 31

Staying Faithful

"Sure it's superficial. I'll be the first to admit that, but superficiality is often the foundation of a long-lasting relationship. It's always been that way, for men and women alike. We pick the cutest puppy in the litter without knowing anything about its personality traits. Appreciation of the finer stuff comes with time. The longer you're together, the longer you appease my superficial needs, the better the chance we'll remain together long enough for me to appreciate your less superficial traits."

There's no denying it, I've gotten rusty around women. It's like I've been on the DL for a couple of months and all of a sudden the coach wants me to pinch-hit in the bottom of the ninth. Sure, I *try*, but I'm flailing away like a blindfolded, drunken frat boy with palsy swinging a broomstick at a piñata. One, two, three strikes I'm out, and as I walk back to the dugout, the fans pelt me with a melange of coins, beer, and half-eaten Eskimo pies.

It's the same way with women. I take my shot, say something hopelessly awkward, and am summarily rejected. As I walk back to my table, onlookers pelt me with coins, beer, and half-eaten Eskimo pies.

It's gotten really bad. I'll be having breakfast somewhere, notice some hottie sitting at a table next to me, and in lieu of being able to think of anything clever or intelligent to say to break the ice, I'll ask, "Would you pass the salsa, please?" Then, just to show her that I wasn't just trying to start a conversation, I'm forced to spoon some salsa on my chocolate doughnut.

I guess the baseball analogy fits because baseball is part of the problem. Ever since the recently completed playoffs and World Series began a few weeks ago, I haven't left the house, haven't had any contact with any living creatures other than my dogs.

Combine that with the fact that I've been working in San Diego—fire-ravaged San Diego, air-choked-with-particulate-matter San Diego—and haven't been able to go outside much in the last week, well then you've got the makings of someone who's been a total recluse for longer than Osama, Saddam, and Chicago Cubs scapegoat Steve Bartman combined.

I finally emerged from my solitude to go to a Halloween party last night and for a while there it felt like the ol' charm was coming back. I was talking to a cute girl and sure, I made some innocent rookie mistakes—like mentioning how my sinus medication causes the teensiest bit of anal leakage—but otherwise I was doing okay.

But then I made a serious error. I leaned over and started scratching her on the side of her belly, right above her low-slung jeans. I guess I'd spent so much time with my dogs that I instinctively reached out and tried to find that spot on her hindquarters where their legs start involuntarily thumping up and down off the ground.

"Yes, she's a good girl, a *goood* girl," I cooed.

I followed that up by offering her one of those liver-flavored Snausages that the dogs like so much: "See? It's a sausage *and* a snack, a Snausage!"

She gave me a peculiar look and walked away. Then I remembered that dogs thump their legs when you scratch them in a certain place and dogs are the ones that like Snausages. I was so embarrassed that I stuck my head in a bowl of vegetable dip and kept it there until everyone went home.

Damn. I used to be so good.

But when I think back on it, I have trouble understanding why I was good. I broke all the traditional rules regarding relationships, but for some reason the relationships were always successful, and by successful I mean that they were generally long-lasting, mutually enjoyable unions where, believe it or not, I remained faithful.

The main rule I broke was practicing complete, total, sexual honesty from day one. I never made any attempt to hide my pigginess.

"Yes, I like porn dear, and no, I will not cancel my subscription to *Cycle Sluts Monthly* now that I've met you."

"But aren't I enough for you?"

"No, you're not enough for me. No woman is enough for any man. No 10 women are good enough for any man, so get over yourself. I may worship the ground you gyrate on, but that doesn't mean I'm not going to do a cervical-spine–wrenching head jerk when some butt cleavage sashays by me on the street."

Amazingly, this sexual honesty made my lust for other women … tolerable. The more I opened up about it, the less it tugged at my testicles.

If we went to see *Cats*, I'd lean over to her and whisper, "Man I'd like to nail those furry little kitties." While it pissed her off in the beginning, she gradually became a partner in my pigginess and paradoxically, it let some steam out of the pressure cooker of my loins. By confessing my lust, I was less inclined to play the field.

I remember the time when a particularly tasty morsel walked out of the gym locker room with a girl I was dating and I asked my girlfriend to describe what the tasty morsel looked like naked. The thing was, her verbal skills were kinda poor so we headed down to the police station where we sat down with a sketch artist.

"Nipples?" he asked.

"Big," she answered.

"Bigger than silver dollars?"

"Hmm, yes, yes, I think they were."

"And the texture? Smooth or a little bumpy?"

"Bumpy."

"How long would it take a blind man to read them? Ten seconds? Twenty?"

"Twenty. Definitely 20."

"And the hue? Pinkish or brownish?"

"A pinkish hue. I remember distinctly because they reminded me of the Alaskan salmon that I like to order from the Sea Shanty on Sheffield Avenue."

I eventually got a reasonable pencil-drawn facsimile of the tasty morsel that I folded up and kept in my wallet.

And in being this honest with all my girlfriends, away went all those white lies that are often part of any relationship. Hell, if I was going to a strip club with the boys, I'd tell her. Not only would she approve, she'd pack my wallet with dollar bills to slide under their thongs. She'd even iron the money. That always went over big with the dancers. ("He's not only a good tipper, but he's so gosh-darn tidy.")

When the evening was over, rather than try to invite the dancers over to my place for some naked Trivial Pursuit, I'd just go home and tell my girlfriend about the evening: "And then, this one girl put a couple of straws underneath her nipples and rotated 'em like propellers so her breasts looked like a couple of dirigibles racing across the room! It was *sooo* cool!"

And because I was free to talk about other women, she got a pretty good idea of exactly what I liked about the way other women look. As such, I never slipped into those relationship phases where you grow so comfortable with each other that you stop caring about how you look.

If your wife or girlfriend doesn't work out, or upon leaving work she immediately slips into stained sweat pants and baggy sweaters that make her indistinguishable from millions of female K-mart shoppers, the urge to stray is going to prey on the mind a lot, as is the urge to run down to Wal-Mart and nab a set of discounted radial tires.

No drab underwear, either! Great underwear! Underwear knitted by the elves of Middle Earth! High heels in the bedroom! Kinky outfits!

Women who do that are as smart as that wonderfully wise AFLAC duck!

And it all spells *fidelity*.

Sure, it's superficial. I'll be the first to admit that, but superficiality is often the foundation of a long-lasting relationship. It's always been that way, for men and women alike. We pick the cutest puppy in the litter without knowing anything about its personality traits. Appreciation of the finer stuff comes with time. The longer you're together, the longer you appease my superficial needs, the better the chance we'll remain together long enough for me to appreciate your less superficial traits.

Besides, the kind of honesty I'm talking about leaches over into all other aspects of the relationship and makes it stronger. A woman is far more likely to get a real answer to the question, "What's wrong?" or "What's bothering you?" if her man has learned that he can say what's truly on his mind without fear of histrionics or reproach.

But listen to me, talking about relationships when I've totally forgotten how to relate to women! I'm like the batting coach who never hit over .200 in the majors telling Barry Bonds how to hit. It's time for me to get in the batting cage and take a few hacks. I may strike out a lot—eat a lot of salsa-covered chocolate doughnuts—but at least I'll be back in the game.

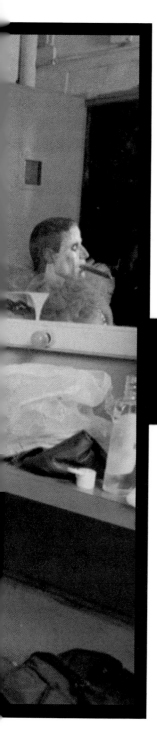

Testosterone
The Essence of Man

SECTION

5

Chapter 32

Alpha Males and Beta Males

"Human males, despite all our pretenses that we're civilized and evolved, do pretty much the same thing. The next time you see two men meet for the first time, take note of their body language. In most cases eye contact will establish dominance, the one who momentarily averts his gaze deferring to the other, more dominant male. If that doesn't work, one or both will stand up straight and stick their chest out to appear more imposing. Physical dominance might be further implied by a bone-crushing handshake or stepping into the other's personal space."

My doctor is a woman. My dentist is a woman. My lawyer, well, he *used* to be a woman, but that clinic in Switzerland took care of that. My barber, my dermatologist, my optometrist, they're all women. If my normally glass-smooth butt needed to be exfoliated, the person who got the job would be a woman.

Why this bias toward the opposite sex when it comes to taking care of my personal appearance or medical or legal needs?

Because most men don't give a damn about my health or making me look good. Most men would prefer that I were in another country, in some other dimension, or even dead. I don't take it personally because most guys feel the same about all men.

That may be a bit harsh, but it's no secret that men are extremely competitive with each other. The root of that competitiveness—at least if you're a strict Freudian man—is sex. It's embedded in our subconscious like the sapphire in Christina Aguilera cute little belly button. All you penis-endowed humans out there are potential rivals for the world-wide Pussy Powerball Lottery.

Don't you see? If there were no other sexually able men around, all the women in the world would be there for the taking. All yours, every last one of them. A good two-thirds of them would probably go lesbo rather than mate with you, but hell, that still leaves a few hundred million fertile females around! Even Wilt the Stilt wouldn't sneeze at those numbers.

Darwin assumed that the concept of natural male beauty arose through competition between males to attract a sexual partner, hence the plumage on male birds, a mane on a male lion, or even antlers on a stag. While human males weren't naturally gifted with any special ornamentation, primitive man got around it by wearing beads or the feathers of birds. Modern man? Well, he puts on a nice pair of Dockers and a shirt from Abercrombie. Of course, what is weight lifting but an attempt to add some ornamentation in the form of muscle?

But the problem with humans—if it's indeed a problem—is that unlike a lot of animals, we can mate any time, even if it's during dental surgery, thermonuclear war, or during commercials for *The Apprentice*. As such, we're constantly in contention with other men. Ever notice how two male dogs size each other up? Their hackles are raised, their tails erect, and they'll posture, chuff, and growl until one's body language acknowledges the other's dominance. Afterwards, they'll usually get along fine. However, if neither is willing to back down, a fight will usually settle the matter.

Human males, despite all our pretenses that we're civilized and evolved, do pretty much the same thing. The next time you see two men meet for the first time, take note of their body language. In most cases eye contact will establish dominance; the one who momentarily averts his gaze is in effect, deferring to the other, more dominant male. If that doesn't work, one or both will stand up straight and stick their chest out to appear more imposing. Physical dominance might be further implied by a bone-crushing handshake or stepping into the other's personal space.

If the dominant male is lacking in physicality and instead considers himself intellectually dominant, he may try to establish dominance through his vocabulary, his position in society, or his wealth. He can do this by flashing a Rolex, rattling the keys to his Benz, or using words like *pusillanimous* or *sesquipedalian*. Of course, if there are any physically dominant men within earshot of words like those, they may jam the keys to the Benz up his nostril so that when he sneezes all the car doors unlock and the trunk pops open.

You see this kind of one-upsmanship all the time in the office, where men will go to great lengths to show who's alpha male and who's beta male. Take my office, for example. Every morning at 9, Tim Patterson comes into my office, unzips his pants, and practices his "urine calligraphy" by writing his name onto my carpet. In turn, I go into the assistant editor's office and blast the ferns off his desk. He then goes into the accountant's office and turns his guppy bowl into a fancy commode. The accountant then marks his own foot, because there's really no one lower on the totem pole. The whole thing is a ruthless, never-ending display of dominance.

Given all that, it's probably not hard to understand why I seek professional services from women. After all, what possible good can come from making another man more desirable to the opposite sex? Sure, they're all professionals who take pride in their work, but they save their best for people who have breasts. Conversely, helping me look or perform better will only increase his competition for access to the people with breasts.

Ever get a haircut from a guy who wasn't gay? Hell, you're lucky to walk out of there with a do that looks better than the one Saddam was wearing when they pulled him out of the spider hole.

Ever talk to a male doctor who didn't treat you as if you were a piece of banged-up luggage? If in the past I wanted to get adequate treatment from a male doctor, I had to hang my pants *and* my testicles on the hook behind the door. I quickly sat down as to not intimidate them with my height or size, didn't meet their eyes for more than a second, and smiled and chuckled like the world's biggest toady.

The last male doctor I had wouldn't even give me a prostate exam during a physical. He literally turned the faucet on partway and said, "After you go to the bathroom, does it shut off immediately or does it trickle out like this?'

"Oh, then you're fine."

Despite his obvious gift as a diagnostician, I now go to Dr. Sheila Blasingame. She cheerfully checks my prostate and, while I may be mistaken, I think she even looks forward to it. Yep, I like to think there's a bit of love riding sidesaddle on that nimble, impetuous little finger.

While some professional men are able to put aside the innate sense of competitiveness and treat all patients or customers equally, it's the exception rather than the rule. Even friendships are plagued by sexual competitiveness. It's usually not overt, but it's there. Male friends take pleasure in your good fortune, as long as you make a little less money than they do and as long as your girlfriend or wife is a little less pretty than theirs.

Having more money and a juicier sex partner tells him, subconsciously, that you're more desirable to women than he is; lets him know you're winning the genetic Stanley Cup, slapping tumescent puck after tumescent puck between the open legs of female goalies. Your very existence decreases the chances that he'll get to procreate with the girl who works at the Dairy Queen around the corner. And while your friend probably wouldn't nail your wife or girlfriend, he thinks about it; he thinks about it a lot. Yep, in his fantasies, she's wearing your Minnesota Golden Gophers sweatshirt and nothing else while he makes passionate love to her right on your favorite La-Z-Boy lounger while you're in the garage building a birdhouse or polishing up your collection of license plates.

As evidence of just how deeply rooted in our psyche this stuff is, research even suggests that the volume of male ejaculate is subconsciously controlled, larger amounts being produced when the male is uncertain about the likelihood of another male having sex with his mate. More sperm and more ejaculate increases the chance of pregnancy, thereby knocking other men out of the procreative picture.

This is presumably what happened to Tim Pattersons's first wife, Jasmine. Her infidelities caused him to experience profound insecurities and when they made love for the very last time, she was literally hosed away, and the milky-white deluge carried her into the waters off the Florida Keys. Her body was never found.

I suppose there's a positive side to this competition for sex. It's probably largely responsible for most advances in human history. Power, accomplishment, status—at the root of all of those lie sex. Without at least a remote promise of sex—somehow, somewhere—we wouldn't even get out of bed in the morning.

Unfortunately, this competition is also responsible for most of the really bad shit too. If women ran the world, the place would probably be a lot happier and everything would run very efficiently. However, I doubt there'd be much impetus to conquer new vistas. Men want to conquer new vistas because there might be some really juicy women on top of that new vista, or news of his new-vista–conquering talents might earn the favors of new-vista groupies.

I've probably made the competition between men sound much worse than it is. Do I really believe men hate each other? No. Do I believe all male relationships–both professional and personal–are tainted by competition for sex? No. Well, unless there are some really gorgeous women in the office or sitting next to us at the ballgame.

In that case, I'm going to do my damnedest to let her know I'm the alpha male and you're the beta.

Chapter 33

The Male Libido

"Having a supercharged libido, at least for a male, is the most distracting thing imaginable. Being a little hungry for food is one thing, but being hungry for sexual release is, at least to me, much more uncomfortable. Not only that, but you keep knocking over your collection of delicate glass figurines every time you turn around too quickly."

I woke up this morning with a *stellar* erection, a real humdinger. I'm not just saying that out of vanity or something because I'm really kinda shy and modest about stuff like that. But you have to understand, this hard-on was particularly noteworthy because when I woke up, my bedroom was filled with a group of local farmers who were pitching horseshoes at what they must have thought was an iron stake, or a reasonable facsimile thereof.

Clang! Clang! Clang!

The noise echoed against the walls, causing my autographed pictures of Shakira and Christina to jar violently each time a farmer hit a ringer.

How the farmers got in I don't know, but they took little notice of me and in between throws discussed the weather, crop conditions, and the price of a bushel of corn. Rather than disturb their game with a lot of fool questions, I instead opted to be a good sport and lie there and ponder the mysteries of erections and, more importantly, the male libido.

I know that spontaneous erections won't occur if Testosterone levels are low, so I appreciate and look forward to their appearances like a small boy awaits sporadic visits from a favorite uncle whose pockets are filled with candy. Yes, a surprise visit from the boner fairy is even regarded by some folks as a herald of good fortune. In fact, one of the horseshoe-pitching farmers just confirmed that a favorite expression among them is, "Spontaneous boner in June, corn be heavy soon."

While spontaneous erections are a barometer of normal Testosterone levels, it's still possible to experience erections from visual stimuli even if T levels are subpar. So if you get an erection from looking at the latest copy of *American Breast Enthusiast*, but not while you're sleeping, it's still possible you have low levels of T.

Regardless, the relationship between Testosterone and libido, and subsequently erections, is mysterious. For some reason, there's a latency period between spikes in Testosterone and elevations in sexual desire. For instance, hypogonadal men who start receiving replacement doses of Testosterone often don't experience a rise in libido until a couple of weeks later, even though T levels hit their zenith a day or two after the injection.

Similarly, bodybuilders or strength athletes who start using anabolic steroids or prohormones often don't get the type of persistent horniness that comes part and parcel with some 'roids until a few days later. Why this latency period exists is somewhat of a mystery.

Personally, Testosterone boosters, along with shots of any one of the Testosterone esters, make me sprout fangs relatively quickly, while many other steroids or prohormones have never had that much of an effect on my libido at all. Sure, it has to do with androgenicity and whether the androgens are particularly progestogenic or estrogenic, but we haven't figured out all the angles yet about why some have more of an effect on libido than others.

But when the libido does come, it comes with a vengeance. Having a supercharged libido, at least for a male, is the most distracting thing imaginable. Being a little hungry for food is one thing, but being hungry for sexual release is, at least to me, much more uncomfortable. Not only that, but you keep knocking over your collection of delicate glass figurines every time you turn around too quickly.

When the collective bunch of us at the office is experiencing unbearable horniness, very little work gets done. You ever wonder why it sometimes takes American workers so long to do anything? Horniness. Unreleased sexual tension. I just know that when our staff is particularly horny, we spend the bulk of the day feeling up the vending machine—the one that has the picture of that cute Little Debby of snack cake fame painted on the front.

(We once caught Big Dave—who works in shipping—with his pants down and locked in a "love embrace" with slot G4. It wasn't until hours later when someone had correct change that we were able to free him.)

Luckily, my partner Tim is cognizant of just how distracting a stoked but not yet stroked libido can be. What Tim did last summer—bless his heart—was hire a very special summer intern from New York to periodically make the rounds between our offices. Some time between 9 a.m. and noon on Tuesdays and Thursdays, Rhoda came to the door of each of our offices, lifted up her skirt, popped her bubble gum and asked, in Bronx-ese, "Can I soyvis ya today?"

Unfortunately, Rhoda looked a little like Bill O'Reilly with tits, so the only guy who regularly took advantage of her offer was Jimmy, the geriatric company swamper whom we once caught humping a wet sponge.

Now that summer and Rhoda are gone, we're back to rubbing up against Little Debby and moaning.

Even among high-T individuals, it's amazing how much libido can vary. For some of us, all it takes to get turned on is to look at a couple of curvy lines drawn on a piece of paper; curvy lines that approximate a woman's hips, narrow waist, and bosoms … heaving bosoms at that, with nipples the size of Volkswagen hubcaps! Hubcaps that are the color of pale, pale roses in springtime! Oh man, where's Rhoda when you need her?

Sorry, I was overtaken by the moment, but I'm okay now. Like Kramer when he lost the bet on who could remain "Master of his Domain" the longest on *Seinfeld*, I just slammed my money on the table.

While some men are aroused very easily, others could be standing security in the dressing room of the Victoria's Secret Annual Fashion Show and instead of drooling into both cups of a spare demi-bra, actually be doing their job and looking for security risks.

Likewise, there's an all-girls private school down the street from the coffee shop where I sometimes meet my cronies. (Think Tony Soprano and the boys sitting outside Santorielli's and sipping on their espressos.)

In an effort to put the kibosh on any budding sexuality, the clueless and T-less school administrators have adopted a school uniform for the females. It consists of a tight white shirt, plaid skirt, knee-high socks, and little black shoes, which, ironically, is the uniform of choice for most of the strippers I've had the pleasure of knowing. Their uniform is the consummate horn-dog fantasy!

When school lets out at three o'clock, a good many of them walk by our table at the coffee shop. Probably half of us look and make noises like Homer Simpson when he's confronted by a particularly tasty-looking donut. The other guys are oblivious! Yes, yes, these are young girls, some as young as 15 or 16, but you have to realize that many of the girls—cock-teases in training—have helped things along by shrinking their shirts, raising the hemlines on their skirts, and wearing heels that are at least three inches high.

It's painful. Most of us at the table will invariably be slamming our money on the table within the next few hours, if you catch my drift.

Anyhow, it's puzzling to me how some of us would look, and some of us wouldn't. And it sure doesn't just apply to the little T-vixens in my neighborhood, either. These same men might not even glance up if the *Girls Gone Wild* people were shooting their latest video 30 feet away.

Is this disparity in sexual interest related to libido, and if so, is libido related purely on a one-to-one ratio with hormone levels? If a group of men of the exact same age had the exact same hormonal readings, and had last had sex at the same time, would they react in similar ways? I'd bet a good chunk of change that the answer would be no.

Many men probably aren't as visual as others, and it takes something very distinct to turn some men on. As an example, I understand that George W. Bush can't have sex with any woman unless her backside is peppered with saddle sores. If, by chance, the sores make an outline that resembles the profile of cowboy hero John Wayne, he's insatiable.

We probably won't know the answers to these questions about libido for a good long time. It's an enigmatic thing, but maybe too much analysis takes away from its magic. Instead, we should, upon experiencing a burst of libido manifested by a proud and tall erection, sit back and marvel at one of nature's wonders.

And, what the hell, if there are some friends around, pull out the horseshoes.

Chapter 34

I'm a Blue Lizard

"The funny thing is, I have a minor in art history, but even so, I'd rather watch nude babes gyrate under neon lights. Now, if you could find me a strip club that was decorated with the works of the French impressionists, I'm there, hurlin' back shots of Canadian Club and getting' pissed when any sumbitch confuses Monet with Manet."

When I went to college, I had every intention of becoming a doctor—not one of them-there *phony* doctors that has a bunch of letters after his name and smokes a pipe, but a *medical* doctor. Science had always been my best subject, and it just seemed like a natural progression. Hey, we're talking about a kid who had a pretty impressive botany lab when he was 10 years old, and who had been known, on occasion, to rip off college-level textbooks from the public library.

A funny thing happened on the way to med school, though. I started looking less nerdy, and for the first time, I was able to meet women and occasionally even talk one into doing unspeakable things in the dark.

I started paying more attention to nookie than classes, and while I still maintained a pretty good GPA, it became clear to me that there was no way in God's creation that I was going to be able to balance my interest in babes with the enormous amount of work required to become a sawbones.

On top of all that, I had this rotten attitude. I didn't like structure of any kind, couldn't stand being made to do something I didn't want to do, and what's more, I had a really, really, bad temper.

I finished college and got a couple of degrees, but only because I liked reading and learning in general. But there wasn't a week that went by without me getting into some kind of altercation. My favorite pissy line was inspired by the *Star Wars* bar scene:

Punk: "Whadda you lookin' at?"

Me: "Your face."

Punk: "My face? Whadaboud it?"

Me: "I don't *like* it."

Yep, I was an asshole.

I had plenty of jobs after college, never staying in any one longer than a year or two because they all made me want to take a high, Greg Louganis triple-gainer out the window. I just didn't like to take orders, and working in a cubicle was like being in a coffin with fluorescent lights and a desk blotter. During work hours, I was a dreary little man, bereft of passion. Come five o'clock, though, I'd try to grab whatever excitement I could; tried to drink up whatever intensity and passion that I could find, which often included staying in the gym for two to two and a half hours at a time—just so I wouldn't feel like Wilson in *Castaway*, an inflated piece of leather with a face on it.

But I'd be back at work the next morning, wishing that my pencil were a steel spike so I could drive it through my heart and end the misery.

I haven't changed much since then. You wouldn't know it to meet me. My friends consider me to be friendly, amiable, and easygoing. That's all pretty much true, until someone I don't know pisses me off, and that's pretty easy to do.

Likewise, I still don't like structure, I still hate meetings and appointments, and I'd much prefer to do things on my own rather than work on a team. Sex still preoccupies my thoughts—impromptu boners were, and are still, my frequent companions—and while you might have trouble convincing me to go to an art museum, it wouldn't take much to get me to go to Bada Bing for a lap dance.

(The funny thing is, I have a minor in art history, but even so, I'd rather watch nude babes gyrate under neon lights. Now, if you could find me a strip club that was decorated with the works of the French impressionists, I'm there, hurlin' back shots of Canadian Club and gettin' pissed when any sumbitch confuses Monet with Manet.)

Anyhow, like I said, I haven't changed much, but at least I have a better understanding of why I am the way I am and as such, am able to curb these feelings, impulses, likes, and dislikes and put them to work for me.

My self-understanding came, in part, from the animal kingdom. Somewhere on this earth lives a species of desert tree lizard named *Urosaurus orantus*. What makes this lizard unusual from a scientific perspective is that the species includes two different types of males. They look pretty much the same except that they differ in their dewlaps, which are the little fans underneath their neck that they flare out when they want to communicate or show off.

One type has a solid yellow or orange dewlap, while the other type has a blue dewlap that's bordered by orange or yellow. The blue lizards compete with other blues and fight to control territory, while the solid orange or yellow ones avoid fights and look for unclaimed territory.

I know nothing about their endocrinology, but I suspect that the blue-necked little buggers are pumping more Testosterone through their scaly skin than their yellow, less aggressive counterparts.

It doesn't take that big a leap of imagination to think that human society has two types of males, too. The one type is much like me in that it's impatient, has trouble conforming or paying attention to rules, and has a very low tolerance for bullshit. Men like us are blue lizards. The other types, the yellow lizards, are very different, and if you look at the Testosterone levels of individuals in various professions, you'll see that there's a strong correlation between T and occupation.

For instance, trial lawyers, explorers, football players, porn stars, firefighters, policeman, and even New York taxi drivers generally have higher levels of T than corporate lawyers, accountants, health-care professionals, computer programmers, ministers, and managers.

Likewise, heavy-truck drivers generally have 25 percent more T than light-truck drivers; advertising managers have 46 percent more than computer programmers; and car salesman have 24 percent more than high school teachers. Blue-collar workers, in general, have 8 percent more than white-collar workers.

Clearly, the high-T types like jobs that require energy, strength, sex, certain mechanical or spatial skills, and flair, whereas the other types gravitate toward occupations that require patience, structure, a team-player attitude, and a willingness to take a back seat to authority figures.

The trouble is, most of these high-T traits don't equate to monetary rewards. White-collar work is boring to a high-T guy. Even worse, these traits make getting an education a little problematic. High-T boys and young men don't want to listen to some teacher drone on all day. (Unfortunately, this trait is often diagnosed as an attention deficit disorder and is treated with drugs that turn young men into focused little Stepford boys.)

Because of a lot of the aforementioned high-T traits, high-T guys are often puzzled about life. They sometimes think of themselves as the proverbial square peg trying to fit into a round hole. They feel as out of place as bodybuilder Ronnie Coleman at a Mensa convention. They don't understand why the majority of the Dockers-wearing guys they know do just fine, settling into boring jobs or long, mutually beneficial (but passionless) marriages while they, the blue lizards, seem to live a life of conflict.

They can't figure out why these other guys, this other sub-species of man, think it's cute when they and their wives wear matching colors; why they don't understand sports; why they get offended so easily at nudity or dirty jokes; why they like cute, fluffy ball-of-fur lap dogs; why they like friggin' karaoke; why they're so in touch with their *feelings*; and why the only time they touch their penis is to wash it and even then, take two quick passes with a loofah and they're outta there.

Likewise, they may wonder why there are so many doves out there that *hrrrummp* mightily when it comes to military aggression, thinking that the best way to battle any kind of transgression is with *hugs*. To a high-T guy—most of whom are hawks—the course of action is clear: Stomp Holy Hell out of everybody who deserves it.

The answer is quite possibly hormonal. The guys that don't seem to fit in with the rest of the world are blue-necked lizards living in an age of yellow-necked lizards. (Ironically, though, war is one time when the blue-necked lizards have a clear function.)

Despite my dire predictions about a blue lizard's lot in life, both financial and personal, it's quite possible for one to be-come successful in all aspects of living. Those that do well either had insightful teachers or parents, or they had the mind power and force of will that allowed them to rein in their passions when needed. And, of course, a lot of them use weights to channel all their aggressiveness, much the same way a physicist uses control rods to regulate the rate of nuclear fission.

Once a blue lizard learns to control that high T, to use it to his advantage, well then you've really got something. It's like a tornado having control of itself and being able to use its tremendous energy at will.

Let me make it clear that I don't consider myself to be a high-T Confucius, Dear Abby, or even Yoda. In other words, I'm not a Testosterone self-help guru, but I do know that being a blue lizard in command of his endocrinology is a great thing.

A blue lizard in control of his blueness can pour all that high-T aggressiveness, drive, passion, intensity, and good ol' fashion flair into studying, pursuing a relationship, working in an office where he's a computer programmer or whatever, and being a team player. Of course, no blue lizard will need to be a team player for long, because if he's truly mastered himself, he'll one day be the boss, with an army of yellow lizards at his command.

Editor's note: The statistics regarding Testosterone levels in various occupations, and the theory that there are two types of men, came from the book, *Heroes, Rogues, and Lovers,* by James McBride Dabbs, McGraw-Hill, 2000.

Chapter 35

Do a Manly Little Dance

"Young men don't know how to act — nobody taught them how to act. There are no rites of passage. No obstacles to overcome, no tasks given, and no contemplation of what it means to be a man. It's just suddenly you're supposed to morph into, starting at about age 13 and finishing up, oh, I don't know, when you're about 80 or 90, if you're lucky. I guess you can tell if someone's become a man by whether or not he's made the decision to swing the bill on his baseball cap forward instead of backward."

Back in April, a pall fell over our office building. And it all stemmed from the emotional vibes of one man—Tim Patterson.

Larry—the character played by Robert Downey Jr. on Fox's hit TV show, *Ally McBeal*—had just dumped Ally. It seemed that Ally was destined to spend another summer alone.

Tim was disconsolate. All he did was stare listlessly out the window, muttering to himself, "Why can't Ally find love? *Why* can't Ally find love?"

His work output stopped, as surely as if he'd been given some sort of paralyzing nerve block by a crazed neurologist. The plans for the new supplement lay strewn about his desk, collecting dust and the residue of spilled Costa Rican coffee. Oh sure, the carbon chains were all neatly lined up on his notepad, but instead of connecting to hydroxy and methoxy groups, they connected to drawings of broken hearts.

And like some horrible retrovirus, the pall spread. Soon, everyone in the office was depressed. The boys in the warehouse, rather than filling Biotest orders, stacked up canisters of protein powder in little makeshift igloos and napped the day away. The graphics guys took all their action figures out of their packages and used them to stage sad little plays where the characters all ended up being phasered by their girlfriends.

I'm no psychologist, but I'll bet you my autographed picture of Seven of Nine that the office was suffering from an epidemic of low Testosterone—low Testosterone brought about by a severe case of the blues.

So rather than see the company get sucked down the vortex of the toilet, I stripped down to my jockstrap and began doing a manly dance up and down the halls, through the warehouse, through the gym, and out the door and around the entire building. Like some Indian shaman, I drove the bad vibes away, and like the sky after a summer thunderstorm, the pall cleared.

The next day, Testosterone again flowed freely through everyone's veins, work resumed, and the company was saved.

I'm a firm believer that mood determines Testosterone levels, and in turn, Testosterone levels determine mood. When bad shit happens, T levels drop and it becomes all that much harder to shake the funk out of your head. I also believe that the mood is contagious.

There's certainly plenty of evidence in nature that T levels are tightly tied to mood. According to a study conducted in 1974 by a scientist named Irwin Bernstein, when two monkeys fight, the winner's T levels rise and the loser's fall. The winning monkey then has confidence for his next battle, while the losing monkey mopes, and rather than fight again, helps his wife pick out some dust ruffles for their bedroom set.

Similarly, when cichlid fish in Lake Tanganyika fight, the winner's skin gets brighter, and he produces more brain cells and more Testosterone. Conversely, the loser's color drains out of him, he dumps brain cells, has his testicles wither, and gets a job greeting other fish as they walk into yuppie fish clothing stores: *"Hi, my name's Morty. Welcome to the Gap."*

Along the same lines, human studies have shown that tennis players who win tournaments experience an increase in T levels, as do winners of chess tournaments.

I scoff at your endgame strategy, castle nuts!

Simply put, winning equates to high T and *more* winning.

Take a look at 2000's National League champions, the New York Mets. Almost across the board, their stats dropped in 2001. The roster is pretty much intact, but you'd never guess that they're the same team. Probably as a result of a poor start this year, they experienced a team-wide drop in T levels, one from which they have yet to recover. Losing caused a drop in T, with its resultant lack of confidence, and the slump became self-perpetuating. As a result, they remain firmly entrenched in next-to-last place as I'm writing this with a team batting average that's among the lowest.

Maybe they should scrap all the blond-hair dye jobs, yank out the earrings, let those silly little manicured goatees spread out across their faces so their mouths don't look like female private parts, rip the sleeves off their unies, and go medieval for awhile. Have the pitchers throw inside and start one of those baseball fights where everyone shoves each other and throws haymakers that miss each other by two feet—whatever it takes to start the T flowing again.

Even those men who witness a victory by their chosen team or favorite athlete experience increases in Testosterone levels. And, conversely, those same fans experience lower T levels when their team loses.

I think it's easy to make a small deductive hop, skip, and jump and assume that winning and losing sports matchups isn't the only determinant of T levels and that victories or losses in business, politics, or life in general affect Testosterone levels and mood.

I think the stock market is suffering from low T. Some stocks dip, investors get scared, and they get cautious. T levels recede like a penis dipped in an ice bath and *whammo!* Recession.

Yeah, that's simplistic, but I'm not the only one who thinks that the stock market lives and breathes with consumer confidence, and confidence, whether fiscal or otherwise, often relates back to T.

In fact, I think the entire United States is suffering from low T.

Young men don't know how to act—nobody taught them how to act. There are no rites of passage. No obstacles to overcome, no tasks given, and no contemplation of what it means to be a man. Manhood is something you're supposed to morph into, starting about age 13 and finishing up, oh, I don't know, when you're 80 or 90, if you're lucky. I guess you can tell if someone's become a man by whether or not he's made the decision to swing the bill on his baseball cap forward instead of backward.

Even so, one thing seems to be clear: The culture dislikes manly men … or does it? Masculinity is celebrated in movies, but woe be it to anyone who acts like that in real life. Grab some punk by the scruff of the neck and shove his head into a pile of sesame bagels for taking cuts in front of that old lady and you'll find yourself in jail, after which you'll be sued by the punk, the owner of the bagel shop where it happened, the bagel anti-defamation society, and probably the old lady, too.

Phooey.

All this indecision about how to act leads to low T, and the low T prevents guys from pulling themselves out of the morass.

Following your instincts—doing manly things—is considered "macho" behavior, macho being a pejorative term. Being aggressive about something is considered juvenile or immature, or the result of "Testosterone poisoning." Liking women, liking women a lot, is considered to be "a propensity to wallow in adolescent fantasies."

Hey, wallow in *this*.

Young boys are being taught to be passive in school, and if it doesn't sink in, they're drugged—better to keep the beasts at bay. Better not be yourself sonny, better not be true to your nature because that would mean that we got ourselves a little attitude problem and we'll have to stick you in that metal shed over there, the one that's in sun so hot it'll bake your brain right in its skullpan as if it were a 'possum pie. That'll get your mind right, boy.

In fact, can you please tuck your balls and penis in between your legs? I mean, I can almost tell that you're a *man*. And you, with the exceptionally long dick, shove it between your legs but maybe jam the head of a cabbage patch doll on the other end where it sticks out so the children won't be frightened.

Sure, the popular culture celebrates manhood, but it's all a parody. We've got *The Man Show* and magazines like *Maxim*, but they make a joke about manhood—a good joke, but a joke nonetheless. The message they give is nothing profound, nothing that changes us in a fundamental way that lingers long after we've turned off the TV or put *Maxim* back in the stack with the other stroke mags.

I think all this malaise is curable, though. All it takes is the occasional lone ballsy high-T guy. In the sports world, having a guy like Michael Jordan on the team was enough to elevate a mediocre band of mostly rag-tag athletes to play beyond what everyone thought they were capable of. Sure, Michael was the greatest player in the game, but his ability, his attitude, his high T lifted his teammates to extraordinary heights. It resulted in a miraculous string of six NBA championships.

I read an article a few weeks ago that described the bad atmosphere in some gyms and how it sucks the T out of the average T-man. I've got no argument with that, but I think that one man can literally change the atmosphere of whatever environment he's in. Back in the early days of Gold's Gym in Venice Beach, California, a certain Austrian would walk in each morning and begin his Testosterone-raising banter. He'd walk in 15 minutes late, throw a towel at the guys warming up in back, and say to his training partners, "Come on, you guys, I'm tired of waiting for you. Let's get *go-ing.*"

He'd begin ragging on his workout partners and anyone within earshot—in a good-natured way—and if his verbal lifts didn't inspire people, the way he exercised did. The place would start to percolate with good vibes. The man was and remains a one-man Testosterone band.

I don't think a guy has to have Arnold's or Michael's charisma to bang the Testosterone drum and raise the spirits of everyone around him, whether it be in the sports arena, the gym, the office, or anywhere. Neither do you necessarily have to drop trou and do a manly dance to exorcise the bad juju.

You simply have to take the initiative. Decide that you're going to shape your environment by making winners out of everyone around you. Do that and you'll have given your life meaning, purpose, and importance.

And, in addition, it'll jack up your own Testosterone, and that ain't bad.

Chapter 36

NPT

"Got dry skin? Fine wrinkles? Nary a pimple in sight? That could also be a sign of low Testosterone. And forgive me for asking, but how's your semen production? Can you only fill a thimble, or can you come damn close to filling up one of those big 7-11 Slurpee cups? If it's the former, compliment yourself on your aim, but realize that your semen production is closely related to T levels."

Most of you probably don't know this, but I suffer from a medical condition known as NPT. It's not life-threatening, but it's forced me to make some adjustments. I wouldn't exactly call myself disabled or handicapped in any way, but it does affect the way I do things. For instance, I can't roll over too quickly when I'm lying in bed, nor can I wear any sleepwear that's too constricting.

And it's my solemn responsibility to warn anyone I'm sleeping with about the condition so that she isn't unduly alarmed when she wakes up and sees me having an attack of NPT.

NPT doesn't have any telethons to support it, nor does it have any famous actors to act as spokesmen. No, NPT, or nocturnal penile tumescence, is a condition that most people won't touch.

All joshing aside, NPT is what clinical types call nighttime erections and they're a good thing. They're a great indicator that my bioavailable levels of Testosterone are up to snuff. If I didn't ever wake up to find myself sporting a flagpole, or popping the occasional spontaneous woodie during waking hours, then I'd probably have to question my levels of free Testosterone.

The same applies to virtually any male.

And being able to achieve erections while looking at erotic pictures isn't the same. Flipping through the pages of *Penthouse* might give you a hardon, but that doesn't necessarily mean your T levels are in a desirable range. It's those spontaneous boners that are really important, clinically speaking.

Similarly, high T levels seem to correlate pretty strongly with sex drive. While individual sexual appetites vary enormously, a man with healthy T levels should probably feel a very strong, compelling, single-minded urge to have sex at least a few times a week, unless his wife or girlfriend bears a strong resemblance to Dr. Zaius from *The Planet of the Apes*.

There are all kinds of ways—aside from lab work—that hint at Testosterone levels, but most are based on subjective feelings like depression or a lack of energy. However, there are lots of physical signs that point to T levels. Most are vague and some are even esoteric, but together they might paint an accurate picture of one's T status. In any event, these physical traits are pretty darn interesting.

For instance, visceral obesity is associated with lower T levels. In fact, in middle-aged men, belly fat correlates *inversely* with serum T levels. That doesn't mean that every fat guy out there has low T levels, but if you're relatively thin except for a Buddha-like belly, you could very well suffer from low Testosterone.

The hairline is also somewhat indicative of T levels. Ever notice that women and boys have straight frontal hairlines? That's because of T, or lack of it. Androgenization, courtesy of Testosterone, is accompanied by a slight temporal recession of the hairline. And, should the predisposition exist, baldness can follow. It's entirely possible that if you're an adult male and your hairline is equal to the kid from *Malcolm in the Middle*, your male hormone never kicked in.

Got dry skin? Fine wrinkles? Nary a pimple in sight? That could also be a sign of low Testosterone. And forgive me for asking, but how's your semen production? Can you only fill a thimble, or can you come damn close to filling up one of those big 7-11 Slurpee cups? If it's the former, compliment yourself on your aim, but realize that your semen production is closely related to T levels.

Now let's take a look at your hands. Hold them up in front of you as if you were commanding Sandra Bullock's wayward bus to halt. Is your ring finger (the fourth finger, counting the thumb) longer that the index finger (the second finger)?

If it is, and you're male, good for you. In the first trimester of pregnancy, when you were firmly entrenched in momma's womb, hormones started to roll up their sleeves to help build your body. It's this early exposure to T that seems to make a difference between the lengths of those two fingers.

Biologists call this the 2D:4D ratio.

No one really knows why this happens, but it's been known for a long time that some bone growth is determined by T; high, chiseled cheekbones, for instance.

One researcher, John Manning of the University of Liverpool, has even done studies that indicate that exceptional athletes and math whizzes have extra long ring fingers (in comparison to their index fingers), perhaps suggesting that they might haven gotten extra doses of T when they were gestating.

Of course, Testosterone isn't the only thing that determines athletic prowess, but it might make a bigger difference than any of us realize. Let's take the flexor digitorum brevis as an example. It's a muscle that helps flex the outer four toes. Experiments with rats have shown that the spinal cord motor nuclei that innervate that muscle are sexually dimorphic, and their size is regulated by T levels. The more T, the bigger the spinal cord motor nuclei, and thus, potentially, a faster, more quick-reflexed rat.

Maybe the same thing applies to humans, and some extra T might have somehow enhanced the nervous system of athletes.

But let's get back to the finger-length discussion. Equally amazing and downright compelling about this whole 2D:4D discussion is the fact that women generally have digits of similar length, with the notable exception of lesbians. They tend to have ratios that are similar to those of men.

It's certainly not foolproof, though. Don't look at your girlfriend's hands, discover that she's got a conspicuous 2D:4D ratio, and automatically start rifling through the drawers of her nightstand in a frantic search for a box that contains sexy pictures of J-Lo and a Martina Navratilova signature-model vibrator. What researchers have found is if they look at hundreds of straight women and hundreds of lesbians, many more lesbians would have ring fingers that were longer than their index fingers.

Somehow, these women might have gotten an errant dose—an accidental tsunami of Testosterone—during their first trimester in the womb. As a result (and this is just one theory), their sexual preferences leaned strongly toward other women. Were it not for their lack of penises, the presence of breasts, and an affinity for LPGA-sponsored events, they might as well have been men.

Many of these examples don't necessarily correlate with your current T status. Some, like an extreme 2D:4D ratio, a masculine hairline, or who knows, maybe even relative strength of the flexor digitorum brevis, might be indications of high T levels during youth.

None of that would necessarily mean that you currently have high T levels. Unfortunately, age hacks away at T levels, along with everything else.

However, if you're experiencing a lack of libido, semen production on par with a hypogonadal hamster, or a little round belly that shakes when you laugh like a bowlful of jelly, then you might want to lobby your doctor for T replacement. Either that, or supplement with pro-Testosterone formulas.

Remember, only you can support NPT.

SEX

SECTION

6

Chapter 37

Lust Out of Control

"You know what's really weird? Go to Las Vegas. There you'll find thousands of middle age, otherwise tight assed couples who'd normally gasp at nudity and sexuality, ogling the naked women in floorshows. Somehow, these people can handle sexuality as long as they can compartmentalize it to Vegas. Or consider the housewives who privately devour romance novels and their ubiquitous rape themes while publicly denouncing extramarital lust."

At any given time, I've got about two or three dozen newspaper clippings lying on my desk. A lot of them have to do with medical research, but a good many of them contain snippets of pop culture because a competent editor gets ideas from anywhere and everywhere.

There's one clipping, though, that I periodically move to the top of the heap. It's a Dear Abby column I read a couple of weeks ago. Every time I go over it again, I can't help but shout out some obscenity, which invariably causes my secretary, Constance, to come shuffling into my office on her five-inch heels to ask what's wrong. (I say "shuffling" because she's got an inner-ear infection that's affected her balance and it's become increasingly hard for the poor girl to stay perched atop her lofty heels and not crash head-first into my file cabinet.)

I tell her that everything's okay and she navigates her wobbly way back to her desk, but not before doing a header into my trash basket. That makes me feel bad, and I briefly consider asking my partner to reconsider the part of our office dress code that requires female employees to wear heels over five inches—or at least make an exception for those women that are over 60, like Constance—but then I remember that damn column.

Here's what it said, verbatim:

Dear Abby:

I am a married man in my 30s, with two adorable little babies at home. My sex life with my wife is very good. I have no complaints at all. My problem is my feelings.

I love my wife and do not cheat; however, I desire other women. I have an instinctual desire to procreate. I can't afford more babies. In fact, my wife and I do not want more children.

Other women—even women I find unattractive—arouse me. As a result, I avoid looking at female co-workers and have become very disconnected at work. Even though I don't act upon my instinctual urges, I still wrestle with them.

Abby, how does a man get past this? Every woman I see makes me feel like I am in heat.

— FIGHTING TESTOSTERONE IN TWIN FALLS

As you might have guessed, it's not so much the letter that bothered me, but Abby's response:

Dear Fighting: Schedule an appointment with your physician to find out if there's a physical reason your hormones are in overdrive. If your problem isn't physical, ask for a referral to a psychotherapist who can help you understand this obsession before it negatively impacts your career or your marriage.

Sweet mother of all that is good! I don't know what's worse, the fact that this schmuck went to Dear Abby to get his question answered, or that Dear Abby didn't know that probably 98 percent of all males feel exactly the same way!

"Fighting" is attracted to other women, even finds something appealing about women generally regarded as *unappealing*, and Abby either wants him neutered or sent to the booby hatch.

How many of the rest of us allegedly psychologically unbalanced or physically ill bastards can go through a single day without mentally boning at least a couple of dozen women? If by electronic magic you could somehow create a video of what each of us had fantasized in an ordinary day, you'd see a trail of sprawled semi-naked female bodies, some bent over mailboxes with their jeans still around their ankles; some perched atop office desks with their dresses unzipped and gathered around their waists; and maybe even an entire row of women at the beauty salon, readjusting their thong panties and smoothing out their skirts in the aftermath of our assembly-line fantasy fornication.

Furthermore, how many of us, even while talking to Shirley in accounting, start to overlook her scraggly hair and Andy Sipowicz honker and think to ourselves, "You know, Shirley's not pretty, but her tits are kinda nice"? Plenty.

Men can be turned on by the slightest of things, the way a woman's eyes crinkle up when she's happy, the way she unconsciously twists her hair around her finger when she's talking to you, or her seemingly innocent habit of pulling off her Calvin Kleins and placing her feet behind her head while making a circle with her two thumbs and forefingers and framing her private parts while winking at you. Yep, any number of cute but innocent maneuvers can make a usually unattractive girl seem attractive to men.

But we're not supposed to be like that. Lust is verboten. We should only have feelings of lust toward one woman, or one man, or the one farm animal you've promised your love. Maybe it's frowned on because of people like Abby. Or maybe it's the end result of all those sexual-harassment suits, the kind where a guy loses his business and ends up putting a bullet through his head so his family can get some life insurance, all because he told some frumpy girl at the office that he liked her dress.

Whatever the reason, it seems that sexuality has been put in the closet. Sure, it's okay to display lust on Howard Stern or daytime soap operas or FOX television, but that's television. In normal, everyday life, men are supposed to be eunuchs, to put their sexuality all tidy-like in the top drawer of their night stand, only to be pulled out when wifey gets an itch.

Never mind that pornography is one of the most profitable businesses in the country. It must be deviant single men buying it all up, because everyone knows that married mens' wives fulfill all their needs and fantasies. Of course, there are probably a few married guys out there who watch porn, but these sick bastards shamefully hide it from their wives on the top shelf of the garage behind the Black & Decker sander and the Bug-B-Gone.

Horseshit!

Abby, chances are, even the most seemingly civilized, dignified man in his tuxedo, if freed from the societal shackles placed on his balls, would confess to his hostess at a dinner party, "A perfectly lovely dinner, Mrs. Kensington, and dare I say that the way your bosom looks in your lovely Gucci gown has caused my member to become so engorged that it looks like the arm of a colicky 18-month-old baby clenching a bright red apple in its angry fist?"

And you know what's really weird? Go to Las Vegas. There you'll find thousands of middle-aged, otherwise tight-assed couples, people who'd normally gasp at nudity and sexuality, ogling the naked women in floor shows. Somehow, these people can handle sexuality as long as they can compartmentalize it to Vegas. Or consider the housewives who privately devour romance novels and their ubiquitous rape themes while publicly denouncing extramarital lust.

If you can figure that out, let me know.

I long for the days when we were able to put Pirelli calendars over our desk, when we could tell women in the office that they looked nice without getting subpoenaed. If I could work my will, I'd have every man in the world unzip his fly right now and slam his dick on the table top in his best imitation of Nikita Khrushchev and say, "We will bury this in you!!!"

Furthermore, I'd sit Abby down in front of me and tell her the facts of male life. No doubt she'd regard me as a real-life Hannibal Lecter:

"Of each particular thing, ask what is it in itself, Clarice ... er, Abby? What is its nature? What does he do, this man you seek?"

"He fantasizes about women."

"No, that is incidental. What is the first and principle thing he does? What need does he serve by fantasizing?"

"Anger. Hatred of women. Psychological illness. A tumor on his testicle the size of a Jell-O mold that causes it to boil over with poisonous Testosterone?"

"No! He covets. That is his nature. And how do we begin to covet, Abby? Do we seek things to covet? We begin by coveting what we see every day. Don't you feel eyes moving over your body, Abby? And don't your eyes seek out the things you want?"

And then I'd eat her liver. No, scratch that, I'd eat *half* of it. I'd take the other half behind a billboard and hump it like Alex did in *Portnoy's Complaint*.

That's right, Abby. We covet. It's our nature. Even Hugh Hefner, who sleeps with seven blonde babe muffins every night, covets the babes hanging on Charlie Sheen's arm. The grass is greener, the snatch is juicier, on the other side. It's the newness of another woman that appeals to us in some primal way that's so basic to our nature that it's almost silly to analyze it.

Whether a man acts on these fantasies or urges is entirely up to him. My argument isn't against monogamy; it's against denying who or what we are, or worse yet, feeling guilty about it.

What we are is clear: we are the beasts in the jungle. Oh, I'm sure that will someday be drummed out of us and we'll all be like the Eloi in The *Time Machine*—passionless, docile folk who pick kumquats off the ground instead of having sex.

I tell you, if that was the case and I was unlucky enough to be alive, I'd raise my hand and shout, "Take me, take me!" when the Morlocks came to eat us.

Now, scuze me while I call Constance in here to take a little dictation. She's old, saggy, wrinkly, and looks sort of like a female Strom Thurmond, but you know, come to think of it, she's got kind of a sexy Cher thing going with the way her gray tresses tumble down her knobby back. Maybe I'll have her set her withered haunches on my lap.

C'mon, Constance, who's your daddy?

Chapter 38

Cybersex

"Shit, I just realized my shades aren't pulled. Who's that looking in the window? Eddie, is that you??? The stupid neighbor kid is out on the lawn looking in at me. Whatsa' matter Eddie? Never seen a grown man naked? Here, here! Is this what you wanted to see? Go ahead, tell your dad! Tell your mom! Have her come over and I'll shake it at her, too!"

I 've got a friend who routinely has cybersex with some woman from the other side of the country that he's never met. Every other night, the two of them log on and use the Internet in an attempt to mutually satisfy each other.

I've always been perplexed by this. I mean, I would at least need a simultaneous live video feed—not because I've got a lousy imagination, but because I'd need to know that the person at the other keyboard wasn't some fat trucker named Earl.

Still, I'm always willing to try anything at least once, so when a female Testosterone reader named Lisa69 sent me a personal email and suggested we find a chatroom and get intimate, I decided to give it a go.

I have no experience with this type of thing, but I played along as best I could. I also printed out the transcript of our exchange, so if you're not 18, quit reading right now, because things get pretty steamy from this point on:

Lisa69: I'm unbuttoning my blouse.

TC: Uhh, okay, I guess I'll take my shirt off.

Lisa69: I just unbuttoned the last button. Underneath, I'm wearing a black satin demi bra. It's a 36-D, if that matters to you. The tops of my large breasts are shockingly white against my tanned skin.

TC: I took my shirt off, but I haven't really been out in the sun much, so I guess my skin's kinda blotchy right now. I'm a little sweaty since I just finished working out, so the thick hair on my chest is a little matted down, too. Looks kinda like the time my old poodle dog got caught in a rainstorm.

Lisa69: Now I'm unzipping my short leather skirt. As I bend over to unzip it, my long, luxurious blond hair brushes against my thigh, which brings goose bumps to the skin.

TC: I'm trying to get my Dockers off, but I think the zipper's stuck. Maybe if I use this metal ruler here to pry it open ...

Lisa69: I'm easing the tight skirt off my firm ass, sliding it over my thighs and calves, being careful not to knock my red stiletto heels off.

TC: Damn! This thing won't budge! I think I've got some pliers somewhere in the desk drawer here.

Lisa69: It's *sooo* hot in here, and I notice some droplets of sweat on my firm, taut, belly. I throw my head back and moan softly as I rub the perspiration into the skin.

TC: Hey, whadda ya know? I found my Bullwinkle Pez dispenser in here. I haven't seen this sucker in years. Did you know these things are worth some money now?

Lisa69: This bra is sooo constricting. I'm going to have to take it off. Although it's warm, my pink nipples are erect, more so than they've ever been. I'm softly teasing them with my fingers, and I feel a small surge of electricity through my loins.

TC: I found the pliers, but I accidentally pulled the head of the zipper off! I think I'm going to have to try lying on the floor and maybe wriggling out of these pants.

Lisa69: Now I'm cupping my breasts in my hands and massaging them. I know I'm naughty, but I just dribbled a little red wine on them, and since no one's looking, I licked them clean, swirling my tongue slowly against first the right, and then the left.

TC: Got those bastards off! Had to wriggle around the room like a drunken worm, and I ended up hitting my head against the bottom of the oak credenza a couple of times, but I got 'em! Where were we? Oh, you've taken your bra off already? I suppose I should take my socks off or something. Okay, I'm slipping them off now. Man, these things are rank. I can't remember if I put new ones on this morning ....

Lisa69: I feel so comfortable with you. I feel completely open, and I don't want to hold back at all. I'm wriggling out of my black thong panties right now, and they've slid to the floor noiselessly. The leather chair feels so cool, yet sensuous, across my bottom.

TC: You've got a leather chair? Get outta town! I got one of these crappy ones from Costco that gives me a rash.

Lisa69: I'm slowly running my hands along the insides of my thigh.

TC: Hey, did you watch that last *Survivor* show? I never would have guessed that Tom guy would win!

Lisa69: Are you as aroused as I am?

TC: Uhh, well, it's a little cold in my room, so I've got to overcome a little shrinkage here, but I'm coming around. Maybe if I take my underwear off and, you know, shake it a little bit. Hey, why is it with old underwear that the area right by the pee-pee always wears away first? These suckers got a tiny little hole right there.

Lisa69: Ohhh, I wish you were here with me. I wish your hands were where mine are right now.

TC: Oh no! What's this little, like, discoloration? It almost looks like a mole or something, but it's kind of white and fuzzy. Oh man, this better not be cancer! Just my friggin' luck! Oh, wait a minute, it's just a piece of lint.

Lisa69: Ohhhhh, ohhhhhh TC, don't stop.

TC: Shit, I just realized my shades aren't pulled. Who's that looking in the window? Eddie, is that you??? The stupid neighbor kid is out on the lawn looking in at me. Whatsa matter Eddie? Never seen a grown man naked? Here!

Here! Is this what you wanted to see? Go ahead, tell your dad! Tell your mom! Have her come over and I'll shake it at her, too!

Lisa69: Ohhhh, omygod! Don't stop, don't stop!

TC: Alright, alright, that's better. I'm getting into it nowww-wwwwwwwwwwwwwwwwwwwwwwwwwwwwwwwwwww-wwwwwwwwwwwwwwwwwwwwwwwwwwwwwwwwwww-wwwwwwwwwwww

Sorry! It slipped out of my hand and hit the keyboard.

Lisa 69: Ohhhh! Oh! Oh! Oh!

TC: I gotta stand up for a minute, my knuckles are getting chafed over here.

Lisa69: Ohmygod! Ohmygod! Ohmygod!

TC: Argggggggh! I kind of rested it against my Epson, and I don't know how, but it got lodged in the paper tray and now there are passages from my compilation of seafood recipes being printed all up and down it! Oh, man that hurts!

Lisa69: Mmmmmmmmmm, I feel so, so, relaxed. Same time tomorrow?

TC: Ohmygod! Ohmygod! Why did this file have to be 50 pages long? Ohmygod! Ohmygod!

Chapter 39

Our Testosterone-Soaked Daydreams

"For some reason, most women haven't come to grips with this simple biological fact: men look. They fail to understand that craning our heads around, with a range of cervical motion previously ascribed only to Gumby, to catch a glimpse of female skin is as biologically engraved in us as the urge to scratch our balls."

S o it's the top of the fourth inning, and the Astros are up. Houston slugger Jeff Bagwell is batting, and he's slamming foul ball after foul ball into the stands. I'm seated behind home plate, but in the loge section, which is right above the field-level seats.

I can take it all in from my elevated seat: the players, the scoreboard, the hot dog vendors, and the apple-cheeked little high school girls who prance onto the field in between innings to catapult bags of peanuts into the crowd.

Bagwell is still hacking away but, out of the corner of my eye, I see a ripple of movement among the fans. "Oh, shit," I think, "those idiots are starting *the wave*." But as I look to my left, I see that it's not really a wave after all. Section after section of men are turning their heads to the right. It almost looks choreographed.

No wonder! There's this glorious mammal walking along the circular walkway that separates the field section from the loge section. She's got this veritable porn star mane of curly black hair, and she's wearing high heels, black leather pants, and a white tube top; you know, typical ballpark wear. Her smooth, flat belly is tanned and each time those long, leather-clad legs take a stride, her ample breasts strain mightily against their nylon-polyester restraint.

She not only has a body that won't quit, but I've heard from reliable sources that it doesn't even take coffee breaks.

As she passes each section, all of the heads turn as if they were watching a tennis match where the ball never comes back to the other side. In retrospect, it was kind of a wave. A horndog wave.

Every male in the crowd has forgotten the game. Bagwell continues to slam foul balls into the audience but, tragically, no one sees them coming. There are foul balls caroming off of skulls everywhere, and the air is punctuated with splatters of blood. It looks like the Zapruder film. Wives wearing pink pillbox hats (with the team logo) are crawling onto the dugout on their hands and knees to retrieve pieces of their husband's brains.

As soon as she walks up the stairs and into the concourse, the sea of heads turns back toward the game, just in time to see Bagwell bloop a single into shallow left field. The endocrinological crisis has passed, but many of us in the crowd will relive that moment time and time again in our Testosterone-soaked daydreams.

I'm sure that most women would be amazed to learn that although we can easily forget some seemingly important date like an anniversary, we can remember, in vivid detail, some little piece of ass in a halter top and shorts that fit like Saran Wrap. Never mind that we only caught a glimpse of her some years ago as we walked into the dry cleaners. We were going in and she was coming out, "two ships passing in the night," but in our imaginations, we turned our ship around, pulled alongside hers, threw out grappling hooks, boarded her, and proceeded to plunder her rich spices from exotic lands again and again and again.

We never even knew her name or anything about her, but re-living that five-second memory is enough to stir Toby from his brief and much-needed nap. "Huh? Whuh? Ya' need me?" he mutters, as he opens his solitary eye and starts to rise.

"Whoa, *easy* big fella." We gently scratch him behind the ear, and he whinnies softly in response. "Go back to sleep, bud-dy," we whisper to him. "Get your rest."

For some reason, most women haven't come to grips with this simple biological fact: men *look*. They fail to understand that craning our heads around, with a range of cervical motion previ-ously ascribed only to Gumby, to catch a glimpse of female skin is as biologically engraved in us as the urge to scratch our balls.

But perversely, cruelly, even though women seem to disap-prove of this fact, they exploit it.

How else can one explain cleavage-enhancing bras and low-cut sweaters? They do everything possible to display their rack, short of building a shelf out of finished mahogany on which to mount their fleshy trophies.

Don't get me wrong, we appreciate the display more than you women will ever know, but why is it that we're not supposed to look at cleavage—? The correct behavior, according to Jerry Seinfeld, is to glance briefly and then turn quickly away, as if looking at the sun during a partial eclipse. If one of us gazes admiringly for more than a second or two, the retinas will start to smolder.

And how in the world are we supposed to talk to you and look you in the eyes when you're wearing something that makes your breasts appear as yummy as a silver serving tray heaped with chocolate truffles?

Even though we're not supposed to look, teams of engineers are hard at work designing bras that will display cleavage even more effectively. Starting in July, the "Nothing But Curves" bra will be unleashed upon the market and the male libido. Twenty designers labored long and hard to come up with a "deep V-bra that manages to create a push-up silhouette without padding and is designed to let women undo one more button on their blouses."

Mother of God, how in the hell are we going to deal with that? If some bra manufacturer really wanted to help us, he'd affix little plastic eyeballs to every bra so we could look into their "eyes" while staring at their feminine glory and carrying on what passes for a conversation.

And this paradox doesn't just stop at the tits, mind you. A lot of women go to extra lengths to display their asses, but again, we're not supposed to notice; it would be rude.

The gym, for instance, is the national repository of ass displaying. Women don't want us to look at their bee-hinds, or so they say, but why then is it damn near impossible to find a woman who wears tights that are more than a molecule of spandex thick?

Young lady, did you do leg curls this morning? Well, then, right now, as you read this in the comfort of your own home, there's some sweaty-faced guy sitting on the toilet, pants down around his ankles, beating off furiously to the memory of your ass pointed skyward, your thong barely visible underneath (you butt-flexing vixen, you).

In fact, it's a pretty safe bet that your ass has been psychically penetrated by *thousands* of eyes. You may feign modesty by wrapping a warm-up jacket around your waist in Starsky and Hutch fashion before you climb onto the leg curl machine, but it's too late. We already caught a glimpse of your mouthwatering declivities. Our eyes will be tunneling through your tights like angry ferrets.

It's our nature to visually devour you, so stop trying to make us feel ashamed about it. It strikes us as the height of hypocrisy to, on one hand, be indignant about our lustful stares, yet on the other, do everything technologically possible to attract them.

Similarly, you wives or girlfriends might cut your man a little slack when he rubbernecks the flesh. You're bucking two billion years of evolution, so if we gave you a wedding ring or let you put a spare toothbrush in our bathroom, you may want to take notice that nowhere with that wedding ring or that toothbrush were our balls attached.

If, in fact, we give you any balls, they're ones that we pried out of our skull at the baseball game.

Chapter 40

How to Please your Man

"Ahhh, to be a male in the '50s! To be treated like a king, to have the respect we so richly deserve! All I can say is, what the hell happened? Okay, so the whole thing seems a little too "Ozzie and Harriet", and I wouldn't respect a woman who subjugated her whole existence for mine (I can't believe I'm saying that...). Even so, there's one thing that seems to be missing from the '50s: sex."

Whether you're aware of it or not, technology is like a feather caught in the jet wash of a Cessna, and those of us in the Western world are like so many feather mites, holding on for dear life. Things are changing so rapidly that it's sometimes hard for really old geezers to fathom it. They're used to a slower, saner pace of life. Those of us who are younger are used to it, though, and we've adapted to this ultra-fast speed of change.

Every year, it seems we're faced with some new invention that absolutely changes the way we live. How many of you had even heard of the Internet 10 years ago? Okay, so you may have heard of it 10 years ago, but who would have guessed you'd be using it every day to download nude pics of Captain Janeway from the cast of TV's *Star Trek: Voyager?* Similarly, cell phones used to be a status symbol owned only by the rich. Now, even homeless people check their voice mail when they come in after a hard day of panhandling. Fax machines, once thought to be the end-all and be-all of business machines, now—for the most part—sit there gathering dust while we simply email documents.

And HDTV? Ha! Give me one of those bad boys, and I'll probably never leave the couch. Won't even work out. After time, my ass will spread to more comfortably fit the contours of the couch. And I don't even need to talk about changes in medicine. Today's cancers will, hopefully, be tomorrow's athlete's foot: pesky, but easy to cure.

There is, however, one aspect of life that might be progressing even faster than technology, and that's the relationship between men and women. Need proof? Take a look at the following list, taken from a 1950s home economics textbook written for high school girls so that they'd be better prepared for married life:

1) Have dinner ready

Plan ahead, even the night before, to have a delicious meal on time. This is a way of letting him know that you have been thinking about him and are concerned with his needs. Most men are hungry when they come home, and the prospects of a good meal are part of the welcome needed.

2) Prepare yourself

Take 15 minutes to rest so that you will be refreshed when he arrives. Touch up your make-up, put a ribbon in your hair, and be fresh looking. He has just been with a lot of work-weary people. Be a little happy and a little more interesting. His boring day may need a lift.

3) Clear away clutter

Make one last trip through the main part of the house just before your husband arrives, gathering up schoolbooks, toys, paper, etc. Then run a dust cloth over the tables. Your husband will feel that he has reached a haven of rest and order, and it will give you a lift, too.

4) Prepare the children

Take a few minutes to wash the children's hands and faces if they are small, comb their hair and, if necessary, change their clothes. They are little treasures, and he would like to see them play the part.

5) Minimize noise

At the time of arrival, eliminate all noise of washer, dryer, or vacuum. Try to encourage the children to be quiet. Greet him with a warm smile, and be glad to see him.

6) Some "don'ts"

Don't greet him with problems or complaints. Don't complain if he's late for dinner; count this as minor compared with what he might have gone through that day.

7) Make him comfortable

Have a cool or warm drink ready for him. Arrange his pillow and offer to take off his shoes. Speak in a low, soft, soothing, and pleasant voice. Allow him to relax and rewind.

8) Listen to him

You may have a dozen things to tell him, but the moment of his arrival is not the time. Let him talk first.

9) Make the evening his

Never complain if he doesn't take you out to dinner or other places of entertainment. Instead, try to understand his world of strain and pressure and his need to be home and relax.

10) The goal

Try to make your home a place of peace and order where your husband can relax.

Ahhh, to be a male in the '50s! To be treated like a king, to have the respect we so richly deserve! All I can say is, what the hell happened? Okay, so the whole thing seems a little too *Ozzie and Harriet*, and I wouldn't respect a woman who subjugated her whole existence for mine. (I can't believe I'm saying that ...) Even so, there's one thing that seems to be missing from the 50s primer listed above: sex. I suppose people had sex in the 50s, but it was probably a pretty sanitized thing, taking place in total darkness between crisp starched sheets, after *The Lucy Show* was over and the little darlings had been put to bed. The female orgasm was just a myth, and the question of whether your wife had been satisfied or not never entered your mind.

Maybe I'm naive to think so, but it seems that sex plays a much bigger part in our lives today. We're pretty sexually uptight in the U.S., but I know we're a lot more relaxed now than we were in the 50s. With that in mind, I'd like to offer the following updated list from a modern home economics book that I'm working on. If you've got a wife or girlfriend, I strongly urge you to have her read it:

1) Prepare yourself

Take 15 minutes to rest so that you will be refreshed. Put on some whorish high heels—flat, comfortable shoes are for lesbians! Hide the pantyhose behind the sacks of fertilizer in the garage. Men hate pantyhose. Go without hose, or put on some of those killer thigh-highs with a fishnet pattern. Remember that he's been looking at office babes all day, and the last thing he wants to face when he comes home is some Annie Hall clone.

2) Make sex more interesting to him

Say, for instance, your man is a hockey fan. Stripping naked and placing a net across your vagina would make for an interesting sexual interlude. For added effect, place a red light bulb in your mouth and have it light up when he satisfies you.

3) Don't speak when your man's watching TV

Ever. Really. If your gall bladder has exploded, wait for a commercial before you let the emergency medical technicians in.

4) Refrain from giving birth during the World Series, Super Bowl, Stanley Cup, Wimbledon, NBA Championships, the Ryder Cup, or any other major sporting championship

He looks forward to these events, and childbirth is often an annoying distraction.

5) Invite your best friend over occasionally so she can join you and your husband in bed for a threesome

Remember, in all likelihood, he rarely gets to sleep with other women. So it would spice up his day (and night) to enjoy another woman without worrying about whether you were going to barge in. Don't be upset if he spends, say, 95 percent of the time with the other woman. This is not the time to be selfish!

6) Before he comes home, tie up the children and quiet them down, using duct tape if necessary

Try to make him remember what life was like before he had kids and ruined his life.

 7) If you walk into the TV room unexpectedly and catch him masturbating to a Victoria's Secret commercial, have the decency to pretend you don't notice

This, in all likelihood, is the only hobby he has. Think of how hurt you would be if he made you feel ashamed for gardening.

8) Don't scold him if, after lovemaking, he inadvertently ejaculates over the carpet or furniture

Remember that his semen is very special to him. If, for instance, he spews on the wall, put a frame around it to draw special attention to it. If he leaves a deposit on the carpet that resembles a bottle of Elmer's glue, erect velvet ropes around it so that he'll feel loved.

9) Practice good grooming

Remember that most men like you to shave or trim your naughty parts. You should not take off your panties and suddenly bear a resemblance to a short Rabbi who just sucked on a sourball, nor should your pubic hair be a haven for hunters and their dogs that are using it as a hairy duck blind.

10) Don't ask him to tell you about work

The last thing he wants to do is relive the hellish events of the day. The best way to help him forget is to turn on the television, pop in a *Three Stooges* tape, and give him a sloppy blowjob. The goal is to try to make your home a place of peace and order where your husband can relax.

All right, so I'm a pig. Here's what the updated home economics book should really say:

Today's men want to be allowed to be men. You should remind them to be civil, courteous, loyal, and loving, but they are what they are. They enjoy certain things that you don't. You can't possibly understand what makes them tick unless you became one, just as they would have difficulty understanding your behavior all of the time. They sometimes enjoy things that seem juvenile to you. That's okay. Trying to change that only breeds apathy toward you, and worse, contempt.

Today's men want you to have equal pay and equal opportunities, but they would like to reserve the right to say "damn, you look good in that tight sweater" without being sued for sexual harassment. Today's men aren't generally as communicative as women. If they don't talk about their inner feelings or cry, it's not because they're inhuman monsters. They're just wired that way. Besides, as Dennis Miller once said, "You hate it when we cry. I've tried crying in front of my wife. She enjoyed it for about 30 seconds, and then started thinking, 'Why in the fuck did I marry this hamster?'"

Today's men think about sex all the time. When you both look at the sun going down, you probably think about the beauty of nature and the transient nature of existence, but most men think, "Man, I wish someone was going down on me."

But face it, you probably think about sex all the time, too. Or you would if you'd loosen up that psychological chastity belt.

So lighten up, and maybe he will, too. At the risk of sounding maudlin, we're stuck on this globe together, for better or for worse (more often for the better). There's nothing better than a good relationship built on understanding and love. Besides, there's no alternative, unless you're into sheep or something.

Chapter 41

The Feng Shui Master of the Soul

"If any wife, mate, or girlfriend out there wants to find their man's secret porn stash, leave the house for, say, at least ten minutes. When you get back, walk up to the DVD player and hit the "eject" button. Odds are a copy of *Lawrence of a Labia* will pop out at you, almost as if the DVD itself had a raging erection."

I was reading Ann Landers' column the other day, you know, because I feel empathy with all the letter writers who share the same problems that I have, from "Never Got Toilet Trained in Tampa" to "Chronic Masturbator in Cleveland."

And when Ann cuts to the tumorous core of these problems and cures them, doing in two or three sentences what no psychiatrist has been able to do for these people over the course of hundreds of hours of therapy, they, and I, are able to resume our lives, once again mentally healthy, morally upright men and women.

Yes, Ann Landers is the Feng Shui master of the soul.

However, as many times as she's rearranged the furniture of my mind so the brain energy can flow unencumbered, she occasionally puts the damn Barcalounger where the love seat should be, and the result is emotional chaos.

Take for instance the following letter, which appeared in a recent column, and which I've edited for length:

"When I first moved in with George, I threw out his collection of pornographic magazines. He agreed that he no longer had a need for them, and it did not seem to bother him when I tossed them in the garbage. Since then, I have caught George watching pornographic movies. I asked him why a married man would engage in such activity when a willing wife was available. I told him it made me feel betrayed and hurt."

"Heartbroken in Idaho" goes on to say that she just caught George reading a girlie mag in the bathroom and how it's "extremely upsetting" to her. She finds the material "disgusting" and a "violation of our marriage."

"George says he loves me and that I satisfy all his needs, but apparently, I am not enough for him ... I cried myself to sleep last night."

Luckily, Ann is no stranger to this kind of deviance. She tells Heartbroken it's obvious that George is "hung up" on porn:

"Accept the fact that his tastes are vulgar, and that he is operating at an adolescent level."

She then recommends joint counseling.

It's a pity that Heartbroken didn't just write me instead. Here's how I would have answered:

Dear Heartbroken:

Excuse me? You thought George no longer had a need for porno? The only way a man would no longer have a need for porn is if he shared a one-bedroom apartment with adult film stars Jenna Jameson and Houston, *and* a squadron of female gymnasts who insisted on using his penis as a pommel horse.

Of course, even that lucky guy probably secretively pops a porn disc into the DVD player when the whole kit and caboodle go to the grocery store to stock up on Pepsi, talcum powder, and condoms.

In fact, if any wife, mate, or girlfriend out there wants to find their man's secret porn stash, leave the house for, say, 10 minutes. When you get back, walk up to the DVD player and hit the "eject" button. Odds are a copy of *Lawrence of a Labia* will pop out at you, almost as if the DVD itself had a raging erection.

Unfortunately, our minds don't work very well when we've got a hard-on, and it's only some minutes later, when we're in the garage pretending to be hammering away on that birdhouse that we've been working on for two years, will we remember that we left the damn thing in the machine.

Heartbroken, you may have the temerity to think that you're "all he needs," and when the gods pulled your exquisite female form from the cauldrons of creation, they said, "Stop, it's been done to perfection; there's no longer any reason to make any more females. No longer will men look at other women, because if they do so, all they will see is imperfection. Quick, make a plaster cast of her breasts and ass so that we can hang them over the fireplace and create envy in the other gods when they come over for coffee and snack cakes."

The truth is, our desire to watch porn has nothing to do with you; it doesn't mean that you have any shortcomings; it doesn't mean that we're "unfulfilled," and it definitely doesn't mean that there's something wrong with us. We are visual creatures, and if we can't have sex, the next best thing is watching other people have sex.

In fact, if the world got smart, we'd take advantage of this urge. Want to increase blood-donor participation? Feature two people humping on a hospital bed in the middle of the Red Cross center. You'd have to turn donors away. People would want to donate all their blood. Want to increase voter turnout? Have a Republican and a Democrat naked on a floor mat in the middle of the high school auditorium screwing each other's brains out. Voters wouldn't care who they elected, but at least they'd be taking advantage of the democratic process.

Of course, Heartbroken, there's always the possibility that maybe you are a little tame in the sack, and your husband's need for dirty movies and mags is a "cry for help." Are you adventurous in bed, or do you lie there like an electrical wall socket, waiting to get pronged? Maybe you should think about becoming a "three-prong socket," if you catch my drift.

Does preparing for sex with your husband involve taking off your discount-bin, whiter-than-the-snows-of-the-Hima-layas, double-reinforced underwear, the kind the fat lunch ladies at my elementary school used to wear? And do you complete the esemble by putting on an authentic, Disney-licensed, floor-length flannel night shirt with a picture of Minnie Mouse on the front?

Maybe, just maybe, George needs a little fantasy in his life because, Heartbroken, you're a little sexually repressed.

You're probably the kind of woman who doesn't want her husband going to strip clubs, either. A lot of women think that it's standard operating procedure for men who go to nudie bars to end up having sex with the dancers. Well, from my experience, that's the *last* place a man's going to get laid.

The women in strip clubs are there to take our money and make us feel really foolish for believing for a moment that we're somehow special—different than the other thousand guys they toy with every night—and nothing else.

Furthermore, a lot of cities have ordinances that don't allow a completely naked woman within six feet of a man, which makes having sexual relations at the bar or, for that matter, at *home*, quite a challenge. Being a law-abiding citizen, I usually have my wife wear oven mittens during lovemaking so we can get reasonably close. Otherwise, I'd have to be six feet away, and that's literally quite a stretch, even for Mr. Fantastic, which is what I call my unusually elastic penis. But I digress.

Ahh, Heartbroken, being disgusted by porn seems strange to me, given that what's actually deemed offensive by society changes from generation to generation. Consider that, in Victorian times, it was indecent for women to show a bare ankle or leg while it was considered proper and even respectable to show mounds of laced cleavage.

Likewise, the ancient Greeks readily accepted full frontal male nudity, but the sight of the glans penis if a man pulled back his foreskin was enough to make proper men and women gasp. "Stripping the head" in public showed blatant sexual intent, while a plain ol', *retracted* penis was fine and dandy, even if it was naked.

Who knows what will constitute indecency in the next generation? Personally, I think full female and male frontal nudity will be quite acceptable. Buck-naked men and women will be seen attending ball games, addressing Congress, standing in line at the bank, and doing all the things that we do today while clothed.

Odds are, something that we consider totally innocent today will be considered obscene tomorrow, the equivalent of appearing in public naked, except for a pair of flip-flops, a baseball cap, and a string of Krispy Kreme donuts stacked on our penis.

So, in conclusion, Heartbroken, relax. The next time George pops in a porn movie, put on a teddy, crack open a Corona, and sit down next to him. You might find yourself enjoying the movie, or what happens soon afterward.

Chapter 42

30 Things Women Don't Know about Men

"Things we find beautiful: a double play; a walk-off home run in the bottom of the ninth; a game-winning three-pointer with no time left on the clock; an 80-yard TD pass in overtime; and oh yeah, sunsets and stuff, I guess."

1. Our balls are living thermostats, rising up and down in accordance with body temperature and climactic conditions. In fact, the astute female would do well to study this phenomenon, as a man's balls provide the most accurate meteorological information possible. For instance, if a man's left testicle is hanging down four centimeters, it means that skies will be sunny and clear, the high will be 82 degrees, and sunset will be at 6:35 p.m.

2. When you get out of bed to go to the bathroom, we put your panties over our noses and start breathing in deeply like the Dennis Hopper character in *Blue Velvet.*

3. Our idea of a self-help book is *TV Guide.*

4. Our penises really do have minds of their own. They also have a nifty little time share of their own in the Hamptons. On any given weekend, you can see scores of them out there water-skiing, antiquing, or lunching on fajitas.

5. If you have any videotapes that contain precious memories, do yourself a favor and knock out that little plastic tab. Otherwise, when our friend lends us a really hot porn video and we want to copy it, we wouldn't think twice about recording over our wedding video.

6. We fantasize about having the ideal family, but our ideal family is the Sopranos. Take, for instance, your sister. If she started yapping about her latest boyfriend or complaining about why we don't get "a real job," we'd have Pauly or Big Pussy rub her out.

7. We masturbate all the time when you're not around. In fact, house dust is nothing but desiccated semen.

8. Contrary to what we tell you, "little elves" have not stolen all of your Victoria's Secret catalogs. In truth, we've stolen them all from your nightstand for the last 10 years and they're piled up in our sock drawer.

9. When we're alone in the house, we grunt, forage for food, and scratch our bodies unashamedly. In fact, when we're alone, our behavior is pretty much indistinguishable from that of Dian Fossey's beloved mountain gorillas.

10. While we like the card you bought us for Valentine's Day, we'd much rather that you shaved your pubes into a little heart and hid chocolate Easter eggs in there, thereby killing two holidays at once.

11. Perfume is fine, but if you really want to drive us wild, rub a gooey cinnamon bun over your neck and ears.

12. For every stuffed animal or ceramic turtle decorating the bedroom, the angle of our erections drops one degree.

13. Chances are, we've stuck our dick through any remotely round object in the house, so you may want to wash out the napkin rings before you set the Thanksgiving dinner table.

14. We pray that your birthday or our anniversary doesn't fall on the day the new *Star Wars* movie opens up, or for that matter, when the NBA playoffs begin, or when it's the day of the Super Bowl, or the first game of the World Series, or the day of the NFL draft, or when TBS is showing *Lethal Weapon* for the 80th time, etc.

15. If we watch *Felicity* with you, it sure as hell ain't because of the story line. The truth is, that curly-haired little vixen kinda turns us on.

16. There's a small erogenous zone about the size of a dime up our right nostril. No, no, I'm kidding. Forget what *Cosmo* tells you about our erogenous zones. We've got one. It's five to seven inches long, slightly reddish and angry-looking, and we prefer you address it as Shamu, Conan, or Two-Ton Tony.

17. Our idea of ballet is the gun battle in any John Woo movie.

18. Screw the romantic meal and the mood music. If you want to be laid properly, screw a red light bulb into your bedside lamp. Either that, or just show up.

19. Our tear ducts are largely vestigial organs, but they do spout a few paltry tears when Old Yeller dies at the end of the movie, and when we learned that Denise Richards married Charlie Sheen.

20. We don't like it when your dildo is bigger than we are ... not that that's possible, no siree, no way.

21. The Corpus spongiosum is not Chrysler's follow-up to the LeBaron.

22. The next time you want to criticize us, please remember that, unlike you, we'll never experience the miracle of birth. (Like we care.)

23. Your Ricky Martin CD is cracked because we used it to prop up our TV dinner tray when you were visiting your mother.

24. Most of us would give up a week's pay just to see the barista at Starbucks in her bra.

25. Men have a sense of smell that's over 1,000 times more sensitive than yours. Oh, wait a minute, I was thinking about dogs. Never mind.

26. We have trouble urinating at ball games. This is either because the alcohol in the beer has caused our prostates to swell (thereby impeding the flow of urine); because the bladder has been stretched too far by all that beer and won't contract properly; or because we have "shy bladder syndrome," a psychological condition that causes our

urinary sphincters to tighten up and prevent our blad-
ders from contracting. Or, it could be that we just forgot
to unzip our pants.

27. If it weren't for women nagging us, we'd never go to the
doctor. Ever. Even if we had an ice pick imbedded in
our right eye.

28. Things we find beautiful: a double play; a walk-off home
run in the bottom of the ninth; a game-winning three-
pointer with no time left on the clock; an 80-yard TD
pass in overtime; and oh yeah, sunsets and stuff, I guess.

29. We have much greater upper-body strength than women,
but our breasts aren't nearly as nice.

30. If we're single, we desperately want to be married. If
we're married, we desperately want to be single. Please
kill us now.

Chapter 43

Bin Laden vs. Big Breasted Girls

"Big breasts are as American as corrupt CEO's, lawsuits, and SUVs. They put a song in our hearts, a spring in our steps, and a happy bulge in our pants. Sure, some say that they're environmentally unsound and making the bras that constrain them uses up too many petroleum byproducts, but big breasts are our God-given right as Americans. Keep your little Japanese or German subcompact breasts and give me some huge, environmentally unsound, oil guzzling American knockers that you can strap a kayak onto . . ."

I'm outraged. If I were Doc Bruce Banner, pelted by Gamma Rays, I'd be morphing into the Hulk at this very instant and the popping of my seams would sound like a reprisal of the Marines landing at Iwo Jima.

Yes, Hulk very angry. Hulk destroy puny humans. Hulk cause lots of property damage and cause insurance rates to skyrocket.

Why Hulk angry? *Hulk angry because of 9-11.* But why, you ask, is Hulk getting mad about 9-11 now, rather than four years ago? Well, much like the Hulk taking a powerful, gamma-ray–powered dump into a placid lake, the effects of that day continue to ripple out and affect us in ways we never dreamed possible.

Something has finally affected the Hulk personally and no, I'm not talking about the economy, or lines at the airport, or even the slow disintegration of personal rights. What I'm talking about is far more insidious and far more hurtful to America and, if true, representative of the evil genius of Osama bin Laden.

I'll stop tap dancing around the subject right now and lay it on you, but make sure you're not eating (lest you choke on your hoagie), don't have high blood pressure, aren't behind schedule on your insulin shots, or are in poor health in general.

Here it is…(deep breath), *big breasts are out of fashion.* Flat chests are in! Flat, in fact, is the "new black" in fashion, whatever the hell that means. And it's all because of 9-11.

Terrorist bastards! I'll kill you all with my bare hands! I'll use your entrails to skip rope!

Bip, bomp, bam alakazam

But only when you're grooving

With the Double Dutch Man

Put on your skates don't forget your rope

Cause I know I'm gonna see you

At my Double Dutch Show

You think I'm kidding, don't you? Well, according to newspaper columnist Catherine Newton of the Fort Worth Star-Telegram, 9-11 caused big boobs to fall out of favor as leadenly as if they'd fallen out of their demi bra after shakin' 'em just a little too hard:

"… it's part of the post 9/11 trend toward cocooning and comfort … The concept is simple: With so much stress and

tension in the world, why exacerbate the situation with binding clothes? It's time to downsize our lives and our breasts."

As evidence of this terrible, soul-wrenching, sans-titties trend, Newton points out the alleged star power of such Hollywood actresses as Gwyneth Paltrow and Rene´e Zellweger. "You don't need big breasts to land big roles," she sniffs. "The look-at-me breasts of Halle Berry and Salma Hayek and poor Jennifer Garner just look so tired, like they're sick of trying so hard."

If you ask me, Ms. Newton seems to be *happy* about big hooters going the way of the small-breasted Dodo. In my eyes, that makes her Osama's henchman, his accomplice, his propaganda minister.

Big breasts are as American as corrupt CEOs, lawsuits, and SUVs. They put a song in our hearts, a spring in our steps, and a happy bulge in our pants. Sure, some say that they're environmentally unsound and making the bras that constrain them uses up too many petroleum byproducts, but big breasts are our God-given right as Americans. Keep your little Japanese or German subcompact breasts and give me some huge, environmentally unsound, oil guzzling American knockers that you can strap a kayak onto, Ms. Newton (or should I say, *Ms. Newton-bin Laden?*).

We're Americans and we believe in wretched excess! When the fathers of the Constitution got around to forming this-here country, they did it so we'd be free to get all silly and drooly at the mere sight of big, gorgeous breasts—along with, I guess, freedom from taxation and discrimination stuff, too. The King of England! Ha! He could keep his pert little fit-in-a-teacup English breasts!

We Americans want big, stupendous, spectacular, awe-inspiring breasts as big as Texas, as broad as the plains of the Midwest, with purple nipple majesties, above the fruited plain. If that weren't the case, we'd all date Keanu Reeves, who, despite being flat as a board, is a good dancer, pretty handy with the George Foreman grill, and sews all his own clothes. And, when you tell him what to do, the bitch listens. In other words, he's a mighty fine catch!

How many of us would give up red meat just to get a look at that cute little aerobics instructor at our gym in her freedom-cut bra? Probably most of us. But ask us to give up red meat for a glimpse of Gwyneth Paltrow in her bra and we'll slap a bun on your head and eat your face, just out of contempt.

If the movie stars you mention, Ms. Newton, have gained some sort of box-office clout, it's because women are dragging their boyfriends and husbands to see these major snorers in exchange for 15—no, 30—minutes of straight oral sex. Either that, or in my best Lyndon Johnson/George W. Texas drawl, the people who go see these movies are just plain *un-Amurrrican.*

I urge all men to do their part in battling this repercussion of 9-11. For one, boycott any new *Charlie's Angels* movies, the stars of which don't have one good breast among them—you'd have to combine all of theirs, place them in a titanium-reinforced Wonderbra and top it of with some ice cream to make just one worthy of our attention.

Secondly, try to find a picture of a big-breasted woman—I think you can probably still find some on the Internet—and hang it on your dormitory wall, inside your locker, or above your workbench to show your support for this oppressed breed of woman.

Sure, it's easy enough to be apathetic about this issue, but remember this: *If the terrorist bombs come, whose bosom are you going to bury your head into, Rene´e Zellweger's or Carmen Electra's?* If you chose the former, you're going to be walking around without ears.

Remember, if big breasts go away—if we allow the terrorists to bring down these milky white, jiggling twin towers—they win.

Okay, so I got off on a tangent, but I wasn't kidding about what Catherine Newton said about breasts. The ma-roon actually said that. But do I take her seriously? Hell no. No more than I take seriously 99 percent of the wannabe-sociologist hosers who blame 9-11 for everything from their impotence to their inability to get a job.

We've turned into a bunch of pussies. We're paranoid bastards who don't address problems, but merely shrug our shoulders and say, "It's because of 9-11." Hulk tired of it. Next time Hulk hear that excuse, he stomp holy hell out of that puny human.

Chapter 44

The Tao of TC

"If you should be lucky enough to get a girl in bed, don't be timid in the sack. Here's a secret I learned: women are nastier than we are. Whatever perverse, dirty, deviant thing you want to try in the sack, they're up for it. Women don't want you to be polite in the sack, asking for permission to insert this here or that there. Just do it. If you ask them, they'll feign shock because, well they're supposed to be ladies and all, or at least fake it a little. No, they want beasts and if what you've done makes you feel mildly embarrassed or ashamed afterwards, you did good, Bubba."

Whenever I see Drew, he's with a pretty girl. Now Drew ain't exactly the stereotypical babe hound. He's tall—really tall—but if he didn't work his ass off in the gym and scarf down prodigious amounts of food every two hours, he'd be downright gangly. While he's lean and muscular, he'd be the first to tell you he probably still needs to pack on 10 or 15 pounds.

I don't think he's tremendously handsome—just an ordinary, okay-looking guy. Think of a taller, leaner, Clark Kent. And, like Clark Kent, he wears glasses that are a bit outdated. The thick frames are black and they look like they came straight out of your dad's high school yearbook:

Drew Katzman

Star Trek Club, French Club, Junior Marketers of America

"Im Klaato barada niktu"

The first time I saw him, I thought to myself, "Oh yeah, this is the guy who walks into the gym one day and shoots everybody because the demons that live under his bed told him to."

But as I got to know him, I realized my initial fears were un-founded. I also grew to like him. He's smart, sincere, curious, and a little goofy, which is okay by me, especially when you have to deal with tight asses on a daily basis.

And like I said, he's always with a pretty girl. For a while I thought it was a *Pretty in Pink* situation, where he's Ducky and the girls he pines for are Molly Ringwald. Molly couldn't imagine having sex with Ducky because, well, he's just a gal-pal. As such, Molly likes hanging around with Ducky because he's safe. Meanwhile Ducky's at home every night sighing and beating off into a sweat sock to ameliorate his unrequited lust and love.

Poor Ducky. Poor Drew.

Turns out, I couldn't have been more wrong. Ducky, er, Drew, is having sex with some of these girls. When I asked him about it, he smiled and said something that struck me at the time as fairly cryptic:

"The Tao of Steve."

"What's that?" I replied.

"It's a movie. Check it out," he answered.

I forgot about our conversation until the following week when I was flipping through the DVD's at Tower Records. There it was, *The Tao of Steve*. For those of you who aren't familiar with Taoism, the word *Tao* refers to the art or skill of doing something in harmony with the essential nature of the thing, as in the Tao of weightlifting, or archery, or whatever activity you're interested in.

I bought it, took it home, and as I began to watch it, I quickly learned that the Steve in the title refers to Steve McQueen, the big-screen actor who succumbed to lung cancer in 1980. The movie's a low-budget film that doesn't feature any big-name actors or actresses. It takes place in Santa Fe, New Mexico, and the lead character is a fat bastard named Dex. Dex works part-time in a daycare center, smokes a bong before going to work, and in general has made being a slacker a religion. He is, however, a student of philosophy.

When questioned about having no discernible ambition, he answers with, "Doing stuff is overrated. Hitler did a lot, but don't we wish he would have stayed home and gotten stoned?" Okay, that's pretty lame as far as philosophy goes, and a lot of his dialogue is similarly tongue-in-cheek.

Anyhow, Dex and his slacker friends devote most of their free time to getting stoned and playing Frisbee golf, but they idolize Steve McQueen. They regard him as the prototypical American male. He's the man on the horse with his own code of ethics and his own code of living, who never tries to impress the girls but always ends up getting the girl anyway.

"Steve," they explain, is a state of mind. James Bond is a Steve. Spiderman is a Steve. Michael Jordan is a Steve.

The opposite of Steve? A Stu. Stu is Gomer Pyle, Barney Fife, or Jughead.

Stus don't get laid, but Steves do; even the Steves in the movie. Why? Well, Dex, the main Steve in the movie, has used his background in philosophy and his admiration of Steve McQueen to come up with a set of rules that allows him to do well with women.

The first rule of Steve is to *eliminate your desire*. In other words, if you want to have sex with a particular woman, you must purge yourself of that desire. "Women can smell agenda," explains Dex. He approaches women as if they were, well, guys. He doesn't think about going to bed with them; he just hangs out with them. He first becomes a gal-pal.

The second rule of Steve is to do *something excellent* in her presence. "This," says Dex, "demonstrates your sexual worthiness."

Good-looking guys don't have to do anything all that swell, but ordinary-looking guys, and particularly fat bastards and the like, have to demonstrate their prowess in something and, as Dex reminds us, everybody is good at *something*.

I don't take this to mean showing her how many olive pits you can shove up your nostril. Rather, allowing her to see you in your environment, the place or activity where you're skilled and doing it in a humble way.

The third rule, which seems almost paradoxical at first, is to *retreat*. Quoting the German philosopher Martin Heidegger, Dex says, "We pursue that which retreats from us." In other words, once the girl seems to show some interest in you or at least thinks there's more to you than meets the eye, you make yourself scarce. "Girls want to pursue a lion or a bear; boredom equals death." What's more, "Men and women both wanna have sex, but they're on different timetables. Women want sex 15 minutes later than men do. If you hold out for *20* minutes, she'll be chasing you for five."

To synopsize, be desire-free, be excellent, retreat.

Sure, you're skeptical, but according to Lao Tse, "When the foolish man hears the Tao, he laughs out loud." So don't be so sure.

It certainly works for the fictional character in the movie, and from what I can tell, it also works for real-life Drew. I'm not sure he follows rules two and three of the Tao of Steve, but I know he follows rule number one. He approaches these women with no agenda and starts talking about, well, anything. The next thing you know, they go out for pizza or coffee. If she makes any remarks about how they're on a date or starting on a relationship, he reacts with surprise and maybe says something about "not wanting to ruin their friendship."

Soon, he's knocking his naked friend's skull against the headboard.

It seems all so brilliant, yet diabolical.

Maybe there's elegance in simplicity, but I've thrown caution to the wind and come up with some of my own rules; call it the Tao of TC. While I may not be an expert on women, I did, on two separate occasions, get a woman to have sex with me without resorting to begging or giving her my MasterCard.

Rule #1. *Compliment them on something other than their looks.* Sure, women are all insecure, but the one thing they're more insecure about than their looks is their (choose one): intelligence, sense of humor, skill in the sack, shoes, hairstyle, body-fat levels, ability to sing, knowledge of the history of Mesopotamia, etc. After complimenting them on one of those things, you can compliment them on their looks, but say something more original than, "Garsh, you're purty." Maybe tell her that she's *fun* to look at and, given the choice of watching her or the cool video of that tiger eating up that Siegfried and Roy guy, you'd really have to give it some thought.

Rule #2. *Show off your gray matter.* I'm not talking about your unwashed shorts here, but your intelligence. Women equate intelligence with earning power and, thus, power and status. And believe me, it's all about power and status. Casually mention, in between bites of your fettuccini, that paleontologists recently discovered the fossilized remains of a giant rat (named Phoberomys pattersoni for its remarkable resemblance to my friend, Tim Patterson) the size of a brown bear. Believe me, it's preferable to talking about sports, beer, or what you ate for breakfast this morning.

Rule #3. *If you observe rule #2 of the Tao of Steve, don't choose weightlifting as your area of excellence.* All women—with the possible exception of porn stars who are used to having high-powered halogen flood lights shined up their hoo-hahs—are a little insecure about their bodies. The last thing they need to know is that you're in better shape than she is. Believe it or not, most women have sex with us because of our personalities and our brains. Physiques usually come in fourth in the male fuckability scale, right after lack of bad breath or body odor.

Rule #4. *Don't talk about yourself.* Every jackass talks about himself. Listen, ask questions, and remain a bit mysterious. And if you do talk about yourself, the completely honest approach isn't always wise. It may have worked for George Costanza, but saying, "I'm unemployed and I live with my parents" is better than nothing, but might not be the best approach. I'm not suggesting you lie, but letting her know that you can't take her home because your mom doesn't allow you to have girls in your room isn't going to score you any points.

Rule #5. *If you should be lucky enough to get a girl in bed, don't be timid in the sack.* Here's a secret I learned: women are nastier than we are. Whatever perverse, dirty, deviant thing you want to try in the sack, they're up for it. Women don't want you to be polite in the sack, asking for permission to insert this here or that there. Just do it. If you ask them, they'll feign shock because, well they're supposed to be ladies and all, or at least fake it a little. No, they want beasts and if what you've done makes you feel mildly embarrassed or ashamed afterwards, you did good, Bubba.

Is practicing some or all of these rules disingenuous? Is it better, as the advice columns recommend, to "just be yourself"? I don't think so. Listen, if we all acted like ourselves right up front, complete with the flaws that are inherent to all of us, no one would want to be with us, let alone some hot woman who makes your member throb like a prospector's divining rod when he stumbles onto some gold.

Following the Tao of Steve, or even the Tao of TC, is simply another way of putting your best face forward. Better to be a Steve or a Drew instead of a Stu.

Of course, following these rules might be why I don't get laid very often, so I could be wrong.

Chapter 45

Young Sexy Girls

"One 19-year-old once told me, matter-of-factly, that she 'doesn't fuck fossils for free'. Apparently, she thought anyone over the age of 30 was a fossil, but regardless, I don't think a silver ring would exactly do the job for her unless it was affixed to some ice. I guess that's one point you can chalk up for Socialism."

Kary B. Mullis, who won the Nobel Prize for chemistry in 1993, once said that a woman's the most desirable when she's 10,000 days old. For those of us on planet earth who measure age in the conventional way, that's equivalent to about 27 years. Mullis argued that women of that age are at the apex of their sexual appeal.

I don't necessarily disagree with Mullis, but I'm hardly as discriminatory. Indeed, I have a little bubble of hot Testosterone in my loins for attractive women in just about any age group. I can tell you, though, that for most men, the cruelest age for a woman is between 15 and 18.

This is when many women, or rather girls, have the bodies of mature females. They've only recently become aware of their sexuality and they're often interested in flaunting it by wearing outfits that if worn by an adult female would cause you to slap down 50 bucks and unzip your fly, a handful of moist towellettes at the ready.

Sure, they wear baby-tees with little silken wisps of bras underneath that do little to conceal erect nipples. They wear little-boy boxer shorts that cause your heart to skip a beat—boxer shorts that are nothing like the poopy ones I saw you wearing in the locker room! They wear shoes with impossibly high platforms! Platforms that raise their pert little asses right up to the sightline of the one-eyed demon that lives in our pants!

It's almost as if they were daring you to take off your pants and run down the street impaling them from behind like so many bits of tasty beef being slid onto a shish kebob stick!

And the way they walk on these towering shoes ... Their long, slender legs, covered with downy blond fuzz, taking tiny uncertain coltish steps as if the smallest irregularity on the pavement could cause them to fall to the ground, their tiny skirts being rudely cast aside by their stumble to reveal carnival-bright colored thong panties with ... with happy faces on them!

Oh, lordy, lordy, lordy.

We try to fool ourselves into thinking that they're too young and that we're not attracted to them by thinking up piss-poor arguments. Sure, their skin is just *too soft* and their breasts are just *too damn perky*, but that's usually when we break down and sob uncontrollably.

The bodies of these creatures indicates they're women and their style of clothing demands that you notice it. Even your frustrated penis begs you to acknowledge what it can so clearly see—even turning its whiny head backwards to look at you with plaintive eye. But of course the laws of man strongly prohibit that you do anything *but* notice, and even that's discouraged.

Abstaining from these tasty morsels is also a moral law, but how then do we explain how some countries, even some states, recognize a young female as being a card-carrying member of adult womanhood when she attains the age of 16 instead of 18?

What the hell is that all about? What we can freely lust over in freakin' England is taboo in most of the states? Who the hell came up with that?

Of course, attempting to define female adulthood—however arbitrary this definition is—was never really attempted until fairly recently. Case in point, writers and musicians in the past often had extremely young women as muses or even lovers. Dante fell in love with his Beatrice when she was nine. Petrarch fell in love with his Laureen when she was 12. Even proto-rocker Jerry Lee Lewis, his great balls obviously on fire, married a 14-year-old.

But it's wrong. We know it's wrong. That's why nature is so damn cruel. It's as if God had a mean streak in him. It's as if he created a world covered with mounds of the most delicious ice cream imaginable, ice cream that's as poisonous as it is delicious.

Thanks a bunch, God. Are you having a good laugh? Well are ya, huh?

Because we know it's wrong, most of us feel tremendous guilt about it. A good friend of mine owns a coffee shop where women abound—women with many of the attributes we superficial males hold so damn dear. Recently, though, a gorgeous mammal that surpassed all others showed up at his counter. She was the Michael Jordan of bootie, the Smarty Jones of assdom … or maybe, because of her apparent youth, we should say she was the LeBron James of ass. And she looked exactly like former child-ass prodigy Amanda Bynes—wearing, of course, those molecule thin, excruciatingly short boy-boxer shorts.

He got goose bumps on his shaven head. His breath shortened. His slumbering penis started thrashing around like a weasel in a gunnysack. But then her mother came in and mentioned they'd just come from a swim meet at her junior high school. Junior high school! The girl wasn't even 15 yet!

O death, where is thy sting?

Those of you who have attractive daughters must live in a special kind of hell. You can't relax, not even for a moment. The men who eye her are like dogs. They know you have a pretty poodle in your pen. The dogs that are her age want her and will do anything to get her. The older dogs, more respectful of laws of man and nature, won't attempt to get her but that doesn't mean they're not fantasizing about her when they're humping that rheumy-eyed cocker spaniel down the street that's just a surrogate for your tasty little morsel in a baby-tee.

And just think, she'll only get more desirable day by day! Can you hear a horrifying laugh that sounds like the late Vincent Price?

You poor, poor bastard.

You might think I'm a pig for even discussing these nymphets, but it's just another painful reality of life. There was even a Seinfeld episode that addressed the same topic, when an angry father catches Costanza eyeballing his 15-year-old daughter's cleavage.

"It's like looking at the sun!" admonishes Jerry. "You're supposed to just take a peek and then look away!"

If I had my druthers, there wouldn't be any 15-year-old cleavage to eyeball. I'd dress them up like they were housing a wounded Harrison Ford in the attic. No budding breasts straining against gossamer-thin fabric, no down-covered half-moons of buttock staring provocatively out at the world, and definitely no velvety-smooth bellies and no tantalizing peeks at the pubic hinterland.

Cover it up! Cover it all up so we can rest!

Cover it up until their 18th birthday, when they can unveil all that glorious flesh for our approval and, if we're lucky, our conquest.

Vladimir Zhirinovsky that semi-crazy former candidate for the Russian presidency, even had a plan for this sexual coming of age. He once wrote that every virgin should have sex with an experienced man. "The man should then give her a silver ring bought from the state as a 'sexual certificate' on which his name is inscribed."

I don't know if this would work in a capitalist society. Case in point, one 19-year-old once told me, matter-of-factly, that she "doesn't fuck fossils for free." Apparently, she thought anyone over the age of 30 was a fossil, but regardless, I don't think a silver ring would exactly do the job for her unless it was affixed to some ice. I guess that's one point you can chalk up for socialism.

There is, however, one thing that saves us. Maybe God, in his wisdom, did give us a defense mechanism, a hormonal governor, so to speak. Comedian Richard Pryor, during one of his monologues, started talking about the physical charms of his 15-year-old daughter's friends.

"Have you seen some of these girls? The titties on them! But thank God they speak ..."

In other words, once Pryor heard these squeaky, immature voices and their inane conversation, his big head and his little head nodded in agreement and went back to reading the paper, finally able to rest.

ACKNOWLEDGEMENTS

Okay, I wrote the articles that make up the book, but a lot of creativity went into its production and I didn't have much to do with that creativity.

First and foremost, thanks to Tim Patterson, President of Testosterone Publishing, for being a big part of the book's design. Secondly, I'd like to thank Philippé Abel, Corey Blake, and Rob Grishow, the highly talented team of graphic artists who put the thing together. And I certainly can't forget Brian Moss, who took all the weird and wonderful photos that are in the book.

Last but not least, I'd like to thank Lou Schuler and Laurie Golder for their suggestions and copyediting.

Now, hopefully somebody will buy the damn thing.